Healing Cambodia
one child at a time

Text copyright © Benoît Duchâteau-Arminjon
Copyright © Editions Didier Millet

Front cover photograph © Krousar Thmey
Back cover photograph © Justin Creedy Smith

The publisher wishes to thank Jean-Marie Dallet for his valuable assistance in proofreading
the original French edition, David Rorke for the translation into English, and James Pham
for proofreading and editing the translated manuscript.

Editorial Director : MCM, assisted by Valérie Millet and Nathalie Barthès for additional
material and editing original French edition.

Color separation: Pica Digital, Singapore

ISBN: 978-981-4385-40-4

Healing Cambodia

one child at a time

The Story of Krousar Thmey, a New Family

Benoît Duchâteau-Arminjon

To Alain and Jean-Marie Le Guay,
to my mother for the kindness and generosity
that she passed on to us,
to the people of Cambodia and Europe who are with me,
to all the children of Krousar Thmey.

TABLE OF CONTENTS

FOREWORD

I just had to meet this Benoît Duchâteau-Arminjon. Actually, this mysterious Bénito baffled me... The former used to work with the ACCOR Group as financial controller, the latter was the founder of Krousar Thmey... Of course, I was to discover that they were one and the same person. Bénito had been very moved by the sufferings of the children in Cambodia following the Pol Pot regime massacres. He decided to give up his job and come to their aid—but all the while respecting their environment and traditions...

This book is Bénito's story, a true story, a very poignant one.

When I finally did meet you, Bénito, you impressed me with your elegant determination and the light that beamed from your heart.

Your story is about how, many years ago, you took it upon yourself to look after "your" kids in Cambodia, how you worked to get them to blossom and to grow up to be responsible adults. I can't say how much I enjoyed the show "your" kids put on, but I saw that they enjoyed it as much as I had when they broke up in gales of laughter! I spent a day with these boys and girls, all so lively and warm, that I just had to meet you, and meet you I did.

When you're involved in a profession like mine, you come to realize that your work isn't terribly important. Perhaps a few people will recognize me on the street, but at the end of the day, I know I haven't made much of a difference. But there you are, Benoît, out doing challenging things, things that are making a difference and that will last. Your reward: the beating hearts of the children, their voices that sing... because of you.

You're just the best. I envy you.

Affectionately,
Gérard Klein

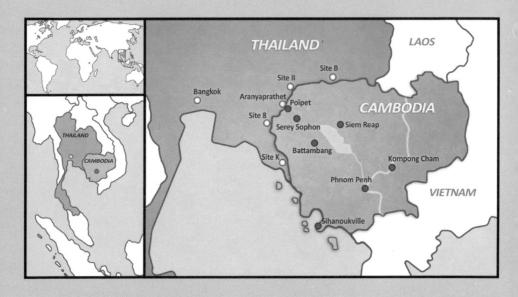

THAILAND

LAOS

Bangkok

Site II

Site B

Aranyaprathet
Poïpet

CAMBODIA

Site 8

Serey Sophon

Siem Reap

Site K

Battambang

Kompong Cham

Phnom Penh

VIETNAM

Sihanoukville

THAILAND

CAMBODIA

PHNOM PENH
(ancient names in parentheses)

Sisowath (Karl Marx)

Tonle Sap

Mekong

Kampuchea Krom (Kampuchea Vietnam)

Monivong (Achar Mean)

Norodom (Tou Samouth)

Krousan
Thmey

Palais
Royal

Mao Tse Tong (Keo Mony)

Tonle Bassac

A BRIEF HISTORICAL BACKGROUND

Although neighbors linguistically and culturally, the Thais and Khmers have never been particularly fond of one another. After the Khmer people had spent centuries as conquerors and empire builders—their territory covered much of what is now Thailand and Vietnam—they saw their vast realm simply melt away. Unending conflicts pitted brothers or cousins of the royal family against each other. In their effort to win, they called on their neighbors for support, in exchange for large tracts of land.

In 1860, France, already present in Vietnam, responded to the king's request and moved in as "protector." France wasn't very proactive in that role, as it had always considered the Cambodian people to be hard to deal with. Contrary to what took place in Vietnam, little in the way of infrastructure was developed. Cambodia remained largely an agricultural country. However, France used military force to get back a number of territories that had come under Thailand, notably the western provinces—Cambodia's rice basket and the home of the magnificent Angkor temples. Cambodia thus grew in area from 100,000 to 181,035 km^2, not far from its current size. But some territories such as *Kampuchea Krom* were left to Vietnam, Cambodia's "hereditary enemy," which has left in the Khmer collective sub-conscience the belief that France's presence contributed to the overall shrinking of Khmer territory to the benefit of its neighbors.

When France became embroiled in the Indochina War, King Norodom Sihanouk, the sovereign chosen by the French to ascend to the Khmer throne in 1941 when he was only 19 years old, secured the kingdom's independence from France. Abdicating in favor of his father in order to comply with the constitution, Sihanouk took the reins of political power and set up *Sangkum Reastrem Nyum*, a sort of socialist system that promoted large-scale public works and development in the country. Cambodia, at that time, was widely considered to be a land of plenty, the Switzerland of Asia.

After France's defeat, the Americans entered the Vietnam War, but they too would sink into the quagmire. While Sihanouk refused to allow American bases to be set up on Khmer soil, he was unable to stop the Viet Cong from taking advantage of Cambodia's position. The opening of the Ho Chi Minh Trail greatly eased the movement of Vietnamese troops from North to South Vietnam to fight the Americans.

In 1970, exasperated with Cambodia's pretext of neutrality while at the same time letting the North Vietnamese cross its territory, the United States facilitated a coup d'état orchestrated by nationalists. Sihanouk was toppled while on a stopover in Russia when returning home from a trip to France. The nationalists installed the Khmer Republic. But things did not go as the Americans had planned, and Cambodia was plunged into war.

The people did not take kindly to the overthrow of Sihanouk, considered as a god-king by many, particularly in the countryside. Furious over his eviction, Sihanouk, from China where he had found asylum, called on the people to join ranks with his erstwhile enemies, that he himself had dubbed the "Khmer Rouge." With the United States supporting a government that most Cambodians rejected, the Khmer Rouge stood for a new ideal, one that opposed this American "puppet regime," and which was seen as a way of getting Sihanouk back in power. Many young people, intellectuals, and idealists thus rallied with the Khmer Rouge guerrillas. Initially favorable to the Viet Cong, the movement solidified under the influence of China, notably under the leadership of a group of young men who had gone to study in France: Pol Pot, Ieng Sary, Khieu Samphan…

Corruption was such that weapons received by the government quickly found their way into the hands of the Khmer Rouge. The latter grew ever stronger and gained positions in the provinces. They bombed the only bridge over the Tonle Sap River, thus cutting the capital off from eastern Cambodia. In 1975, the Khmer Rouge finally entered Phnom Penh. The jubilant citizenry welcomed them as liberators. But the atmosphere very quickly changed and the people realized what a mistake they had made. Claiming that the Americans were about to bomb the city, the Khmer Rouge had it evacuated. Some two million inhabitants and refugees, under threats from teenagers armed with AK-47s, were forced out into the countryside so that a "new order" could be established.

The Khmer Rouge declared money to be valueless, abolished personal property, emptied the pharmacies, destroyed banks, and burned up paper money in huge bonfires. They rejected any form of contact with the West and all modern items, except for anything flashy—expensive watches in particular—for which they had a strange fascination. All recalcitrants were summarily executed; hospitals were emptied with patients simply tossed out the windows in some cases. The disabled were shot on the spot. A mass of humanity in indescribable chaos was driven out onto the roads leading to the provinces. Family members lost touch with one another. In just 48 hours, Phnom Penh, a once bustling and thriving city, was turned into a ghost town.

The people were scattered into labor camps, fed very meager rations, and forced to perform grueling work in subhuman conditions. Men were teamed up like oxen. Men and women toiled in rice paddies, the production of which was destined for China. With the support of Chinese advisers, the Khmer Rouge ordered a crackdown unrivalled by anything in the Chinese Cultural Revolution; emphasis was on cutting down, not building up. *Angkar's* focus was not re-educating unpatriotic elements, but annihilating any individual not bearing the seed of the New Man. So what if one third of the population was eliminated? According to current estimates, in three years, eight months, and 21 days, the Khmer Rouge exterminated approximately 2 million of Cambodia's population of 7 million at the time. Many died from starvation; others were purged as enemies of the revolution. Cambodia thus lost most of its human resources, including virtually all of its intellectuals.

But in their attempt to take back *Kampuchea Krom*, the Khmer Rouge provoked the ire of pro-Soviet Vietnam. So with help from Russia, the Vietnamese communists decided it was time to overthrow the pro-Chinese Khmer Rouge. They liberated Phnom Penh on January 7,

1979 and drove into western Cambodia both the Khmer Rouge and any who refused to accept Vietnam's presence. An anti-Vietnam resistance was thus born, of three different stripes: the Khmer Rouge (the most powerful and best structured), the nationalists (loyal to Marshal Lon Nol under the leadership of HE Son Sann), and the royalists (faithful to Prince Sihanouk).

The Cold War was waging and the United States feared that expansion of Soviet-style communism, which had already taken power in Vietnam, Laos, and Cambodia, would reach into Thailand. Against this backdrop, American and Chinese aid came to the rescue of the three resistance networks, with a preference for the Khmer Rouge, as they were better organized and ideologically more effective against the inexorable advance of Vietnam, going so far as to offer Cambodia's seat at the United Nations to the Khmer Rouge, in spite of the undeniable record of genocide committed by that regime.

Even though intellectuals, mainly leftists, among them Jean Lacouture, took it upon themselves to hail the Khmer Rouge's rise to power in *Le Monde* and other newspapers, the forced population displacements, the organized horror, and genocide in Cambodia were soon common knowledge due to firsthand accounts collected and recounted by Fathers Venet and Ponchaud. Waves of refugees then flowed into such camps as Sakeo and Meyrouth, effectively removing any lingering doubt about the Khmer Rouge atrocities. In 1979, many Khmer Rouge took flight ahead of the arrival of the Vietnamese and were among the first refugees accepted by Western countries, led by the United States, Australia, Canada, and France.

When the Vietnamese entered, refugee camps were set up across Cambodia's border with Thailand, under the aegis of the United Nations. But the Thai were wary of the armed incursions on their territory and feared the influx of these thousands of Cambodians reduced to little more than skin and bones. In the very early stages, they refused to allow Cambodians in and turned them back, sometimes with extreme violence, to the minefields on the Cambodian side.

So refugee camps were set up on the Cambodian side along the Thai border. They were controlled by the Cambodian military leaders of the three resistance factions and were relocated depending on where fighting was taking place. Additional civilian deaths in the many attacks on these camps were in the thousands. Nevertheless, the camps enabled the families of the fighters alongside the refugees to receive international aid. This situation prevailed until 1984 when, in reaction to violent Vietnamese offensives against the resistance and its camps for internal refugees, the United Nations got Thailand to agree to the creation of camps for displaced persons all along its border. These were not refugees in the meaning of international conventions—accepted by a country under United Nations protection with the possibility of immigrating to a third country—but were displaced persons, that is, accepted for a limited time by a country other than their own (Thailand) until a decision was made to send them back to their homeland or to have them accepted by a third country.

This situation that was imposed, so to speak, on Thailand by the United States and China was also an opportunity, that of getting heavy investments out of the international community, both for displaced persons and local communities under hardship, and that proved to be a windfall for Thai trade and commerce. For the larger powers, this human belt was a means of checking the expansion of Soviet communism. For Thailand, it was an opportunity to get China to put an end to its support of the Thai Deng, Mao communist resistance fighters. The camps were therefore organized and controlled by armed factions, with assistance from the United Nations, but under Thai supervision. Some of these camps, such as Sites VIII and K, were run by the Khmer Rouge, others, like Site B, were run by royalists, and still others, such as Site II and Sok Sann, were under nationalist influence. At one point, they collectively held as many as 375,000 persons.

So it was that under American orders, the nationalists under HE Son Sann, former prime minister under Marshal Lon Nol, took over the largest camp, Site II, a veritable second capital city of Cambodia with a population of 215,000 inhabitants. Located on 7.6 km^2 of barren land, it was home to refugees on Thai soil from various Cambodian camps. Site II North took in Ampil, Dangrek, Nong Chan-Nam Yoeun, and Sanro, while Site II South got Rythissen and O'Bok.

After years of poverty and emergency relief, one failed peace negotiation after another, these camps started to get organized. Many humanitarian organizations began donating food, sanitation supplies, and medical aid, along with education and training for adults.

TWENTY YEARS...

It's 7 a.m. on April 6, 2011. Stuffed into my navy blue suit, I feel a little stressed out. We had been working for months on our 20th anniversary and in just a few minutes, the ceremony will begin. A double line of pupils dressed in blue and white flank both sides of the highway for several kilometers—an honor guard awaiting the signal to wave flags and hold up portraits. At my side are many friends, former volunteer workers, and helpers from France, Switzerland, and elsewhere on hand for this historic moment. On hand too is the Australian team under Jack Thompson who had produced a documentary on the repatriation 18 years ago. The spacious schoolyard is filled with thousands of children from our programs, hailing from all the provinces of Cambodia.

The security department is nervous. Any minute now sirens will sound and the official convoy will enter our newest school for blind and deaf students to celebrate Krousar Thmey's 20th anniversary. Twenty years! What an obstacle course it has been! But the looks on the faces of these children and their support team members are proof that our energy has not been expended in vain.

Let's go back over the road we covered—a journey full of surprises, many pains, and unbridled enthusiasm.

A VISITED VISITOR
(August 1990–March 1991)

On August 3, 1990, after quickly dropping in at ACCOR's Asia Middle-East Office on the 23rd floor of the Wall Street Tower, Suriwongse Avenue, in Bangkok's financial center, where I work as a financial controller, I rush to pick up my bag in my Sala Deng apartment, jump into a taxi, then speed on to Mo Chit Bus Station in the northern part of the capital.

The monstrous traffic jams of the Thai capital and its unending suburbs finally give way to a highway running along a khlong, nothing more than an open-air sewer. An hour and a half out of the city, the countryside begins to unfold in a checkerboard of manioc fields and rice paddies. The closer one gets to the bus station, the more police and military checkpoints there are. They are looking for illegal Cambodians going home from Bangkok. This plentiful and cheap source of labor nevertheless makes a valuable contribution to the Thai economy, to its farms, and to its rapidly expanding building sites.

Another five hours on a good highway brings me to the center of Aranyaprathet, the last town before the border. Using the little Thai I knew at the time, I ask how to get to Ta Phraya, a small village 50 km further north. I get off the relatively comfortable Bangkok–Aranyaprathet bus and board a local bus. In Europe, this bus would have been sent to the scrap yard; here, it's part of the landscape. Totally battered and with windows agape, it's already filled. The people here are poor country folk, of darker skin color.

What happened to the immaculately dressed secretaries, the school children in dazzling shirts, the militiamen dressed to the nines? It's a different world out here. The soil, of redbrick clay, is poor and unproductive. People chew on quads of betel nut (areca nuts mixed with lime and rolled into a betel leaf) and spit the juice right onto the wooden floor of the bus. The local people speak a mixture of Khmer and Thai. They're of Khmer origin but of Thai nationality. Here, you just grab what you're carrying—chickens bought at the market, bags of fertilizer, etc.—and pile onto the bus.

The driver is leaning over his steering wheel. Over his head a fan feebly stirs the humid air. Talismans and wreathes of dried jasmine hanging from the rear-view mirror caress the Buddha stickers plastered onto the dashboard. From time to time, he wipes his forehead with the back of a face towel that doubles as a rag to shine his steering wheel. His assistant is doing his best to fill up the rooftop baggage carrier with luggage and rice or fertilizer bags, woven from a type of red plastic ribbon. The engine runs in fits and starts. Whenever it sounds like it's about to die, he opens the throttle.

Three horn blasts rouse the passengers sipping on sugarcane juice or catching a cigarette alongside the bus. And, with a snort of black smoke the bus lurches northward bound. We go along the border to our right, sometimes a few hundred meters from it, other times a few kilometers. The road is in rather good condition, and the bus services various hamlets made up of a few houses. Their roofs are clad in sheet metal, their walls are of roughly hewn boards nailed over each other regardless of size, the disparate lengths seemingly rendering them useless for other purposes. Undoubtedly the squatters living here to escape the fighting of the last 20 years are looking forward to being exiled somewhere else.

Fifty kilometers go by and the driver signals my stop. It's a small village with no more than three main streets, two parallel and one perpendicular. At the entrance are the offices of the Catholic Office for Emergency Relief and Refugees (COERR), a Thai Catholic organization, and one of its staff points out the blue house in front of which I'm to meet Gilles de Noblet.

But there's no one there. I'm too early. I wait patiently over a beer in the local convenience store, an ordinary house with a refrigerator and all manner of items hanging from hooks above, from bags of soup, snack biscuits, and condiments to detergent and a variety of small household goods. About 5:30 p.m. a car drives up and a passenger waves to me from inside. It parks in front of the COERR office. Out steps a young blond man smiling broadly, wearing slacks and a green polo shirt, a colored scarf around his neck—the quintessential Khmer krama, a multipurpose piece of cotton cloth that Cambodians use for just about everything: a hammock for the baby, a rag to wipe off the table, a bathrobe, or a sack for groceries.

I was given Gilles de Noblet's contact information by my friend Olivier Dauphin who had encouraged me to do a sponsorship with a child welfare association. Like me, Olivier is a French national service volunteer, and coordinates sponsorships for this association out of Bangkok. He's one of the first people I met in Thailand in December 1989. I was already sponsoring a Tibetan child in a refugee camp in northern India, so Olivier had no problem talking me into doing the same thing for the refugee population in the Thai camps. I've a comfortable income, so it's quite easy. Sponsoring a child appears to be a gesture of generosity, but as I would find out the hard way, it is, in reality, a good idea that goes wrong in the field of humanitarian aid.

Gilles had a brilliant scholastic record at the École centrale but was declared unfit for military service. Feeling that he owed a year to his country, he decided to spend this time volunteering to assist refugees in the camps. A Jesuit father helped him get a job through COERR as a math teacher in a technical school on Site II camp. He agreed to take me on a tour of the camp the next morning, Saturday.

Out of the blue huge speakers begin playing the Thai national anthem. It's 6 p.m. Passers-by and motor vehicles alike come to a one-minute halt. It's the same everywhere in Thailand. The highly respected king has ordered the anthem played every day at 8 a.m. and 6 p.m., suspending people's lives for a minute each time. King Bhumipol has been on the throne since 1950 and is adulated by his subjects. He acts as mediator when military coups take place. His authority is uncontested in the country. Anyone daring to do so would quickly end up in jail.

Gilles suggests that I freshen up. It's a welcome idea, and I proceed to take a shower, Thai style.

Using a plastic dipper, I draw water from a big tank in the corner of a spacious washroom and pour it over myself. The water falls directly onto the concrete floor and runs out through a hole to the side. The reservoir holds nearly 500 liters of water. The bottom of the tank is muddy. Water is supplied by the village for an hour in the morning and an hour in the evening... unless there is a cutoff. When it comes out of the pipe, it's still murky. Using a cake of alum, the dirt particles settle to the bottom after a few hours. Beware of being too energetic and stirring up the water! On these scorching days, it's so nice to have a source of virtually clear, cool water.

It's only 6:30 p.m. and already dark. In the tropics, night falls in about a quarter of an hour. As the year goes by, there is little variation, exactly 30 minutes between June and December, with sunrise at 6 a.m. and sunset at 6 p.m. We're off for dinner in a small restaurant frequented by the Ta Phraya volunteer workers. Nurses and doctors from *Médecins Sans Frontières*, Americans with the Red Cross, Belgians in charge of camp hygiene, many French, some Australians, and all sorts of nationalities who are similarly attired: shorts and T-shirt, rubber sandals, and a canvas backpack. The expatriate population accounts for 25 percent of the people in town and is a boon to the village economy. Nearly all of them work at Site II camp, 22 km from Ta Phraya. There are those working on a fully volunteer basis, others on a meager allowance, but they collectively contribute to the livelihood of a lot of local families. As is true throughout Thailand, people don't do much cooking at home. There are food vendors on every street corner. For a pittance one can buy all manner of spicy dishes, packaged in plastic bags sealed with knotted elastic bands. Or one can eat out in small plain restaurants. It often costs more to do your own cooking.

The only ones who aren't part of the restaurant scene are the junior evangelical crowd from America, zealous proselytizers, who live in group homes. In addition to doing humanitarian work, often of commendable quality, they try to convert the Cambodians. But the new converts are not very interested in Christianity per se. Most Cambodians adhere to so-called *Theravada* (Lesser Vehicle) Buddhism. If not drawn to the perks on offer (health care, clothing, education, equipment, and so on), Cambodians often convert to escape their karma. Indeed, according to the Buddhist religion, a person inescapably suffers the consequences of his acts in previous lives. So those who were involved in unmentionable conduct during these years of trouble hope they can avoid the consequences thereof by changing religion… And what better religion than the one whose God is forgiving?

While at dinner, I meet a number of young men like Gilles who are putting in a year to help people on the other side of the world. Others, often women more mature in age, have been working as volunteers or on a very small allowance for many years for one association or another in the area. Secular nuns, you might call them. They give me more objective background information than the rather overdone accounts of freshly arrived volunteers.

Gilles has been here for 11 months now and is winding up his contract. He is still pondering whether to sign up for another year or head back to France where his girlfriend is waiting. Most happy with his teaching year, he gives me some details about his experience—the camp, the refugees, life at the border, and Cambodia that seems so distant despite being only a few kilometers away. I'm enthralled. How could a guy just 24 years old, rather than embarking on the career that his *grande école* had prepared him for, decide, after putting forth so much effort, to just put his life on hold and take a sabbatical year so often frowned upon in the corporate world, winding up at the end of the world with its water buffaloes, spiders, and giant cockroaches, to give a helping hand to a people with whom he has no particular bond? Some, driven by their religious convictions, have a clear motivation, while others are simply altruistic. Why? I listen to him talk for a good part of the evening in an attempt to understand.

In Bangkok, I spend my time recording figures, filing information, reviewing financial data, comparing results, drawing up tables of percentages, commenting on trends, and the like. I love my work, particularly when a job comes to an end, when the results are straightforward, and a file can be closed. My office is perched aloft in a glass-enshrouded high-rise tower where expatriates push into the elevators in the morning and are just as pushy when they go down for lunch or head home after a day's work by taxi or in insufferably crammed buses to their luxury condominiums, under the scrupulous care of plethoric but solicitous security staff.

The European, fastidious for efficiency, is often irritated by local customs and annoyed with the slow Oriental pace.

So it is that foreigners and Asians rub shoulders but never really communicate with each other.

This evening, I'm meeting someone who I could have crossed paths with in my glass tower but who has chosen a harsh but fulfilling life. To me, it looked like the volunteers were actually happy to head to the camp early in the morning and return the village at night. I just can't get enough of it. I feel like I've just crashed down to earth; I was on the wrong track. Yet, there is time to change direction. But can I? Don't I have a vital need for comfort, ambition, stress, competition? We talk on until very late and Gilles concludes by saying, "Just wait until tomorrow; you'll see."

The alarm rings at 6:30 the next morning. But a rooster had crowed long before that. Did it ever stop? I find out here that even the headlight beam of a passing car or motorbike gets the cock crowing. We down a quick breakfast, some tea, and bread at Kim Kim's, a store in Aranyaprathet that learned what it takes to satisfy foreigners. Even when their means are limited, they still look for little treats: whole wheat bread, jam (even the horrible stuff from Bestfood is just great), Nutella, Cheez Whiz, and the like. On any run from Ta Phraya to Aranyaprathet, one has to stop at Kim Kim's.

The volunteers going up to the camp this Saturday morning are mustering at COERR. Gilles tells me that I need to pick up a pass. The camp is restricted and only volunteers with a pass can get in. So I pick up a pass that's just sitting there. The picture doesn't look like me, but so what? I'll be blond for once in my life. Gilles tells me that the chance of a check is rare, all the more so because Father Vincent is driving. The driver turns all of the passes over to the Thai police for them to check the dates and make sure that the number of passes matches the number of passengers. At any rate, they have trouble telling white people apart from one another, something like us with them.

The pickup takes off at 7:10 a.m. There are 11 of us: three in the leatherette-covered front seat, four in the back seat, and four on benches in the modified back. The road is windy but good for the first

15 km. We are overtaken by vehicles belonging to the United Nations Border Relief Operation (UNBRO), the UN agency in charge of problem management in the Thai border camps. They come up from Aranyaprathet, a more developed town where businesses and restaurants are more readily available. But they have to do 72 km both morning and evening. So they're often in a hurry to get there.

Over the next few kilometers, we weave around potholes gouged out by tank trucks. Initially used to haul gasoline, these red vehicles are now all battered and take out their vengeance on the road. Despite drilling attempts, there's never been enough water on Site II. When the camp was first opened, the Thais purposely chose land that had no water to be sure of holding a trump card to play when the time comes to have the refugees repatriated.

One more checkpoint and we are alongside the barbed wire fence surrounding the camp. Here and there children are slipping through holes to pick up sticks or gather plastic bags blown about by the wind. Nothing is lost; everything is recycled. Three kilometers further, we gain official access to the place. After a turn, the road splits around a large bamboo guardhouse tended by some relaxed-looking officers in navy blue uniforms. Welcome to Site II…

It's August 4, 1990. The Displaced Persons Police Unit (DPPU) checks vehicles going through. Several years earlier, the DPPU, a special police force funded by UNBRO, replaced the black-uniformed Task Force 80 border guards who were routinely accused of rapes, acts of brutality, and murder committed against refugees. The DPPU officers are more disciplined, less corrupt, and show greater respect for the refugees.

The officer on duty asks for our passes. My heart starts beating faster, but there's no problem. In we go.

The first thing I observe are the deeply rutted red clay dirt streets. Bamboo shacks are lined up as far as the eye can see. They are no more than little huts with thatched palm leaf roofs and walls. Scattered here and there are more impressive administration, school, and hospital buildings. No concrete; no permanent buildings. Gilles de Noblet explains that they don't want the Khmer people to feel too much at home. Everything about the camp breathes of the transient, the fugitive, the degradable. After all, the refugees are nothing more than displaced persons sponging off the Thais and who are supposed to go back home as soon as possible. This temporary state has already dragged on for six years.

Since 1984, when the camp was established, no solution is in the offing. At every new conference about Cambodia, negotiations flounder. Many children were born in the camp, born prisoners, so to speak, and know nothing more than their barbed wire horizons. In fact, children under 14 make up half of the camp's population.

As we walk along, they pour out from everywhere, most of them bare to the waist, in ragged shorts, noses dripping, hair tousled. Yet, what radiant smiles! Some of them are carrying a simple stick to which a rusty can is tied, their only toy. Many have a key around their necks. Is it for the door to their homes or a fetish to protect them from evil spirits?

When foreigners go by—*barangs*—they start waving and calling out "O.K. Bye bye! O.K. Bye bye!" We encounter two pickup trucks belonging to humanitarian organizations, a water supply truck, and a few bicycles with an upholstered board mounted on the luggage rack. "Bicycle taxis," proffers Gilles. "They come in handy to get around the camp." Indeed, under the merciless sun with no shade trees around, it's good not to have to walk too far.

The COERR offices are no different from the administration buildings—bamboo structures held together with wire and nails. The walls are of woven bamboo and the roof is made of palm leaf panels. The floors are packed dirt, that red dirt from which a pervasive fine-grained is dust blown in by gusts of wind. Desks, tables, and chairs are also made of bamboo, varnished in a yellow or purplish color.

It's just 8 a.m. and the heat is intense. The sun is already up high and is scorching the earth devoid of trees and greenery. I'm making my way through a desert with a human population of 215,000. Although this is the monsoon season, there hasn't been any rain for two days, although it had rained a lot in the last few weeks. In the distance the Dangrek Mountain range is visible, covered with jungle, marking the Thailand–Cambodia border.

Gilles takes me to his school. A few meters away, a crowd of men, women, and children carrying pails and bamboo yokes stands waiting for the water truck. Jolting its way along, a battered tank truck pulls up and stops near the approximately 1m3 galvanized iron tanks. A Cambodian man jumps from the truck, pushes his way through the crowd, grabs a pipe, hooks it up to the valve, and drops the end of it into a tank. He next fires up a small gas motor and water gushes from the leaky pipe. The children leap into the spray, jumping and dancing under the welcome shower. Once the tank truck is empty, two Cambodian men take out a list and call up the families one by one to get their daily ration: 20 liters per person, that's it... for drinking, bathing, laundry, and dishes.

Some Cambodians in the camp receive assistance from more fortunate family members who emigrated to the United States, Australia, Canada, France, or Switzerland, and that upgrades their daily lot. For a few Thai baht, the currency of the camp, they can buy up the rations of the poorest of the poor who are short on cash. Despite the extreme poverty of a refugee camp, I take bitter note of long-standing disparities. For instance, some have made it their specialty to carry water, some of whom are 12-year-old children. A yoke over one shoulder and a pail hanging from each end held by a wrought iron hook, they walk like disjointed puppets, swaying from one step to the next, digging their heels into the ground to keep their balance as they ply under the weight of the water. Quite a feat as they try not to scrape the skin off their shoulder or to spill the precious contents!

I'm dumbstruck as memories of my own childhood come back, of the days when I used to play with my siblings. We would drench each other copiously as we filled up our plastic swimming pool. What a difference!

Gilles invites me to follow him into the spacious dirt courtyard where the school buildings stand. Each has three classrooms with dirt floors. From doors to windows, everything is of bamboo and thatched palm leaves. Some buildings have fuchsia pink or sky-blue curtains that add a touch of color to the scene. The Dangrek Technical School is subsidized by the Konrad Adenauer Foundation and sundry other donors, French in particular, and provides instruction to students in math, chemistry, electricity, and mechanics.

I'm surprised by the range of ages, from 17 to 45. Officially, no one is allowed to work in the camp, so adults make time each day to attend these training sessions to keep their minds occupied, thus finding a way out of the futureless daily grind and getting a break from the endless expectation of peace that just doesn't come.

Some of the students greet Gilles with a bow: "*Bonjour, professeur. Vous allez bien?*" Gilles explains that these are his engineering students. They're studying chemistry this morning.

We enter the classroom and 20 or so students, mostly male, give me a smile:

"Allo! What you name?"

"Benoît."

"You French? You come work Syte too?"

"Yes, I'm French, but just visiting."

"You friend my teacher Zil?"

"Yes."

"Welcome engineer school!"

The interchange ends with bursts of laughter.

Before sitting down, the students give the tables and benches a brushing off with the back of a notebook. A cloud of dust ascends from each table. One of the students wipes off the blackboard before the volunteer teacher begins the class. With mischievous big smiles and beaming with intelligence, they all bid me *au revoir*.

We continue our tour. To the left, a large room is filled with engine bodies that the students are taking apart and reassembling. The teacher, wearing red coveralls, proudly tells me that he received training in a factory and takes me to admire the Peugeot engine religiously enthroned on a dismantling table. In the middle of the schoolyard, behind a classroom off on its own, the Dangrek school has one of the rare buildings made of non-temporary materials. Built of breezeblocks for a degree of coolness, it houses a computer room equipped with old IBMs, donated by a company. The room has fans and even an air conditioner. A generator is used to supply electricity, but during class time only.

Site II does not have electricity. Some better-off families have used money sent over by relatives in other countries to pay off the Thai police and get a car battery or, for the really well-off, a small generator. I then come across a system that I would later find everywhere in the remote countryside: an inverting unit that transforms 12-volt current into 220. I'd never seen such a great thing before. But 99 percent of the population is plunged into darkness when night falls. Now I understand why, with families crammed into quarters where they share just one bed, there are so many children!

The tour has ended and Gilles invites me to have a drink at Thavy's. Just a few meters from the technical school, in the shade of the only tree on the street, at a table made of disjointed planks, around which are placed some old bamboo chairs and a plastic chest, soft drinks are available. Thavy, a charming Cambodian girl, speaks a smattering of French. Her shop is in a good location next to COERR. It's a watering hole for the volunteer workers who stop and talk with her, teaching her some basic French in exchange for beautiful smiles and saucy Khmer expressions.

It's barely past 10 a.m. and the earth has already absorbed an unbelievable amount of heat. Overwhelmed by the sun, we would like to just stay here and sip our drink. But I've a meeting with Mr. Samnang, in charge of the Cambodian Red Cross. I'm a little apprehensive of the formalities, but am welcomed with open arms, with this smile that seems to be the trademark of Cambodians.

The local Red Cross office has no affiliation with the International Red Cross. It's just an office opened by the camp administration to help out families, notably by means of sponsorships through the organization that Olivier looks after. The people in charge were told I was coming and are happy to tell me about what they're doing both in the camp and in Cambodia, in what they call "liberated zones." Indeed, all along the border, sections of Cambodian soil remain under the control of the resistance armies. Whenever the Cambodian army pushes them out, the resistance armies cross over the border undisturbed by the Thais before simply reoccupying those zones.

The fall of the Berlin Wall and the collapse of the Soviet bloc dried up grants to countries like Vietnam, who withdrew its troops. So the government army is finding it increasingly difficult to maintain its positions near the border. With no headquarters, enjoying no support from the people, and viewed as a puppet in the hands of the Vietnamese, it ended up abandoning the whole area north of Sisophon. The three factions share this zone, each one trying to turn it into a showcase for its party. The Red Cross on Site II camp claims to be active in areas close to Thma Puok, a few kilometers from Ta Phraya.

Inside the camp, the Cambodian Red Cross helps families, mostly through individual sponsorships. This was the context in which I became the sponsor of a young Cambodian boy. I'm taken to his family by one of the officers. As I go down the narrow alleys, families look at me and laugh. Women wearing kramas on their heads cover their mouths as they titter away.

The homes are minuscule, with one large bamboo bed and little or no furniture on a packed dirt floor. The windows are often blocked off by a rectangle of blue plastic to keep the dust out. Some of the fancier homes have a remnant of nylon cloth for a curtain, pink or blue, the flashier the better. Some have a plastic-coated picture of a flower-bedecked Swiss chalet above their doors, their dream home! Others glue magazine pictures on cardboard to make a partition. An old woman is curled up asleep on an old bamboo bed in the shade of a porch roof. A skeleton-like man with a toothy grin moves lightly about in a piece of navy blue fabric girded on with a length of string. Armed with an axe, he's chopping some kindling wood to light a fire. Here and there dogs bark and boys kick them away. Some kids are tossing their flip-flops at an indistinct target. Others are playing marbles with flicks of their index finger. Chickens are pecking away at piles of rubbish. Little girls jump over an elastic skipping rope; a closer look reveals it is made of dozens of small rubber bands knotted together.

I thought upon arriving that I had seen children and life along the well-laid out dirt alleys and in front of the proper rows of dwellings, but never did I imagine such a glut of people. One step down a lane and there's a tangled mass of shacks. Thousands of children at play, not a care in the world, oblivious to the obvious. It's as if the poverty and hopelessness of exile had no effect whatsoever on their happiness to be alive. And most of them know nothing more than this barren tract of land at the Dangrek foothills, alternately stricken by drought then drenched with torrents of muddy water. The water doesn't penetrate; in copious free flow, it washes away everything in its path. And too bad for anyone who tries to grow anything. The land and the water are unfriendly to man.

Yes, those beautiful smiles astonish me as I pass by from house to house, from one bamboo wall to the next. Smiles of children whose teeth are already stained; the toothy smiles of the elderly, definitely not older than my father but who look twice as old; the shy smiles of women who cover their mouths with their hand; the red betel nut smiles of old shaven-headed women.

But where are the men? Men aged from 20 to 50, although occasionally seen as one goes along, are conspicuously absent from this incredible human density. Many are off serving in a resistance army in an ongoing fratricidal war pitting Cambodian against Cambodian. The fighting is endless, stoked by a Cold War version of international aid.

Imagine a city of single-story structures. Of bamboo and thatch huts flimsily built right on the ground.

In less than ten minutes, I've already gotten an eye full.

As we reach one narrow lane, my guide informs me that we've arrived. A dwelling much like the others. I am greeted by a father who hugs me like a savior. He calls his wife and children, but soon the whole neighborhood invades the house—dogs, hens, and rooster to boot. Compared to the others, this place is quite large: two bedrooms, girls and boys separated, a common room wallpapered with posters pasted on salvaged cardboard, Thai movie stars, and those ubiquitous Swiss chalets bordered with flowerbeds. Maybe 40 m² altogether. One community toilet for each group of houses. The kitchen? A cubbyhole outside with a fireplace on the ground, on top of which a teakettle is perched. A few utensils blackened by the charcoal smoke, strung up on wire. A wicker basket holds fish to dry in the sun. Flies are a permanent fixture of the decor.

I'm given a motion to be patient. I eventually understand that they've gone to look for the boy I am to sponsor. A lad of about 12 years old makes his appearance, wearing pants from a navy blue uniform and a yellow T-shirt. His skin is very dull in color and he's almond-eyed like most Khmers. Unlike the Chinese who are light-skinned and slant-eyed, Khmers are quite dark and rather square faced, with heavier lips and eyes with little slant. When one looks at the Khmers, one can guess the diversity of the migratory flows that populated Cambodia. Whether from India, Malaysia, or Indonesia, immigration was massively from south to north in Cambodia. On the other hand, Vietnam is marked by north to south migratory flows, therefore predominantly Chinese. Hence the name Indochina.

He's come from an arithmetic lesson. He smiles, but doesn't dare come forward. He's pushed against me as if he belonged to me, as if I was expected to grab him and take him abroad on the spot. Everyone wants to be beside me. They touch me, feel my arm, and give a little pluck on the hair. I'm a curiosity, a mascot that has to be touched to bring good luck. I feel uncomfortable. I'm suffocating. The heat, the dust, the smells, and the emotion of touring the camp are already quite overwhelming. I suddenly need some air.

My guide gets the picture and asks the neighbors to leave. I'm invited to sit on the bed next to the kitchen. That makes it easier to talk. I'm brought some fruit, a supreme luxury. I'm hungry but dare not eat more than one. I imagine that when I came they had to borrow some money to buy fruit in my honor. I'm given a glass of boiled water. Although the water is warm, it has a pronounced chemical taste from insecticide put in the earthenware jars to keep dengue-bearing mosquitoes from breeding. I feel better despite the heat. I'm shown a big blackboard with today's date written in French, beautifully formed in white chalk, something like our old primary school teachers would have done. They're proud to have their French sponsor in their home.

And as for me, I feel ashamed. Ashamed of this pedestal they put me on in exchange for a monthly amount equivalent to one of my meals. Ashamed of this exhibition. Ashamed of this possession that I'm being pushed to acquire. Yet, I cannot deny my wealth, my designer jeans, my clean shirt, or my Docksides that stand in stark contrast to their poverty.

I gather that the family is trying to learn French. I recognize some of the words they are struggling to utter. Laughter and smiles, universal modes of communication, relax the atmosphere to some extent. Quite a while goes by with nothing understood between us. The guide invites me to join his family for lunch. I feel even more awkward; they're going all out to offer me their best. I prefer to go back with Gilles and make an appointment to meet up again in the afternoon and go for a walk through the camp with the children.

I confess to Gilles how embarrassed and frustrated I feel. I'm shocked by their poverty, yet I realize that this family is not among the neediest. I saw smaller houses all around and people in greater poverty. I feel terrible! Here I am creating scales of poverty…

We have fried rice for lunch. Relieved to share my impressions with veteran volunteers, I have my homework cut out for me. I get information about these refugees, their living conditions, how the camp is operated, the rationing system, the different organizations working in it. All of this fascinates me.

Rations are distributed by UNBRO to any person registered by the camp administrators, based on the family book. Actually, politics often comes first, humanitarian assistance second. I'll understand the reason for this later. These family books are the key to their identity. Most people lost everything and have no way to prove their civil status. Neighborhood surveys are therefore taken as the basis. Birth dates vary. If one can pass for younger, it might be easier to get into school or to improve one's chances of leaving for a third country. And some Cambodians have their name changed. In a family, the name derived from the paternal ancestor may vary. It might be the father's, the mother's, or the grandmother's. No big deal. As for given names, many are very similar: Sokly, Sokny, and Soky; Chamroeun, Chamrath, and Chamrong; or Bouny and Boumy. Some children born here are named Site II! This vagueness in matters of civil status perplexes us. How many Cambodians go overseas with an identity and age that differ from the reality? Some individuals get registered in a number of family books to increase their rations. Others have forged a new identity for themselves in hopes of effacing an ignominious past…

The right to rations is a real bargaining chip. The family book can be rented or used as collateral for a loan. The rates are exorbitant, as much as 20 percent a month. If the amount borrowed is low, the rations picked up by the lender will be used for interest; otherwise, often bigger sums are required to repurchase the book. Some borrow to make an attempt to get to Thailand or to pay go-betweens who are supposed to facilitate approval of overseas departure applications. In either case, failure is the general rule and the borrower loses his family book. The camp is the mirror of a society restructured on different bases. The strong exploit the weak. Those who want to get out of it, to start a small video or vegetable selling business, are often under obligation to deal with the Cambodian administration of the camp and the Thai police. And the place boasts of a courthouse and even a jail. Um-hum, a jail within a jail.

I learn of the existence of a red light district in Rythissen, referred to as Section 7. A trick goes for half a dollar, and is sometimes shared amongst several customers, spreading AIDS, which is already wreaking havoc in Thailand.

Impressed with the well laid out camp and the beaming smiles, one almost forgets that all of these families have been condemned to idleness for years. They have nothing to do but wait, continue to wait, and then wait some more. Escaping the Khmer Rouge horrors did not lead to a much better life. After fleeing westward with emaciated bodies, crossing seemingly endless minefields where many watched helplessly as those close to them died, then were pushed to flee again because of the incessant fighting, the Khmers feel they have been cursed. As if beaten to an excess, many just fell to the ground without the strength to pick themselves up. Since the 1970 civil war, the majority have experienced nothing but one violent event after another, a stream of disasters and horror stories. Their daily fare is war.

How can one not see in this, as the Khmers often do, the mark of bad karma, the fate of a people that is paying for sins committed in another life and that makes any happiness impossible, while life smiles on others?

I'd psyched myself up, but my protective dike crumbles and the millions of cubic meters of observations on the woes of the Khmer people are going to swallow me up. It's not a gentle shower; it's a tidal wave. I'm positive by nature and refuse to let things get me down, and despite this information overload, I ask to find out more. Even though tempted to go off and have a quiet beer, I want to get more out of this initiation. I want to understand.

The children offer to take me around the camp. Okay! At 2:30 p.m. I'm at the *Médecins Sans Frontières* hospital, at the corner of two main streets. I get there early, but the children are already waiting for me. The Swiss are renowned for their punctuality, but the Khmers are punctual too; they often arrive early for appointments.

There are five of them. The brother and sister are joined by three neighbor children that were seen in the morning. Communication is a matter of smiles, undecipherable attempts at the spoken word, and a great deal of laughter. We barely understand each another, but we walk and we smile. We sometimes come across a water truck or bicycle taxi. If it's a motorbike, it'll belong to a DPPU officer or someone from the Khmer People's National Liberation Front (KPNLF). The camp's infrastructure is functional. Although invariably of bamboo, the administrative buildings—hospitals, schools, sub-camp offices, health services, international organizations—are conspicuously located on the main streets.

International organizations distinguish themselves with eye-catching logos or flags bearing their emblems on their vehicles and buildings. Both sides of the street have wide ditches to collect the torrents of rainwater that flow into a large water reservoir. Next to it is the famous fire tower, from whose top the horizon can be scanned to spot fires before they burn out of control. A few gardeners are growing rows of lettuce or water morning glory. We go through a small local market under plastic tarpaulins where women sit crouched selling fruit and vegetables.

A Cambodian man notices my communication problems and asks:
"You American?"
"No, French."
"Ah! Are you working in Site II?"
"No, just visiting."

Proud of being able to converse with a foreigner, he follows me. He relates that at the big Thai market, one can find vegetables, fruit, kitchen utensils, and the like brought in directly by Thai merchants. The little market, like others sprinkled throughout the camp, is Khmer. Small-scale merchants retail produce that they buy at the Thai market.

Yes, one can find small packets of shampoo, cut up fruit, tiny bags of palm oil, dwarf sachets of salt, MSG, pepper, or sugar, such as I'd never seen before. Another way of measuring the poverty level. People buy their staples in 20- or 30-gram amounts in a country where the cost of living is already very low. It's the thing about poor countries. When a daily staple is sold in single doses, it's obvious that the buyers have absolutely no cash flow. There's nothing else one can do but pay an excessively high price for everything! Where money is in short supply, prices go up!

Clearly, this camp tour has given me a different view of the world. I was the visitor, but here I'm being visited! I want to stay, to go into other sections, see a hospital, visit schools… But this is Saturday and it's already 4:30 p.m. And the camp is only open to outsiders from 7:30 a.m. to 5 p.m. Every day it's the same thing for these thousands of refugees. At 5 o'clock the humanitarian vehicles go back to Ta Phraya or Aranyaprathet, taking with them the barangs that help them, give them health care, and bring them a little comfort. When they leave, night falls and with it fear returns. Fear of bandits, fear of Khmer or Thai soldiers, fear of a return to violence.

After extending my warm thanks and promising to come back soon, I leave my sponsored child and his friends. I was happy to have been able to meet him, to put a face on a file, even though I feel that I wasn't referred to people who really need my help. I go back to COERR where Gilles is waiting. He watches me arrive with his good-humored broad smile. The dust, the heat, and the smell of the camp have changed me. Is the young managerial level employee who got off at Ta Phraya this morning the same person? Did he vanish in just one day? The external change is nothing compared to the change going on inside.

I'm exhausted and would like nothing more than a good shower and a cold beer. So many images, so many feelings swirling about. A tempest in my brain. That's the best way I can describe it.

We cover the 22 km between Site II and Ta Phraya without me realizing it. Before entering the blue house, I buy some cold beers at Sri Sovann's, a Thai neighbor and primary school teacher who provides a great service for foreigners.

Gilles lets me shower first and I happily accept. The water in the tank is a delight. The earthy color that put me off the night before looks familiar. I use the plastic bowl and dump large amounts of water over my torso. The temperature difference is surprising at first but one quickly gets used to the dousing of cool water. The nylon brush feels abrasive and almost burns, but it's not overkill when it comes to scouring off the caked on red clay. I dry myself off with a blue and white checkered cotton Khmer *krama* and put on clean clothes. The Spartan conditions of this house, full of dust and cobwebs, now seem to be a great privilege in contrast to the miserable conditions of the Khmers just 22 km away. Here, we have electricity and, although turning on the big fluorescent light draws in a host of insects, I appreciate its luxury.

Gilles asks me how my day went and goes on to tell me about how he got started, his projects, anecdotes about his students, about Thavy, and talks about his family... I look at him impressed, spellbound. More so than yesterday, I appreciate his courageous choice, but also sense the tremendous satisfaction he's getting out of it. Going to the camp and each day, observing the mix of suffering and joy, hopelessness and a zest for living, the abject poverty and merriment of the refugees. I understand why he's tempted to stay on. We talk at length about his commitment. What strikes me is his belief that he has received more than he has given.

I don't believe it! A few hours after my visit to the camp and here I am already imagining what I could do. Is it the concern for others' interests that my mother imbued in me or the entrepreneurial spirit that is already trying to come up with solutions to the problems of these refugees? The poverty of the people and the smiles of all the children give rise to an irresistible desire to act. A desire to give them a chance, the chance we had of choosing our life.

But how?

I reminisce on my hours of discussion with Alain Le Guay and Véronique Tauvel, close friends from business college. They had shared a few weeks in the life of Tibetan refugees from Dharamsala. We spent many a dinner talking about what could, should, or should not be done, about human rights, development aid, in a word the great problems of this tottering world. For the most part, it was just parlor chat. At the time I had never experienced any physical or moral suffering and I couldn't really understand what they were on about. I jokingly compared their attitude to that of a butterfly fluttering from flower to flower and seeing an anthill being helplessly drowned out of existence by a flood of water. Véronique was wavering between a career as a financial controller or going into humanitarian work. As bright as she was efficacious, she had what it took to be a moneymaking link at the corporate level or a worker bee in an NGO. It was then that we decided to sponsor a Tibetan youth through an association. That was the extent of our hands-on participation.

What Gilles is saying is realistic. He's doing his little bit on the ground, not remaking the world, through things commensurate with his ability. He's teaching math to young Cambodian would-be engineers. That's all. True, his instruction goes over their heads at times and he knows it. But even if this knowledge isn't going to be of immediate use to them, it's nevertheless an intellectual exercise, an opening up to the world, an escape from the monotony of the camp, the promise of a better future. Many of them have been there since 1984 and, before Site II, they lived in other camps. They have known nothing but war, the fear of landmines, the absence of future.

In Site II camp, a person could wonder if the moral deprivation—a lack of hope and future—is not worse than the material poverty. If so, the educational role of foreign volunteers is vital. Site II is a giant learning camp. The inmates aren't permitted to work. The only activities allowed are educational. True, there are handicraft projects, but very few and often of poor quality. When on tour there today, I visited the Dangrek Technical School, but I heard about many other schools or institutes—a policy and management institute, a nursing school, a school to train medical assistants, a law and economics university, English, French,

Japanese, and Thai language classes, a baking school...

The UN and many American or pro-American foundations are investing plenty of money in education on Site II in order to qualify elite students for government posts in Phnom Penh. Political motivations lurk behind the good will and the humanitarian ante. Site II has already merged several other camps so that as many displaced persons as possible come under the control of nationalists, more aligned with the American government.

In animated conversation, we forget about the advancing night and with it our need for sleep. I was baptized and brought up a Catholic, but am not very regular at Mass or other religious events. Nevertheless, I accept Gilles' proposal to go to Sunday morning Mass on Site II, to be said by a very interesting man.

On Sunday, August 5, 1990, after sleeping in till 8, we leave for Site II. We pick passes out of those available. I again change identity. I'm becoming a Khmer. The highway seems deserted. The administrative and humanitarian vehicles are off duty and supply trucks are rare. This morning, it's mostly the French who are heading up to the camp to meet Khmer friends, picnic at the edge of the reservoir, or simply attend Father Pierre's Mass. Pierre Ceyrac is a Jesuit. After doing several years in India, he's looking after the Vietnamese community, traditionally more Catholic than the Cambodians.

If a person didn't know Father Pierre and his kind nature, you'd think he was a Santa Claus in front of whom the faithful bow or receive money. Here and there he's passing out envelopes or small packages. Surprised by so many transactions, Gilles tells me that Father Pierre is a go-between for many refugees who receive money from overseas. Prohibited from leaving the camp, refugees who get a check from abroad have to give it to a *barang* who will get it cashed by a Chinese money changer. Based on a procedure of dubious financial merit, an electrical goods shop in Aranyaprathet cashes checks—for a commission, of course. This system based on trust works very well. However, should the check bounce, the foreigner who handled the transaction has to return the money unrightfully paid, and he sometimes has a problem getting it back.

Father Pierre, known for the somewhat blind trust that he bestows, is often asked to cash checks. So each time he comes, he brings the amounts he was able to get for this one or that one. He adds little things that lack. A good word for one, comfort for all.

Although I don't share his way of giving to those who stretch out their hand, I must admit that he's quite unusual. As such, he's the happiness postman, so to speak, delivering in large measure to those around him—money and gifts, yes, but also joy and serenity. He is often moved to the point of tears, but radiates an inner joy.

Every Sunday, Father Pierre celebrates Mass in a small section of the camp occupied by the Vietnamese. In an uncomfortable position due to Khmer racism against them, the Vietnamese on Site II are as if "punished" here. After refusing to be transferred to another camp, thinking it was a maneuver to send them back to Vietnam, they've seen their peers go abroad while they been languishing here for years. Confined to a small section of Site II, they scrape by amid a population largely hostile to them.

Fervent Catholics, they built a bamboo church crammed with religious knick-knacks, a veritable monument of poor taste. But they put a choir together that transforms the nasal twang of the Vietnamese language into lovely singing.

I walk out of the church deeply moved by the fervor of this small, close-knit Vietnamese community united around Father Pierre. There I meet Olivia, a tall beanpole not unlike Fifi Brindacier, perpetually assailed by a horde of children. Each of her words is like a theatrical exercise. Her expressions and sweeping gestures convey bubbling optimism. She teaches French for a small organization, SIPAR (*Soutien à l'Initiative pour l'Aide aux Réfugiés*).

Mass over, I pick up my things at Ta Phraya. I catch a ride in a car going to Aranyaprathet for a few errands and some photocopying, then board the bus back to Bangkok.

On Monday morning, I wake up in my Sala Deng apartment, put on my suit and tie, and head for the 23rd floor of my glass tower. Just like I did three days earlier. But I feel that something isn't right! That weekend, more than I could have imagined, has totally changed my outlook. Suddenly the hotel figures, the reports, the financial data, all has a different meaning, that of a meaningless duty. Conversations with my colleagues, especially the newly arrived French deputy chairmen, sound empty. I've exited their world. Their petty whims, their expense account reimbursements, their spats with the ever so kind Thai employees, and their whininess annoy me. I no longer share their convictions.

However, my relationship with my closest coworkers grows stronger. The girl from Myanmar who experienced many trials, understands and encourages me. I now discover the true face of my Pakistani colleague, a grouchy, uncommunicative accountant. He had carefully hidden his big heart. He tells me about the long years he spent helping a bunch of Pakistani kids with their studies. My boss' assistant then comes forward with an unexpected display of generosity. She was one of the first to offer me financial assistance for the refugee children. I feel as if I'm casting off the moorings of my expatriate comfort.

For several weeks now, I have spent Thursday mornings at Lard'hyao Prison visiting French prisoners, most often sentenced for trafficking or being in possession of drugs. My role is not to feel sorry for them—they are not necessarily worthy of such—but to help them to be hopeful by keeping in touch with the outside world. I also get a lot out of these visits. This new look at people does something for me. I don't know what I'm going to do yet, but I do know that my life is going to take a new direction. A complete break?

Two weeks later and I'm back at Site II for the weekend to learn more about the camps, the refugees, and volunteering. To listen and understand, then act. I take advantage of the opportunity to bring French products available in Bangkok like wine, Ricard, and sausage for French volunteers at Ta Phraya.

Welcomed with open arms, I make acquaintance with volunteers that I'd met before, nearly all of them teachers of math, chemistry, economics… Graduates of engineering or of business schools like me, they've come to teach for a year. Many have a background similar to mine: good family, raised Catholic, decent education… And off they are to give a year of their lives for others. Easy under such conditions, some say. Maybe so… But you've to get out and do it.

I'm impressed. I wonder if I'll one day find the courage to do the same. No, they aren't out to save the world, but are doing something concrete to make it better. As usual, I change identity to get into the camp. One day blond, another brown, with a round nose or a flat nose, all kinds of eye shapes. Stacking my different ID cards gives me a Picasso head.

I rush over to my sponsored boy's family with a few clothes from Bangkok for each one, as promised. But I'm still ill at ease. I feel that I'm doing the wrong thing, that I'm not helping the right people. Volunteers tell me that the program is mainly supporting people close to the nationalist party. It's obvious that they are not the worst off. Such favoritism upsets me.

I go back to the technical school, then visit an MSF hospital, and question the volunteers. At the big Thai market, I find a bunch of kids begging or eating spoiled fruit. Some are picking up old plastic bags that they wash and sell back to the merchants for reuse. The muddy, stinking alleyways of the market stifle any urge to buy food there.

I'm dumbfounded. How can it be, in a refugee camp where rations are supplied free of charge by the United Nations, where every individual is accounted for, that these kids are doing the rounds of the garbage cans to feed themselves? My dismay grows even more when I see trucks loaded with rice come in, but also leave loaded with rice. I'm told that this surplus is because of fake family books. The rations are resold by the administration and the proceeds used to buy ammunition and food for the guerilla forces.

How were these refugee children reduced to begging? Is poverty bottomless?

Many families are so poor and helpless that they throw their children out on the street, especially the children of a different mate. The new spouse dismisses the children of the first marriage… until it comes time to register them in the family book and qualify for rations. So it is that many kids loiter about, beg, or pick through waste at the market… But in a refugee camp, how much can garbage be worth? Do they go to school? They're not wearing the mandatory uniform. They wander about by day and sleep in the market stalls by night.

These little beggars are naturally inclined to petty theft. If caught by the Khmer police, they're arrested and held at the police station at the Thai market until a relative comes to get them.

This morning there are a few of them at the police station, wearing just a dirty pair of shorts, their legs pockmarked; they're terribly skinny. But what upsets me the most is their young age. I would say they aren't more than seven. Excessive crying has left a lighter colored furrow down their grimy cheeks. They have a vacant stare; their noses are runny. Behind bamboo bars like wounded animals, they resignedly wait for someone to come and fetch them.

And if no one comes? Most often, word gets through from a neighbor or another child and one of the parents or a relative comes. After being lectured, he or she takes out his or her wrath and shame on the child. Some of them are not picked up. After two or three days caged up in the sight of all, they are shipped to an orphanage. The situation appalls me. I can't stand the idea of a child being subjected to such an ordeal and I want to understand.

Out of curiosity, I ask to see one of these centers. Some large orphanages come under the political administration of the camp. Often overseen by ex-soldiers, they house from 100 to 150 boys. Discipline is strict. Since the war ended, they are given schooling. Previously, they would have been taught to hold a gun and used as reinforcements in the resistance ranks. As for orphan girls, they are generally taken in by families as servants.

The Ampil orphanage, like the administration buildings, is of bamboo and thatch construction. Inside it has a large dormitory, the beds in neat alignment. Above each one is a small shelf held up by wire. A few notebooks, a folded mosquito net, and a salvaged cardboard box to stuff a few clothes in. That's all. Boys aged from 8 to 16 come and go, seemingly unoccupied. They greet me and exchange a few words in English with me. There are no supervisory staff to be seen. A small group is playing sey, a shuttlecock hit with the back of the foot and that must not be allowed to touch the ground.

I'm impressed with the size of this enormous dormitory. I meet the director. He complains about the lack of resources and staff, the shortage of food for the children and teenagers who need nearly 700 grams of rice a day to satisfy their appetites. Seven hundred grams. In Europe we reckon 90 grams per person per meal! But, of course, the meal is almost exclusively rice. And the Khmer word for eat is "eat rice." The young people do the cooking. Very little meat, a few vegetables, and giant pots of rice.

I leave with a feeling of sadness and outrage. What I just saw is more like a farm than an orphanage. Despite the never-ending smiles that, for Cambodians, often express awkwardness, the scene is pervasively dim and grim.

What can be done? How should one react or, better, act?

When I get back to Bangkok, I decide to talk it up all around me, to make my expatriate colleagues aware. I'll look for funds to get something done. What? I still don't know, but the lack of resources will not be an excuse.

Camp volunteers asked me to pick up a volunteer who is coming to teach at the Dangrek school for a year. As soon as he arrives, I commission him to put together a project for the market children. Not a long-term project, but an operation around Christmas, for instance, which is a good time to raise awareness throughout my network of relations. Fortunately I have a large, caring extended family. Might as well tap into them. No qualms, I'm not doing it for me.

In no time word comes back from the camps. After École Polytechnique which left him with a military demeanor, Alain Goyé was recruited to come and teach math at the Dangrek school on Site II. With almost transparent white skin, a deep, almost mystical look, he sometimes breaks out of his deadpan seriousness with a hesitant thought, that a quirk of the lips lets us know is meant to be a joke. Alain Goyé, who took over from Gilles, got in touch with a Cambodian man in charge of youth. In response to my proposal, Ouk Sinath asked Alain to provide school uniforms for 200 to 300 young orphans.

I like this idea. In these countries of Asia where every pupil wears blue shorts or a blue skirt and a white top, the uniform gives a measure of dignity to all of them. I like the word; I like the concept, especially for children who have nothing. Such as those children at the market or held behind bamboo bars. I can just imagine how happy they would be to put on a uniform just like the others. It occurred to me that it would be more logical to buy the cloth and have the uniforms made in the camp. It would be something for the refugees to do and get more people involved.

This way, the budget for 200 uniforms could be stretched to allow 330 to be produced. But where will the money come from? I had been in the position of the one giving, and here I am on the other side of the wicket... the one asking. You don't become a beggar, even if it is to help others.

Initially, I get my peers excited about this aid project for refugees. Others just find it amusing. Whenever we go to a restaurant to eat and it comes to splitting the bill, I always ask for it to be rounded up and I pick up the difference for the uniforms. Every time we go out, I bum some money off this one or that one. Sometimes it goes from amusement to annoyance. Even though some have trouble getting out of their comfort zone, their leisure activities, their weekend of golf or diving—and I knew I was upsetting them—I was overall quite well received by the French expatriates. Many support and encourage me.

I'm a member of a little theater company. Most of the members, teachers at the *Alliance française* or French *Lycée*, tell me to put on a show. Since I look a little like Bozo with my bushy hair (which I had at the time!) and large-rimmed red glasses, they suggest I do a clown routine with another Frenchman. A costume of colored cloth swatches, like the one my father made me for a birthday, would do the rest.

A few weeks later, we put on the show for over 200 French and Thai children. It's our first fundraising show. And it works. We laughed a lot and got people to laugh ("raising fun for raising funds").

The budget is in the bag and "Operation School Uniforms" becomes a reality. Preparation work started on Site II and distribution is set for December 22.

That day I'm out at Site II. Alain Goyé and others come with me. Cambodians in charge of the Dangkrek sub-camp make the operation official. Three hundred and thirty orphans donned in rags are on hand, nicely lined up, boys on one side, girls on the other. The ceremony gradually gets underway, orchestrated by Sinath. He's of average height, his face is a little haggard, but he's always smiling. Ouk Sinath seems only to see solutions for all the problems he's faced with. His black eyes sparkle with intelligence and he's of infectious good humor. Being at ease with foreigners and his communication skills help overcome his so-so English. Wanting to honor and thank us foreigners, he's pulled out all the stops. Everything is oiled to perfection. Too organized, too official for me, but it's no doubt important for the children.

I'm handed a list and I attempt to read the names that I have difficulty to pronounce despite their approximate phonetic representation. Everyone bursts out laughing. The children whose names are called don't understand. I turn the mike over to Sinath and, as the children come forward, we extend to them with two hands their new clothes. Even though the gift of this little uniform fills the kids with an ineffable joy, I'm uncomfortable with this cliché of the White donor. Taking advantage of a talent acquired from my neighbor's hens, with each handout, I squawk like a chicken before and after laying an egg, which dispels any remaining solemnity from the ceremony.

The children, proud of their uniforms, rush to try them on. Some modestly keep their clothes on and just wear the uniform over top. No doubt about it, happiness prevails, unstrained, and it's a great reward. The patchwork of faded colors and dirt is transformed into a mass of white and blue graced with broad smiles. So it is, with next to nothing, a few meters of well-hemmed cloth, a ray of happiness is generated. I delve deep into my childhood memories to find an equivalent; I remember what it was like to get all kinds of goodies at the start of the new school year, but I couldn't remember such joy.

The ceremony ends with the serving of a generous snack of cake and cookies, bananas, pineapple, with, of course, drinks of flashy-colored fizzy Fanta that the kids go wild about.

All the way home, the smiles stay with me and, as soon as I get to Bangkok, I rush to the photo shop. Two hours later, the pictures are developed and I can share the joy of the children with all who contributed to the operation. I also come to realize that the help I was giving to my sponsored child was meaningless and I decide to discontinue my sponsorship. My financial support can be better invested.

Haunted by the image of those kids scouring garbage cans to get their lunch, locked behind bars in the uncertain expectation of a relative's arrival, my thoughts turn to what to do next. Could something more sustainable be done than this donation of uniforms?

In those last days of December 1990, my hesitation is considerable. At times I dream of leaving the suits and ties, the air-conditioned offices, the seaside weekends, the restaurant outings, the jaunts up north… In a word, move from the glass tower to barbed wire. At times I think about going back to Paris, to a successful career as a financial controller, to my friends, my studio apartment in Ménilmontant, my weekends in Noisy…

The alternative is constantly on my mind. On the one hand, I've the option of doing what Gilles and so many other admirable volunteers have done. On the other hand, the easy life of the expatriate in Bangkok. I think about the choice Véronique Tauvel made, starting her working career as an auditor. With awe-inspiring efficiency and speed, she threw herself into a corporate job and went on to blossom. I think about my late friend, Alain Le Guay, who left us right here in Thailand with a lot of embryonic projects on the roster. Here I am, two years later, at the same crossroads.

I'm obviously in the grips of a challenge. The easy thing would be to stay put with ACCOR. Leave, fine, but where to and for how long? The challenge or the career?

The question has been on my mind for some weeks now and I even contacted various humanitarian organizations. I met the people in charge of French NGO who think they might have a job that would suit me. Its main thrust is teaching French, and it's planning soon to start a project to train small entrepreneurs, right at Dangrek Technical School on Site II. The organization is looking for someone to teach accounting and management. My profile suits them because of my education and corporate experience, particularly in Asia. But my independent character has them worried. They hesitate.

Shortly thereafter, some family members come to visit me, one of my sisters, her husband, and my mother. We decide to tour Thailand, with a focus on the north. I share my misgivings with them. I'll never cease to amaze them. When I was in high school, they saw me, a callow youth, out in the market selling pizzas that I'd made the night before, hawking shirts and leather jackets, taking on the advertising department of a little Savoyard bimonthly, going into politics... And now I'm wavering about doing humanitarian work for a year. After financial controlling, a humanitarian multinational? Yes, but not just any humanitarian work. Training neglected youth and helping Cambodian officials to get a handle on things. I don't want to fall in the trap of expert help and pure charity. If I'm going to get involved, I want it to be serious and long-term.

My mother has no worry whatsoever that one of her sons is putting his career in jeopardy and lends her support to my project. An open, generous person, she gives my venture her full stamp of approval. ACCOR agrees to take me back after a sabbatical year. One night, after working late on an urgent file, the Asia branch boss comes into my office. He knows that I've been very different since my camp visits. He had always supported what I was doing with the French prisoners and let me have Thursday mornings off to go to Lard'hyao Prison. He's a businessman, but very much a human. I tell him of my hesitation and ask: "If I leave you to work for a year as a camp volunteer, would you give me my job back?" He replies with an immediate yes, but on the condition that I extend my contract so I can coach the auditors until the mid-March accounts closure.

A few days later, I make my decision. If I get the job with SIPAR, I'm off. As I'd hoped, I get a positive answer. But it's nuanced. Yes for a job with local status, but with a three-month trial period. No problem, see how it works out. I have a foot in the camp and I'll work the rest out later.

I right away start building castles in the air. Sinath, my Khmer partner in Operation Uniforms, would like to open an orphanage for these children. On Site II, I talk it over with him and meet other specialists in child welfare. What traps must be avoided? How should we go about it? It's very nice to want to help, but how can mistakes, issues of jurisdiction, and family tensions be avoided? I'm still knocked out by the memory of the boy I'd been linked with as sponsor being pushed into my arms so I could get him out of the camp. I also hear of a family that set up the adoption of their own daughter by an American family! I'm offended by this casual attitude of parents towards their child. Without being judgmental, I refuse to support it.

I lose no time in asking Sinath to put together plans to open a center of manageable size for 30 or so children, boys and girls. How many people would be needed to look after it? What levels of approval would be needed? Where could it be set up?

After the success of Operation Uniforms, my colleagues in Bangkok no longer see me as a dreamer but as a pragmatist. Based on the preliminary information, I can immediately start collecting funds to start up the center. Since my mother came and saw pictures of the December 22 operation, I know I can count on my family. With my mother pitching in, help is not long in coming, from my siblings, uncles and aunts, grandmothers, and cousins.

Leaving Bangkok is now just a matter of time.

To get around more freely, I plan to buy a motorbike. I didn't have a motorbike license, but fortunately, due to a translation error on my Thai license, it includes motorbikes! I just have to buy the beast… A friend of mine is leaving Bangkok soon. I'm prepared to buy his Honda 250XL off him provided that he brings it over to my place. I've never driven a motorbike and the chaos of Bangkok scares me. But it would be a good place to learn to drive. No mistakes allowed; drive your vehicle carefully. I've never had an accident.

The last few weeks at ACCOR drag by. The accounting department is taking on an auditing team that's having a hard time figuring out how a multinational works with hotels in several countries, offshore companies, and a regional office in Bangkok. I spend my time rehashing the same information. Moreover, ACCOR's Asia Middle-East facility was recently extended to the Pacific, including Australia. Several deputy chairmen were recruited, all provided with a big Volvo, a driver, a secretary, a rented house, school for the kids… They weigh down the office atmosphere. They're supposed to develop the zone, but end up adding to the material problems and sensitivities to be accommodated. For some, there's always something that isn't right.

The February 1991 coup d'état leaves them in a cold sweat. Yet, the Thai government was toppled without bloodshed. I learn of it when a panic-stricken friend phoned me from France. I go out. The streets are bustling. People are shopping in Silom as they do every Saturday… But French television has exhumed archive images of tanks in the streets!

I look forward to my departure with relief. It was nice to work with a small close-knit, easygoing team, but it's hard to put up with the new administrative lead weight. It's time to move on.

Meanwhile, I try to find a place to live at the border. Many organizations have headquartered in Aranyaprathet.

This border town has businesses and good restaurants, like that of the International Red Cross, and is easier to live in. International Red Cross people on long-term stays usually set up on in a good location a little bit out of the way, on a large piece of land. They opened a rather cheap restaurant featuring some Europeanized food. That may not seem very important, or even out of place, for a visiting guest, but it is important when you're far from home and working in makeshift conditions. And then there's always this charming train and the direct bus to Bangkok, linking the border to the Mo Chit Bus Station north of Bangkok, taking four and a half hours on a very acceptable highway.

There are many reasons for me to settle for Aranyaprathet. SIPAR's weekly meetings take place there and I'm told by the people in charge to stay away from Ta Phraya, even though their vehicles go through the village every day. I also know that I'll have to make frequent trips to Bangkok. I've left behind many friends, I'm a party animal, and I want to keep up my visits to the French prisoners.

But I just can't see myself living in Aran. To me, it's ridiculous to travel 72 km in the morning and again in the evening. With my motorbike, I wouldn't be a burden for vehicle planning and I would be independent. And it was in Ta Phraya that I had my first contact with the refugee camp volunteers. The atmosphere and spirit of self-sacrifice appeal to me. Ta Phraya is only 22 km from Site II and despite the fact that it is a small village with little to offer, it has a friendliness to it that I like.

Alain Goyé agrees to help me find a place to rent. I don't feel I'd like to live in the blue house as many volunteers do and where Gilles de Noblet used to live, nor in one of those dark, dingy houses. Life will be hard enough and I think that to keep my balance I'll need to get a good night's rest in an inviting place. And I have a motley collection of items, including furniture, figurines, a computer, a fax machine, etc. that I would like to gradually move over to make me feel at home and allow me to give my attention to fundraising. My idea is that while working as an accounting teacher, I'll continue to work on my project for abandoned children. Fortunately, a house is soon to be completed and I entrust the job of negotiating the best price to Alain. The owner is a friend of Sri Sovann, the delightful Thai teacher who is always with the volunteers. The owner is a little cash-strapped to finish the place, and I agree to advance several months' rent in exchange for a better price. Alain assures me that I'll not be disappointed.

March 14 is my last day with ACCOR. The audit is over and my mind has already left the office. Stéphane, who quickly became a close friend, took over my apartment. It works out well, because I can cut baggage down to the strict minimum. After all, it'll be my first trip by motorbike.

Healing Cambodia—One Child at a Time

AN UNSTOPPABLE SHARPSHOOTER
(March–December 1991)

On the morning of March 15, 1991, with one bag firmly secured to the luggage rack, another to the handlebars, my backpack slung over my shoulder, and police helmet on, I hit the road.

The maps show that the bus route is not the fastest. In fact, it is the most dangerous. The eastbound highway via Min Buri and Chachoengsao is less travelled by semi-trailers. In Asia, the pedestrian has to watch out for the bicycle, the bicycle for the motorbike, etc., up to the jumbo trucks. The strong look down on the weak, especially two wheelers. But what I thought was going to be a real expedition went without a hitch. In four hours, I reach Aranyaprathet, and just 40 minutes later I'm here in Ta Phraya. I follow the directions Alain gave me and go straight to the house.

A little off the beaten path and quite impressive, it faces out to a red clay dirt road. It's 10 m wide with a ground floor of breezeblock walls. The second floor is in wood and covered with a sheet-metal roof. Huge iron gates open up to a giant cement-floored storehouse. I cannot contain my surprise; I don't recall having rented rice storage space! Happily, to the rear left, a varnished wood staircase leads up to a commodious room with wide plank flooring. There are two adjoining bedrooms. A set of windows lights the room on three sides and gives depth to the floor. Alain did it right; I'm going to feel at home here. It's undoubtedly the nicest house in Ta Phraya and one of the rare ones with a telephone. When I decided to rent it, I asked Alain to have the telephone put in… It wasn't that easy in this village cut off from everything and right next to the ongoing border skirmishes, but the line is there. I can hook up my telephone-fax machine and keep in touch with friends in Bangkok, family in France, and especially Béatrice Le Guay, a regular pen pal. I treasure her support. I love her refined writing style and her detailed descriptions that enable me to vicariously experience each season in Europe. Here, there is a contrast between the rainy season and the dry season, but I really miss the distinct seasonal changes.

In the afternoon I get some mattresses and pieces of foam, order cushions, and replace the horrible fluorescent lights which attract insects with incandescent bulbs recessed in conical fish trap shades. The warmth of the fabrics, the subdued lighting, and arrangements of knickknacks bring the house to life.

The next morning, the SIPAR team comes to pick me up. There are ten of us including another Benoît. Word has it that a third Benoît will be arriving imminently. So to avoid confusion, I take the old nickname given me by my siblings: Bénito. And Thais have an easier time saying it. That name has stuck.

SIPAR is active in the border camps at the request of the Ministry of Foreign Affairs. Ms. Petitmangin, its chairwoman, had set up intake center and integration networks for Cambodians in France in the early 1980s. The French government quickly realized that it would be easier for refugees to fit in if they already knew some French and assigned Magali, who put SIPAR together, to put on classes of French as a second language in the camps. Her husband, former CEO of *Charbonnages de France*, came to assist her when he retired. He's not particularly qualified to teach French, but sensing he might have to go back, suggests that his wife set up a small business school project to train adults in the basics of marketing, accounting, law, and the like, and thus prepare them to start up their own business or company. That got me a job on a trial basis as an accounting teacher. I'm happy with that, even though with my two years of experience in Asia I find it a little unfair to be on probation. My maverick streak must scare them. So what! At least I'm able to get into the camps and work there.

I'm taken to the Dangrek Technical School where the SIPAR pilot class is already operating. Damien, the coordinator, introduces me to my future students. I then go to visit the building where most of SIPAR's French classes are held, as well as the Faculty of Law and Economics at Rythissen. I'll be going there to do some management auditing and cost accounting classes. During the lunch break, I rush over to see Sinath, in charge of Operation Uniforms, with whom I'm continuing to develop a project.

SIPAR has a temporary pass issued for me, which allows me to come and go freely. Back in Ta Phraya, I continue setting up the house where Alain is already living. We pick up the beds and tables ordered from Sister Ath's "Bambou Project." Sister Ath is a Catholic nun, a pleasant, go-getter type. She's the brains behind a bamboo furniture-making project that employs disadvantaged persons. Unlike so many other aid projects, Sister Ath's approach appeals to me because it's can-do and realistic. Just because workers are on social assistance doesn't mean that quality can be sidestepped. The result is that Sister Ath's products are in high demand and the waiting list is getting longer. This gives the workers a sense of pride in accomplishment and dignity. Nearly 20 years later, I'm still using some of those items of furniture.

I also use this weekend to work with Sinath. With funds donated by my family, expatriates, and friends in Bangkok, including my going-away present, he was able to get construction going on our bamboo orphanage building. This welfare center is soon up and running, but the number of openings is purposely limited. A former landfill site was cleaned up and made available by the Dangrek camp administration, with which Sinath is well connected, and we are starting with a basic facility for 35 children, with a dormitory, a small classroom, a dining room, a kitchen, and a spacious recreation area.

In the following days, 1 finish getting settled in Ta Phraya. Neighbor seamstresses made large cushions with the silk I brought from Bangkok and the house has become a home. I then arrange a housewarming for the volunteer workers in Ta Phraya, from COERR, the public administration institute, and the incredible Marie-Claude, the spellbinding teacher for many Khmers on the border. Marie-Claude is sort of a lay nun, of plain figure, both discreet and obliging. An expert in both the Khmer language and culture, she's a real inspiration for the Ta Phraya volunteers.

On housewarming day, the criticisms fly: 'Why so many creature comforts? Why the telephone?' I get a laugh comparing their reaction to the way my Bangkok friends put it, 'How can you take being so deprived?' So be it. When you're all over the place during the week, you need something to come home to. The welcome mat is out for guests passing through to wet their whistle with a glass of beer or *Mekong* (a Thai rice alcohol). The telephone-fax machine that some felt was a needless whim comes in handy for visitors. I even have to charge a 20-percent fee to cover unpaid calls.

Very quickly, life in Ta Phraya starts falling into place. We leave for the camp about 7 in the morning and I come back home after class with the SIPAR teams. I teach a total of 20 hours a week in three different locations: Dangkrek Technical School, with the business school project, 25 students; the Rythissen law and economics faculty, 80 students, almost my age; and a hotel business class in O'Bok for older refugees, one of whom claims to have served General de Gaulle when he came to Cambodia.

In late March 1991 I get clearance to use my motorcycle for travel to and from the camp. This is a timesaver and gives me independence. My big bike, easily recognized by the DDPU, helps me enter and exit the camp and get around in it.

This loose schedule allows me to go back to Bangkok, collect funds, and meet up with friends. By stacking my classes early in the week, I succeed in getting away on Wednesday afternoon to catch the last bus for Bangkok. This way, I can drop in and visit "my" prisoners on Thursday morning. I go by ACCOR to do some writing for presentations about my project with Sinath.

The weekend, I take the overnight bus to Chiang Mai, buy a bunch of handicraft items and return in the opposite direction packed like a mule. While in transit in Bangkok, I pick up an old IBM computer donated by a friend and get back on the bus to Aran at Mo Chit, then hit Ta Phraya. As soon as I get back, I display the handmade items that might catch the eye of my visitors. The proceeds of the sales are turned over to our project.

The next day, after the morning classes, I pay a noontime visit to the building site. As the Khmer New Year approaches, the heat gradually intensifies and becomes absolutely stifling. A scorching wind stirs up dust, and one can cut the air with a knife. The earth is packed rock hard.

At one corner of our lot, above the canal, workers are drilling. Sinath, aware of the water rationing problem, fears that the children won't have enough. The well won't provide unlimited water, but a welcome extra.

During a break between classes, I go back to the construction site where the workers are plugging away. Sinath greets me, beaming; a little girl named Panha is nestled tightly against him.

Sinath got news of her this morning. A woman had transported this 10-year-old girl out of Cambodia to be resold in Thailand. An orphan, she'd been passed from hand to hand, from supposed aunts to presumed aunts, Khmer-style, where everyone is someone's cousin. Sinath had learned that smugglers were moving her through Site II on the way to a Bangkok prostitution ring. On the strength of his connections with administration, he's taking Panha temporarily to his place pending completion of the facility.

Pitch-black hair, slightly slanted eyes, wearing an orange flower print dress and a white blouse, she looks out of place amid the bamboo poles and workers. She won't let Sinath out of her site, but hounds him with questions. He introduces me to her, but since I can't speak Khmer, we just look at each other and laugh. Sinath translates. Panha, without a care in the world, babbles on and on, gives her opinion about everything, and chides the workers. Sinath laughingly says she comes from the line of Khmer women of strong character, the kind that boss their husbands, as the saying has it, "When the husband is commander, the wife is general!"

Indeed, Cambodia is a matriarchal society. The arrival of a baby girl is a more joyful event than that of a boy. Boys are good-for-nothings, Sinath adds, tongue in cheek. They spend their time at play instead of helping their mothers. When they get older, they're more often at the coffee shop than at home. When a girl gets married, she cares respectfully for her parents, affectionately for her husband, and tenderly for her children. The boy only looks out for himself. When he gets married, he leaves his family and joins his wife's family, where he's an extra pair of hands to help with the plowing. Rare is the abandoned girl who doesn't find a foster home. Panha's case is typical. When she was smaller, she did housework from family to family until becoming of age to attract the interest of prostitution rings.

Of age? Why, Panha is only ten! I choke up.

Over the next few days, she gradually lets go of Sinath and mixes with the orphanage staff: Mrs. Touch, the cook and her daughter, Mr. Ly and his wife, as well as Cham, Sinath's assistant in charge of screening and monitoring children that are not accommodated in our center.

During my free time, I think about the approach our orphanage project should take. The more I learn about Khmer customs and culture, the more it becomes obvious that an open, small-scale facility is the way to go. There's no problem taking children in, but you have to ask the right questions.

Should a child be admitted because the family asks us to?

Because a neighbor declares that he / she is an orphan?

Because the child is referred to us by an official?

Or should we be cautious of everything and everyone, and check out every piece of information?

With Panha in, Cham and Sinath give me a list of children that they would like to have enrolled in the Dangrek orphanage. I balk at the word 'orphanage.' Doesn't it lock children into a rigid status? Seal their fate? I think about this for a long time. The Khmers are calling it *Mondol Koma Kom Prier*, literally "center for children with no parents, deceased or not." Europeans have a more restricted notion; they apply the term to facilities for children whose parents have died. I feel the word smacks of pathos—defining children by what they don't have. I don't like the word. But I won't go against the Cambodians who are for it. Words have their meaning, but the main thing is the facility's operation and purpose.

I'm handed 20 or so applications. Sinath tells me that they are all orphans. I look them over one by one and try to grasp the background of each. Most of them are not clear-cut. The Cambodian personnel are happy with the information given by the children or neighbors and don't bother checking it out. Am I driven by my training as an auditor or simply by my curious nature? I quickly see the implausible nature of some of the accounts. The European volunteers have taught me to be wary and to always ask questions. But for Asians, particularly Cambodians, it isn't proper to ask questions. You always have to word the question so that it is open-ended and get back to the issue using a different approach to avoid any misunderstanding. A Cambodian, especially if he feels inferior—and many Cambodians feel that the white man is superior, no matter where he's from—generally responds in a way that the questioner expects him to. To keep him or her from losing face? Because the truth is unknown? What does it matter! The big thing is failing to have an answer. And if the person is caught saying something wrong, he will multiply unverifiable details and it becomes hopeless to ferret out the truth.

If I ask: "Is the mother actually dead?" the person won't contradict me. If my question is: "What evidence is there that the mother is dead?" I have a chance of finding out much more about the mother, maybe even where she is living. In the Cambodian mindset, an orphan is not a child who has lost father and mother... Rather, an orphan is a child who has no family support—driven out, a runaway, or simply in search of a better life.

As an experienced volunteer explains, you have to really have your wits about you to determine if a child needs rescuing "because if you're not careful, all the children in Cambodia could end up in orphanages. With or without a father or mother, Khmers feel that such a facility, especially if run by foreigners, is an educational opportunity not to be missed. And for the parents, it's one less mouth to feed."

I first take this as a joke, an empty comment made by an embittered person... But I learn the hard way that vigilance is the watchword. With this cynicism that helps us come out on top of challenging situations, we'll laugh about it later when asking orphans how their parents are doing... And it turns out that in some cases I've dealt with, when I've requested information to round out the woefully scanty background, great has been my astonishment to discover that sometimes the mother of a child had died before it was even born...

It takes a lot of time to crosscheck information, reword questions, and interview a child. There are no registers of civil status, no ID papers.

The only document that can be used to certify a family name and given name is the family book issued by the Khmer camp authorities in liaison with UNBRO. Realizing that Khmers can change their names several times, ostensibly to get away from bad spirits that are attacking them or just to cover one's tracks, whitewash an inglorious past or deeds, it is understandably difficult to get reliable information.

Though my assistants are great people, they lack training and are being pressured by friends, officials, and families to accept this child or that one. I realize that strict control is needed, no matter how much I trust my teams. So I'll give them some training in making up questionnaires and becoming investigative officers. Then, to avoid admitting children that could stay with their families, biological or not, another solution comes to mind—support the child right in his or her home. We will call those our outside cases. This will help keep the child from being abandoned and encourage foster families to take in children.

About mid-May 1991, what with errant children brought in by Sinath and his assistant at the Thai market, refugees from Cambodia brought in by the administration, and those picked up by the police, the center is almost full. Whenever I have a free moment, I review new cases and outside cases with Sinath. After being asked more detailed questions, some children accepted initially are returned to their families but with on-going support from us. After these basic training sessions, the teams realize how important the family structure is, that our facilities are just a stopgap and not a permanent answer even though they are small and manageable.

Although we have a few girls, most of our charges are boys from 9 to 13 years old. They typify the children loitering about the Thai market. Problem boys, petty thieves, always ready for a scrap, sometimes lazy, but not bad. Often mischievous, they immediately create an atmosphere of play and friendliness.

Vasa is a boy about 12. He was arrested by the police after stealing fruit from a merchant. He has a family but his alcoholic of a mother doesn't look after her children, especially those from her first marriage. She spends most of her time playing cards and her gambling debts forced her to pawn her family book. Vasa's father died and the new man in his mother's life rejects him, sending him out to beg, beating him if he doesn't bring enough in. So Vasa prefers the rough life of the market, the spoiled food, sleeping on bamboo racks, and the routine arrests. The police who turn him over to us say that Vasa has often been arrested and no one would come and get him.

When he first came, he was wearing nothing but a pair of shorts so dirty that you couldn't tell what color they were. No flip-flops or T-shirt. His skin was filthy black, covered with pockmarks, especially his legs, like most street children. At first fearful, he quickly gains self-confidence. The door is kept wide open and Sinath tells the boy that he's not in a jail but in a place where he will be able to grow up, keep clean, eat, play with his friends, and make up for his lost schooling. He's given a *krama*, a pair of thongs that fit, a pair of shorts, and a green and white striped T-shirt. Then he goes for a shower, dousing himself with cool water out of the earthenware jars. Proud as a peacock in his new cloths, he is astonishingly bright; his black eyes look everywhere. He observes everything and mixes with the boys kicking a soccer ball around before lunch. Actually, here he meets up with his earlier companions of misery, children wandering about the Thai market also brought in by the police. Winning their confidence, it's no time and Vasa is part of the gang.

When the old car axle used for a bell clangs out, the children rush to the dining room. Vasa takes a huge plate of rice and sits down at a bench. I observe him from a distance, ready to bet that he won't finish it. Not only does he gulp down his big serving of rice but goes and gets another one. The broken rice meal comes with a soup made of scraps of meat and vegetables, but is nevertheless quite substantial. When I eat at the center, I can hardly put down half a plateful. But for him and his friends, it's a real feast. It's a lot better than the regular fare of many Cambodian children. At siesta time in the large open dormitory, he goes straight to the bamboo bed that he was assigned.

My afternoon is divided between accounting classes at the technical school and a class at Rythissen. Before heading back to Ta Phraya, I make a quick stop at the center. Sinath tells me that Vasa has gone on and on asking about the *phou barang* (literally the French uncle).

Vasa is put in a remedial class. He is illiterate and can barely form some basic letters of the Khmer alphabet and pronounces them falteringly. Yet, education in the camps is the pride and joy of the Khmer administration and the UN. Totally free of charge, schools are everywhere. Only a few kids with no family slip through the net. He is seated beside a poor little tyke who likewise comes from the market. Not far away, Panha is zoned out. Vasa catches sight of me and waves, ready to bounce, but the teacher kindly tells him to calm down.

The class is barely over and our Vasa has already jumped on my Honda, nearly knocking it over. Happily, the kickstand is well placed. He impudently gestures his point that he will not get off until I take him for a ride. I have to give in, while the other kids laughingly call him Bénito's boy.

True, I'm not at ease with special bonds, but having favorites is unavoidable. They are often the most difficult. Of clownish nature, Vasa uses his sharp mind to grab attention. Ever ready for a game of soccer or badminton, he has problems staying with things or turning in his homework. But because he is clever and observant, he quickly catches up.

Panha, on the other hand, is rather slow, has a hard time to grasp what she's being taught. She used to have something to say about everything but now seems a little lackluster. As if, lost in the group, she is no longer unique.

Overall, the remedial classes are very successful and facilitate the children's integration into the local schools. We feel it's important that the children in our care mix with the others and that they not be stigmatized as orphans.

These sweltering hot days get the Cambodians worked up. The last marriages are celebrated before the rainy season. In Cambodia, marriages are most often arranged by the families and the date set by a seer, always in the dry season. It's a very costly affair and money is not easy to come by in the camp, because work is not allowed except for humanitarian organizations. That's because the Thais have a "deterrence policy," not wanting the Cambodians to take root on their soil.

As this dry season ends, several tragedies strike. Aside from mortar blasts often heard on the border, sometimes even at the edges of the camp, there are frequent attacks by bandits. One morning, we learn that Thavy's family suffered a grenade attack. She has relatives that emigrated to the United States and send back money, allowing her to own a small TV. In the evening, she uses an inverter, a car battery, and video cassettes from Cambodia, turning the house into a fee-paying movie theater. A speaker brays out distorted audio. Hong Kong movies with terrible dubbing in Cambodian, always featuring great effusion of blood, are the constant billing. Without much else to do, people crowd in.

This showy success arouses envy. The foreigners have it that Thavy's family is under military protection. Several people including a little girl died in the attack and other members of her family were wounded as a warning to get her to pay up.

A few weeks later while on our way back to Ta Phraya for the night, the UNBRO radio broadcasts that an entire neighborhood of Site II is afire. We try to go back to help but are refused entry. I have to wait until the next morning, pick up Cham on the way to the orphanage, and head in as soon as the camp opens. Despite the firefighters' intervention, hundreds of homes have gone up in smoke. Thousands of families have again lost everything. There is nothing but a desolate waste of blackened earth. Hundreds of refugees are poking through the ashes in hopes of finding anything. Children are picking up charred iron scraps for resale by weight; nails, wire, anything used to fasten the bamboo, are collected. Everything is marketable in the camp, even if for just a few pennies. Bottomless poverty.

The only things left are the cement crocks, a testimony to the density of the houses. One jammed next to the other, they caught fire in one fell swoop. The dry season and lack of water compounded the firefighting efforts. Many people are crying.

A mother stands frozen, staring into empty space, one child bawling in her hands, another clutching her leg. She has no strength left to cry. She lost everything and was unable to save her precious family book. Her identity lost, she's no longer entitled to rations.

The UNBRO is an old hand at emergency situations and has blue plastic tarpaulins distributed in no time. Bamboo is ordered, but it'll take several weeks. Fortunately, the rains have not yet started. Given the extent of the disaster, UNBRO presses the camp authorities to issue new family books. Some take advantage of the opportunity to pick up an extra issue—for financial consideration. Even in poverty, the strong get stronger, while the weak, annihilated, bow their heads in silence. Where are the bonds of Asian solidarity I've heard so much about? The more I observe, the more I see a dog-eat-dog existence in this society. As for peace, still no hope on the horizon.

The center is working and so are my classes. They're not getting any smaller and I enjoy the esteem of my students. After teaching in French with a translator, as requested by SIPAR, I elect for English to satisfy the students, also with a translator. Most of the students speak some English and aren't very keen on instruction in French.

That puts me at loggerheads with SIPAR. My subject is management, not French, and I feel that the important thing in my course is for me to be understood and for the students to enjoy it, so I teach in English. But we are being paid by the French Ministry of Foreign Affairs, so we are supposed to teach in French. The issue is a thorny one. Are we there to give them the help they need or the help we think they will be better off with? I understand SIPAR's position and its commitment to promote French, but for management courses, wouldn't it be better to give greater attention to comprehension, especially where young motivated adults are concerned, among whom one can sense the early vibes of nationalism?

The classes in Rythissen are particularly animated, even noisy. It's hard to keep order in the classroom. The 80 students, all about my age, are male in an overwhelming majority (only three female). They've moved quickly from being passive listeners to talkers, which I have encouraged. I welcome challenge in my classes to arouse their critical mind. Cambodian teaching is mostly lectures. The teacher pontificates to his class and the students daren't ask anything that might be interpreted as questioning his authority; if he makes a mistake, he mustn't be made to lose face.

I fully realize that my approach is specific to Europe, France in particular. My classes have therefore turned out differently. Given free rein, the students let go, sometimes too much. It could be dangerous if things get out of control. During one exercise, Savouth, a student with a bit of an attitude, catches me off guard. He claims that my model answer is wrong. The class erupts in laughter and the din gets louder. I have a hard time keeping it together. So I ask him to come up to the blackboard and go through the problem again. He then acknowledges his error: he had missed part of the statement. I crow in victory and the class gets back to an even keel. My authority is now firmly established and as for Savouth, he's been nicknamed Mr. Rooster!

After three months, my probationary period with SIPAR is ending and I'm to be inspected by the board of directors. I know that they're not very happy with my stand on a number of issues, notably my using English. And they find out when they visit that I've set up an orphanage. They aren't comfortable with one of their volunteers in the camp carrying out other activities not under their control. Yet Martin, our coordinator, and the other volunteers are familiar with the center.

I am ordered to put the orphanage under SIPAR's banner or hand in my resignation. I categorically refuse to do either. I want to continue teaching while remaining free to develop the orphanage. If I resign, my situation will be untenable. I need visas and passes to get into the camps. COERR then informs me that it might agree to sponsor me, but I want to keep teaching. I love my students and I love teaching. A real dilemma. I receive support from Father Ponchaud, who appreciates what I'm doing, as well as from the teams in the field. Magali Petitmangin, chairperson of SIPAR, may be strong-willed, but she's a lucid, big-hearted woman, and accepts the status quo. She even lets me go back to France to raise funds.

That's a relief to me, all the more so because with Sinath, faced with the scope of the street children problem, we have plans to open a second identical facility elsewhere, in O'Bok. Rather than expanding the existing facility, it seems more effective and humane to open a second structure of human dimension. As a child in a big family, I learned to live tribally, so to speak, but with a place for each member. I want to keep the children from becoming numbers and the staff, deprived of responsibility, from being reduced to simply performing a duty dictated by schedules.

Another orphanage had opened in Rythissen camp, not far from the bakery. But, overwhelmed with other responsibilities, the woman who founded it gave up. The Italian volunteer directing the center is short of funds and properly trained staff. The orphans in their orange and white plaid uniforms stand out too much. I fear stigmatization. They aren't like the others; they're the kids from the Rythissen Center...

Moreover, there's getting to be a hundred or so of them, an unmanageable number in my opinion. Observing how they run things, I become even more convinced of the principle of keeping the facilities small. Rather than expanding, it's better to swarm, open a new center far from the previous one so that the children don't form a human wall in the neighborhood. If one can't do it this way, it would be better to stop taking in children. Otherwise, those already in the center will suffer.

Opening the new center in O'Bok means funding. Donations from expatriates in Bangkok and the sale of sundry handicraft items are no longer enough. And my personal reserves are melting away.

I'm not keen on opening an independent organization because I'm not yet sure how long I'll be staying. There's already a plethora of NGOs, so why set up my own? I made a commitment for one year and, for now, I'm not looking any further. The future of the camps is uncertain; all attempts at reconciliation have failed and nothing points to the end of a conflict that has been raging for 21 years now. Indeed, the collapse of the Soviet bloc and the fall of the Berlin Wall resulted in the withdrawal of the Vietnamese in 1989, but, save for what are referred to here as "liberated zones" that remain out of its control, the Cambodian government has its hands on virtually the whole country. The international community is ratcheting up pressure to get the four factions to reach an agreement. One feels that the long-awaited peace is close but so far away. The refugees, who have been yearning for it for so long, now fear it like poison. They know that they will not be welcome in Khmer territory.

I plan to put in place a revolving fund system for the orphanage that will not depend on how long I'll be here. The food needs aren't covered under the UN ration scheme because we're not yet officially registered. In addition to salaries, albeit modest, and clothing, supplies of staples have to be paid for. Prices in Thailand are very affordable, but the budget keeps spiraling.

Many of my French friends are anxious to help. My family too. The people in my home village and parish of Apremont, nudged by my mother, are already gung ho. But sending money is complicated. Without a proper way to transfer money, collecting it in small sums shoots up the transfer fees.

The organization with which my friend Olivier Dauphin is working naturally comes to mind. When he got back from Thailand, he became the director of communications with Enfants du Mékong. Despite the bittersweet memory of my own sponsorship with them—of being set up to help a family that is better off than many others—this strikes me as a good channel to receive regular income. Enfants du Mékong has a rock-solid reputation and is well seasoned in this approach.

I meet Yves Meaudre, who I had already come across in Bangkok. We agree that Enfants du Mékong will manage my sponsorships for me and the donations that I generate. That rids me of one niggling problem. My Dangrek orphanage files are ready and I'll send him the rest this summer. I'm also mulling around an article on my project for its magazine, also named *Enfants du Mékong*.

Among all the friends that I get back together with, I am particularly happy to find Jean-Marie Le Guay. Since the death of his son Alain, he keeps abreast of what I'm doing and supports me like a father. He has me on his newspaper cutout mailing list. We look together at the terrible situation the refugees are in. He helps me to step back and analyze rather than judge. I go out for dinner with my business school alumni. Our interchange bears fruit. Excited about my projects, they unhesitatingly offer to help. All will become sponsors. But, as happy as I am to see them again, I feel out of place. I'm no longer in their world. A sharpshooter who is far from the front lines, I don't feel on top, but rather sidelined, on the margins, out in the boondocks. When I think of it, less than two years ago, I was the very one advising Véronique Tauvel to stay away from humanitarian work!

Each talks about his or her occupational status, the obsession of climbing the corporate ladder. Some are thinking about marriage, while others already have their first child in arms. I no longer share their concerns for accommodation, transportation, or consumer goods. I feel that the material problems, the race for comforts, beating the system, are ancillary. Despite the mild, late-June weather here in France, I do miss Asia, the camps, the children. I was happy to get back to my home country, but less than three weeks have gone by and I can't take it anymore. I look forward to my return to Ta Phraya, where my heart is aflame for a cause, one whose rationale shines brightly.

When I get back, the dry season is winding up. Early rains have brought a timid green to the countryside. The wet season will make it harder for me to get around, reining in my independence. The day after my arrival, at the crack of dawn, I go full speed to see the children before my classes. I've regularly received news about them. They're all there, in great shape, and welcome me jumping with joy. I do the same. They pinch me and poke me. I had forgotten that they were such teases. Sinath is happy to see me back. One or two new faces, one of which a boy whose hair is almost blond. What? It wouldn't have surprised me if some volunteer in the early days of the camp had something to do with that, but Sinath tells me that such discoloration is caused by a dietary deficiency.

My arms are full of packages. In Bangkok, I snapped up some bargain cloth in Yaowarat Chinatown to have clothes made for those who will play in the *chayam* (traditional drums) folklore group that Sinath plans to put together. I collected enough money to buy drums and a few other instruments. I hope that in addition to school activities, the children can get back to their roots through such things as traditional music and dance. Jean-Marie is with me all the way. We do a cost estimate and a dance teacher is recruited.

At the Dangrek school, my students display similar joy at my return. It's good to feel that one matters. While I was away, the curriculum featured other subjects, so I can easily pick up from where we left off.

At lunchtime, I go back to the orphanage to eat with the kids. It's so good to be back with them. I'd forgotten how much life and energy we get from the children in this little bamboo center. The cloud ceiling has sunk very low; the heat and humidity make the atmosphere oppressive; the smell of a thunderstorm pervades. Insects fly helter-skelter about us. The excitement of the children wells. They seem to smell a rainstorm like the kids in Savoy smell a snowstorm. I try to make it through my afternoon classes. The chalk wetted by my own perspiration hardly makes a mark on the blackboard. The students pant like marathon runners at the end of the race. Perspiration rolls down their arms and drips onto their notebook pages. They wipe one another off from time to time with the back of a *krama*. I let the unhappy group off early. Not a breath of air in the stifling heat. You could cut it with a knife. The heavy black rain-laden clouds bear down on us. The storm could burst forth at any time. I take care to wrap my course materials in a plastic bag, slide it into my satchel, and hit the road.

I go 10 km and the wind begins to lash in gusts, as if some mysterious force had awakened. What a relief when the early drops of rain spatter the grey pavement and turn it black. I love the dusty smell exhaled by the asphalt. It's like our thunderstorms back in Savoy. The first drops evaporate and form a layer of light mist for 20 cm or so above the road. Then, suddenly, it's a liquid sheet that descends. The delightful coolness of the first drops gives way to a sense of being enwrapped by the voluptuousness of the rain. There's no way out of it. The streaming water makes its way under my motorcycle rainwear. The plastic, no longer watertight, becomes waterlogged, clinging to my body, sticking to my torso. And the water gleefully infiltrates along my skin with no respect for my privates. I flatten out against the motorcycle. Passing vehicles send up a giddifying spray from the pooling water that slaps my body, giving me a bath from head to toe with my clothes on. I'm totally drenched; my shoes are overflowing. I'm shivering from the cold. I don't dare go too fast with my vision dually handicapped; I can see but 5 m ahead and I had to take off my steamed up glasses. Fortunately, there's hardly anyone else on the road. The last curves tell me Ta Phraya is near. I slow down, my teeth chattering. The main street is empty. Taking shelter under the eaves, the Thais are chattering away, but their words are drowned out by the racket of the rain on the corrugated tin roofs. They contemplate the rain while filling up large crocks varnished with arabesques of dragons. The poorer houses have large concrete tanks. Some Thais have gotten hold of some of those 1m3 galvanized containers that the UN had put in the camps. The rain is a blessing for all. Life is renewed. The life-sustaining rice paddies quench their thirst. As for poor little me, I'm coming down with a cold.

At home, with the gate open and the motorbike inside, I'm hit by the earsplitting din. The drops strike the tin and make it resonate like a drum in this large empty storeroom. I remove my sponge-like shoes and take off my dripping wet togs. The deluge broke its way into the kitchen and flooded the floor. The water in the bathroom storage tank feels warm. What a pleasure to slop the tepid water over me, as if the heat accumulated over the last few days was there to relax my taut muscles. My feet skid on the varnished wood floor and, upstairs, where the wall planks overlap horizontally, some of the celestial flow has infiltrated. The floor is soaked. Windows left open for air circulation invited the rain to feel at home and it stretched right out over the living room couch, not missing the silk cushions.

By the time I sop things up, wring out the wet items, and finish cleaning, the rain is over. As if drawn by a stage hand, the sheet of rain moves its show to the south. The clouds dissipate and the jeering rays of the sun project themselves over the still damp air. The heavy atmosphere has been washed; a fresh, very pure radiance succeeds it. In the golden light, there is a gleam, a sparkle, about everything: a piece of metal, a scrap of a tire, a shard from a broken crock… In front of the house, a farmer prods his water buffaloes home. Under the translucid rays, they acquire a mythical look. The road is steaming. The heat of the day evaporates the water, not giving it the leisure of seeping away. The gold flooring shines brightly. The varnished staircase railing shimmers at me. I blink one eye, then both of them. I have an immense sea in front of me!

In the calm of the evening, I finish up some files on the computer. I also draw up a budget for the O'Bok center, to be built of bamboo. A director has been found, a friend of Sinath, who's in charge of youth issues for the O'Bok camp, just the man we need. Although not as sensitive, he's better organized. He's gotten a pile of child applications ready for me. I'll wait for Cham to check them over to be sure that they meet our standards and that they can't be handled any other way. It'll be run just like the other center—35 children at most, under the care of Cambodian teams within the center and others accepted from outside families to prevent them from being abandoned.

The next day, back at Site II, the heat returns with a vengeance, as if yesterday's retreating storm had surrendered. My day goes by without a cloud in the sky. At 3 p.m., after my classes, I pour myself into the new center with Sinath. The air gradually gets heavier. The children are bubbling over with excitement. Half an hour later, violent gusts of wind begin lashing. The thatch walls sway, followed by the bamboo crosspieces. In the yard, dust clouds swirl. The children run to collect their laundry. From a very tender age, they are accustomed to looking after their own things. Everyone does his own washing.

Seconds after the first drops fall, the downpour spews over the camp. The wind drives the rain diagonally, sometimes even horizontally. The boys tear off their T-shirts and skip nimbly about under the deluge, at times skidding, doing pirouettes, or somersaulting in the mud; the girls, more reserved, their tops buttoned up, enjoy a shower under the sheets of water pouring down from the roof's edge. Soon, torrents of red water gush over the embankments, filling the side ditches. The camp turns into a giant paddling pool. Everywhere, the children splash around in the water. Where the road is badly rutted, veritable swimming pools form and they happily slather themselves all over with mud. Scrap blue oil containers from the U.S. are passed on from one person to the next; the adults use any available receptacle to capture water from the roofs and pour it into earthenware jars. Love you, rain!

The wet roads are slick, slowing down my trips to and from Ta Phraya. It rarely rains in the morning, but in late afternoon, all my clothes have to be wrung out. So I drop my trusty motorbike and don't object to a friendly car ride. The trips are loud and long with discussions on Cambodian politics and the international community's involvement.

In mid-July 1991, the now finished center in O'Bok opens to the children. Things are calm. More children are coming in as brothers and sisters, fewer seem to be from the big Thai market. They do better scholastically. We're situated some distance from the camp's center, almost giving the impression of being in the suburbs. Nevertheless, there are frequent interactions between the two centers, especially on jaunts to the reservoir or at soccer games when excitement runs high. Not being much of a soccer fan, I seldom join in.

In mid-August I find myself completely wiped out. Headache, muscle and joint pain all over. What's with me? Always with energy to spare, here I am drained, exhausted, wrecked, out of commission. My students think I'm joking. I'm diagnosed with dengue fever. Wiped out by a pesky striped mosquito. No medication, no treatment, just wait it out. Patiently. At home. Absolutely no blood-thinning aspirin. The big risk with dengue is internal bleeding, very frequent in children but rare in adults. Okay, provided that I haven't stayed too much of a child. Light is hard to bear; it hits my eyes like a ton of bricks if I can even open them. One week in bed, two weeks before I am back in shape, three weeks of forced vacation…

With the rainy season now in full swing, summer in France has opened the way for batches of volunteers to come and help for a few weeks. We are somewhat apprehensive of this cloudburst of humanitarian tourists.

The Cambodians are totally enthralled with their fast-track teaching, a novelty for them. Our year-long classes are dropped in favor of their courses that vary from a few days to a few weeks. This is compounded by the fact that the Cambodian officials, prone to whip up competition between educational organizations, require that diplomas be issued for these fly-by-night training sessions. And Cambodians love diplomas, even more than the education that they are supposed to symbolize. In a society where appearance is everything, the diploma confers more prestige than the actual knowledge acquired.

Although I share the reservations of the long-term volunteers about the onslaught of summer volunteers, I agree to have some of them stay with me. At the very least, they can help out with my rent. One pleasant evening in mid-August, Rémi and Isabelle Duhamel arrive with a cohort of other volunteers. A quick, very civil introduction ensues. I offer them a drink, but they're teetotalers; besides, they have an appointment elsewhere. Over the next few days, I see them discreetly leave their room in the morning and go out; they come back just as discreetly at night. They share leisure activities and meals with other one-off volunteers. That puts me off. No interchange, no discussions…

However, one evening when I'm sprawled out in the living room indulging in some Thai music, Rémi comes over for a visit. He's heard about what I'm doing and offers to shoot a short-length film about the center. He accepts a drink and we talk. His proposal comes just at the right time. When the next school year begins, I'm supposed to do a conference tour in France and a film would be most welcome. The next few days, Rémi scouts the orphanage with his little camera. He's there for the arrival of a COERR vehicle from which emerges a buxom Dutch woman followed by a Cambodian boy who struggles to get out of the car. It's Wanna.

Wearing a T-shirt with the word "Jesse" emblazoned across it that hangs down to his knees, Wanna is blind. He's about 10. We know nothing about him, except that he had been left at the Rythissen hospital. His arrival evokes curiosity, even wonderment. He always looks directly at the person speaking to him. One glassy eye seems to look for light; the other one is more closed.

Sometimes a blind adult has gone through the camp begging, led by a child. But neither the kids nor I have ever seen a blind child. Sinath asks him a few questions. He says that he had been looked after by a family who took him to the hospital and left him there. He doesn't know where he's from and has no name other than Wanna. While Sinath is questioning him, Wanna goes over to him, feels his face with both hands, grabs his hand, gives it a sniff, and lets it go. He then starts talking, his eyes raised and his little face lit up with a big smile. Sinath introduces me and he touches me as well, smells my hand, plucks on the hair on my arm, and lets out a laugh. In no time he is talking a mile a minute and if he isn't listened to attentively, he jumps from one foot to the other and waves his arms impatiently. He needs an audience.

He doesn't know where he's at and what he might stumble over, but is guided to the canteen for lunch. He dives right into the full plate of rice he was served and gets it all over himself. Sometimes he wipes his face with the back of the spoon to glean the errant rice grains stuck there. After lunch, he refuses to take a nap. He wants to discover everything, to play, to talk, talk on and on. The in-house rule is explained to him—at least 30 minutes. Cham shows him where he'll be staying: a bamboo bed, a mosquito net, a blanket, and a small pillow. He touches everything, traces the edges of the bed with his hand, strokes the lathe work. He takes ownership of his new space, but doesn't sleep. Ever restless, he moves his head from left to right, as if scrutinizing the place. Nap time over, his hands go to work, feeling out every nook and cranny. Of course, he bumps into a bed, a door, a partition. No problem. The children follow him around, mesmerized. Packed around him, they readily give way so as not to hinder his exploration.

A sudden inspiration has one of the boys putting on a blindfold and groping around. He bumps into everything. Gales of laughter. Everyone wants to find out what it's like to be blind and it ends up in a game of Blind Man's Buff. From now on Wanna is the center's mascot. Never left out of games, he is accepted and protected by his new friends. Whether it's a game of soccer or riding a bike, Wanna is fearless. He takes a kick, in hopes of touching the ball, but strikes nothing but air. He tries again and again, moving along, guided by the shouting, and finally kicks the ball, sending it way off. He jumps for joy and his triumph is met with applause. His face brightens and he congratulates himself. He wants to try everything, undeterred by falls, bumps, or bruises. The others love him for his intrepidity. I spend hours observing him, admiring the strength of character of this little man, his thirst to try, smell, and feel what he cannot see. I have unbounded awe for him. What a lesson about life!

Rémi and Isabelle, who witnessed Wanna's beginnings at the orphanage, are deeply moved by his courage. They become his sponsors. Wanna is the key to the involvement of Rémi and Isabelle, who turn out to be my most consistent supporters in France.

A few days later the long-awaited news arrives: UNBRO and the Khmer administration are giving us ration rights. Our food budget can now be partially reinvested. Even though the quantities are not sufficient for fast-growing children, the rice, vegetables, and other canned food from the United Nations will be welcome. The savings will enable us to redouble our efforts to teach Khmer music with the purchase of more *chayams* and dance costumes.

Wanna learns to play the *chapey*, a traditional Khmer instrument. This two-stringed lute is often played by itinerant blind musicians, alternating with vocal improvisations. Wanna soon wins the admiration of all. Our child musicians do so well that they put on a few shows outside of the center. The loud applause of their peers makes them very proud. But the most impressive outcome is the sudden confidence acquired by the children; they gain a self-assurance that sets them up for life. That's really something for children marked by unspoken traumas, who are withdrawn and experiencing learning difficulties. Panha, for instance, after something clicked, just started learning overnight. For many, the results are spectacular.

I then have a feeling that a cultural activity such as traditional music would have a decisive impact on the psyche of the children. Our impassioned exchanges on this topic with Jean-Marie now take on added meaning. There are no psychologists in Cambodia. In Khmer culture, you don't talk about yourself or your problems. In such a context, what is available to help a child overcome the trauma he has experienced? Part of the answer lies in taking up an artistic activity. The cultural dimension therefore becomes a key ingredient in all of our projects.

When the cultural activity is linked to tradition, this gives the child identity and dignity; it makes him feel that he fits in. With a newfound identity, the child's dignity is restored and he becomes capable of fitting in with his own country. These three values will form the cornerstone of our activities.

Very quickly, I have to give attention to funding diversification. On my way to France, I make a stopover in Bangkok and go to the French school to talk to the pupils about our two centers. The thrust is two-pronged: open the minds and hearts of the somewhat overprotected French children, and generate funds. I receive a warm welcome from both teachers and parents. It is even decided to go further and a youth exchange is scheduled for the end of the school year. It's important that my conferences not only raise money, but also get my audience to reflect on humanitarian work and its purpose. In the camps, an act of generosity can miss its mark and an initiative that is not controlled can feed corruption. There is no end to stories of dual sponsorships. Medication may be immediately resold, clothing kept by the people in charge, operating expenses bloated; the abuses are many. Humanitarian work is not sustainable where there is laxity. At the modest level at which I am working, I think it is possible to change the minds of those who hear my conferences.

It was while on a tour in France that I learned that peace agreements had been signed.

Expectancy had dragged on for over 20 years. On October 23, 1991, in Paris, the four factions agree to a ceasefire and sign a peace agreement: Messrs. Hun Sen, Heng Samrin, and Chea Sim representing the government of Cambodia (installed by the Vietnamese); HRH Prince Norodom Ranarridh, son of Prince Sihanouk, representing FUNCINPEC (the royalist party); HE Son Sann, president of the KPNLF (the nationalist party), a carryover of the former Marshal Lon Nol government; and finally Mr. Khieu Samphan, representing the Khmer Rouge.

A powerful wind of hope is blowing over Cambodia and in the camps. Emergency care situations can now give way to a reconstruction process. A humongous peace-keeping operation is put in place, including the UN peacekeeping corps, or Blue Helmets, and deployed throughout the territory, to ensure its success by negotiating the disarmament of the factions. Free elections will lead to the appointment of a new government. And this operation will, of course, include the massive repatriation of refugees.

Where will the refugees be relocated? How? Will they go back to their land? Will they be allowed freedom of movement? After the jubilation of the peace agreements, such questions cause the refugees to wonder nervously. Departments specializing in mental health see their consultations double.

An insider gives me some details on the otherwise very nebulous operation. Nothing is known about the nature and scope of the resources. It is known that elections are planned for May 1993 and that some 375,000 displaced persons herded into camps at the border must be repatriated first. But how? Rumors run rampant, with little means of verifying any of them. Everyone claims to have privileged information.

UN-run committees are set up to index the problems and possible solutions. As the person in charge of two orphanages, I'm allowed to attend these steering committee meetings. Although pleased with being viewed as the man in charge of an organization and having my two facilities fully recognized, I seethe with impatience in these unproductive meetings that are held in Aranyaprathet, far from where I live. Between teaching, fundraising, managing the centers, and corresponding with sponsors, sticking to my schedule becomes a juggling act.

Meanwhile, sponsorships have gone full circle. Friends and family members well aware of our situation agree to become sponsors for a first batch of files. However, a third of the applications are assigned to sponsors unknown to me and who do not fully understand the situation on the ground. Despite my articles in *Enfants du Mékong*, dozens of sponsors ask for photographs, letters, or news from the child they are sponsoring. Some are already sending gifts. This makes me uneasy. Why would one get a gift and not another? The letters have to be acknowledged, translated into Khmer, the translator has to be paid, the letters forwarded to the children, the children have to be asked to reply although some have never written a letter in their life—it's just not a cultural thing—then get it translated and checked. If the answer has nothing to do with what the sponsor asked, I have to ask for the letter to be redone, translated, approved and... sent off.

I thought that sponsorships would be a rather easy source of ongoing funding. I was wrong. Aside from the translation and postage costs, there's a tremendous follow-up job. But money is coming in, and that's what I need.

Another brief trip to France confirms that Rémi's film is working. After a showing in Apremont and an article in *Dauphiné Libéré*, I have a stint in Paris. Olivier introduces me to Francis and Dominique Letellier.

We're immediately on the same wave length. I see them again with Jean-Marie and we tend toward the same conclusions. They promise they'll visit Cambodia. A pleasant surprise, they donate 50,000 francs to the project, a sum that will certainly come in handy with the repatriation process. At the same time, I meet the first Mission Bamboo, a group of young people from good families that Enfants du Mékong wants to send to the camps for a year. They're unprepared for what is awaiting them. They have a rather idyllic view of humanitarian work, as if they'd been born for the refugees. I attempt to open their eyes. I don't mince my words, which upsets some of them but amuses others. I agree to help them with accommodation and to adjust to living in Ta Phraya as it's going to be a hard landing for some. The stark reality will likely be a far cry from their dreams. Three of them who share my sense of commitment agree to help me before they leave, then go on to set up an exhibition project developed with Jean-Marie.

Meanwhile, I phone up a Cambodian refugee in France, Sor Si Savang, author of the book *L'Enfant de la rizière rouge* (Child of the Red Rice Field) that had a real impact on me: "Hello Savang! You don't know me. You're a Cambodian living in France; I'm a Frenchman living in Cambodia. Your story really fascinated me and I would like to meet you." At Montparnasse, we can't decide on French food or Asian food, so we opt for something in between—couscous at Bébert's. Savang is captivating, riveting, even disconcerting. Getting right to his book, he says that Jean-Claude Didelot, chairman of Enfants du Mékong, got him to write it. We see eye to eye. I belong to a big Catholic family with five uncles in the priesthood and am allergic to fundamentalism. To people who critically say I'm no longer a believer, I retort that I am a practicing unbeliever. We exchange views for three full hours, laugh, talk about Cambodia, and enjoy a copious meal. The hunger Savang experienced under the Khmer Rouge has left its mark on him; he insists that we clean up every last grain of the gargantuan couscous.

We agree to meet again. I need him. And I want to be there when Savang gets together with Jean-Marie, a man of respect and openness. I'm sure they'll hit it off.

We realize that we need to prepare the children for the repatriation. Not just those with us, but all of them in the camps. And what could be better than a substantial exhibition on Khmer culture? The young people we met will be in a position to help us, Savang too. Actually, many children born in the camps don't know a thing about their country, or even about growing rice. Some think that rice grows in UN bags, even though most of their parents are farmers. Traditions, both agricultural and cultural, have been lost. A travelling exhibition seems to be the best way to remedy this ignorance of the world to which they are about to return.

Jean-Marie proposes to play the role of point man in France. He meets specialists from Cambodia and purchases an impressive quantity of books. We don't want the exhibition to be overly specialized, but we do want quality. Designed for children, it should first and foremost be educational. It must be a factual introduction to their culture and identity. Jean-Marie taps the brains of the Khmer world, both foreigners and Khmers. There are researchers with the *École française d'Extrême-Orient*, alongside ethnologists such as Jacques Népote, Madeleine Giteau, and delightful Solange Thierry. The *Association des Amis de l'Orient* proves very helpful. Also of real help are the library and publications of the *Centre de documentation et de recherche sur la civilisation khmère* (CEDORECK). Its president Nouth Narang fills in the gaps in our knowledge. Agronomist François Grünewald shares his deep insight on Cambodia. He had long worked for GRET in Cambodia, acting informally as the agent for France at a time when it did not yet have a representative office. Along with them are many Khmers in the camps with a background in the University of Fine Arts, the Disabled Persons Center, and the like.

The exhibition has a dual objective: prepare for the return and facilitate integration. Actually, it seems just as fundamental to familiarize the children with modern-day Cambodia as to root them in the culture on which their identity is pinned. They have to get used to the idea that they are full-fledged Khmer children. The exhibition will have the theme *Rizières: deux cultures à découvrir* (Rice Paddies: Two Cultures to be Discovered). It will put as much emphasis on the agricultural features of a farmer's life around the rice paddy as on the culture, customs, rites, and beliefs of the people. Some 80 percent of Cambodia's population lives in the rurals and most people living in its cities were originally farmers. If the country is to be rebuilt and its wounds healed, Buddhism, the official and traditional religion, is the natural binder between the refugees and contemporary inhabitants of the country. But this does not leave out other religions and beliefs, among them animism, Taoism, Christianity, and Islam.

One team is working on Site II, liaising with the monks, the elders, and scholarly types; another team is working in France with Jean-Marie and Savang as focal points. Back at the border the pace is picking up. As promised, I find a house for the young people from Mission Bamboo. Exactly 30 m from my place, a big building is going up. Khmer resistance soldiers are now logging massive amounts of precious wood to meet the demand in Thailand. The wood is cheap, but under Thai law, the origin must be identified. So for many, the best way to stock up on precious wood is to build a house in Ta Phraya.

Furthermore, according to a strange rumor going around among the Thais, thousands of Europeans will soon be coming to live at the border to work for Cambodia's development. So some are getting a jump on this influx that, predictably, never materializes. The house is made of quality wood. The owner is a madam and obsessed with Rococo sculptures and glossy varnished furniture, but it's the right house for the group. Early on I do legwork for the newly arrived Mission Bamboo people.

Days and weeks go by with endless coordination meetings with no results. The only real decision is the date of the next meeting. The stagnation exasperates me. An idea emerges out of the blue: prepare those running the camps for the repatriation. They have to be in tune with the current reality of Cambodia and visits should be planned. Now you've got me interested. Before preparing the children, let's prepare the leaders, whose opinions matter. The best way to prepare is to go and check things out. But how?

But rather than planning a trip right away, the talk goes on and on. My call for for efficiency is taken as naivety: "Oh! It's not as simple as all that! We have to check with the UN first, then the government in Phnom

Penh, plus the local governments…." The discourse is interminable, the action nil. Okay, I'll try something else. "Every problem has a solution. If there's no solution, that means there's no problem," so a Cambodian man told me.

A border market just opened on the weekend. People are allowed to cross into Cambodia. It's a big drawing card for Thais throughout the area. Featured are alcohol, cigarettes, secondhand clothes, and plenty of dodgy or smuggled goods. Volunteers regularly go over. Could we use this market and jump the border? Legally, no. The border is closed and only people going to the market are allowed to cross. I would be in an illegal position and the many checkpoints would hinder the trip, especially for a Big Nose, as we are called here. According to UN workers who just got back, Poipet, a settlement over the border, is in a disastrous state. But for the Khmers, it's business as usual. The Thais say it's hell, but from their point of view, anything from the other side of the border is evil. The camp dwellers and volunteers are all ears for the resistance propaganda passed on by the international community; in Cambodia, except for the liberated zones, everything is communist and the people are living in abject poverty. And researcher Raoul Marc Jennar, from his vantage point as witness to the political change in Cambodia while serving as adviser to the Cambodian chief of State, was just in Aran to appeal for help for Cambodia still under the American embargo.

The only one way to find out is to go and take a look.

With help from his FNLPK contacts, Sinath gets a passport and a permit to go to Bangkok. Overland is out of the question; we have to fly. Only one plane does the Bangkok–Phnom Penh route. A two-way ticket costs a fortune… skyway robbery.

The Ministry of Foreign Affairs issues visas. Cambodia is closed tight to foreigners. A few months earlier, one of my ACCOR colleagues was expected in Phnom Penh for a hotel opening, but was turned back by Cambodian immigration because he didn't have approval from the ministry. A quick fax over my priceless telephone line gets me an official invitation a few days later. I buy tickets for Sinath and me.

"A HUMANITARIAN WITHOUT
HUMAN KINDNESS?"
(December 1991–April 1993)

It was a putdown, but the way my friend Alain Goyé said it didn't hurt my feelings: "A humanitarian without human kindness." I found it rather amusing, even flattering. I've often been criticized for being hard, judgmental, unyielding. It's true. I want to move fast and I don't like being bogged down by a Plan B. I avoid being paralyzed by angst and always try to focus on the overall operation of the organization.

One female volunteer was so upset when confronted with the reality of the camps that she was in tears from morning till night. 'Let her go back home!' was my reaction. To those who feel that I'm harsh and heartless, I answer that the more heartrending we find the misery of the camps, the more we need to keep our cool. The enormous repatriation process, our ignorance of Cambodia, and the paucity of our resources leave no room for pussyfooting.

In mid-December 1991, I'm with Sinath in Bangkok. The next morning, we head north to Don Muang Airport. It's the first time Sinath has been on a plane. Although trying to hide his apprehension with a smile, he's obviously on edge. As for me, I'm excited about discovering this forbidden land. I feel like I'm reliving the Checkpoint Charlie experience of my first trip to East Germany ten years earlier, leaving the free world to enter a world of jail-like surveillance. As we were informed by the travel agency Transindo, there's no announcement for the flight to Phnom Penh. Thailand and Cambodia have not restored diplomatic relations, so there's officially no flight to Cambodia. No information on the monitors, not a sign of any kind at the check-in counters; it's a ghost flight. Yet, one hour before departure, a clerk carrying a small cardboard sign marked "Phnom Penh" takes our passports and leads us to the domestic airport where a bus takes us out to a Kampuchea

Airlines plane, an old Russian Antonov. The two propellers gradually start spinning, the plane shakes, and takes off. After five minutes of unbearable heat, the air conditioning kicks in, emitting a thick smoke-like mist. A foreigner expresses some worry and a Cambodian woman reassures him: "If it doesn't smell bad, there's nothing to worry about."

Immense rectangular fields and irrigation canals surround Bangkok. An hour and 15 minutes later, we have flown over the mountains without seeing a soul and descend toward Phnom Penh. Tiny fields form an immense puzzle of totally disparate pieces. The land looks sun-parched. Around the stilted houses, sugar palm trees and scraps of bushes add a touch of green to this mosaic of sunbaked rice paddies. There's only one aircraft on the tarmac, a Vietnam Airlines plane. Along the walkway we pick up our luggage from a pile on a cart.

Sinath is worried. His smile does a worse job of covering his fearful excitement than at boarding. He's not the Sinath I know as he cowers behind me like a child in want of protection. I self-confidently hand over both of our passports at immigration, along with a copy of the fax from Foreign Affairs, the forms, and ID photos. They ask, "Where are you staying?" to which I reply unhesitatingly "Cambodiana Hotel," a luxury establishment at the so-called Four Faces, the confluence of the Mekong, Tonle Sap, and Tonle Bassac Rivers. ACCOR opened it while I was still working in Bangkok. I know the director, which might come in handy in the event of a problem. But at $200 a night, it's way out of our range. Sinath has to look for a place near his family where we can stay. After much ado over the passports, there's the sound of the stamp and, much to my relief, we are allowed in.

I was thinking we'd have to take a taxi, but to our surprise we are met by a Cambodian Red Cross official from Site II, a gesture that bodes well. The airport is virtually deserted. In the parking lot are some hefty UNAMIC Land Cruisers and a green-plated Volga government vehicle. His little car quickly covers the 8 km. In Phnom Penh, the roads are clear save for the odd cyclo, a few motorbikes, and even fewer cars. Empty lots and shacks here and there line the road. We go by a market with its telltale worn-out umbrellas under which sellers squat with trays of fruit and vegetables on their knees. I see dozen or so pop bottles filled with a pink liquid on racks. A local drink? No, bottles of gasoline. The few fuel stations have no pumps in working order. One sometimes sees a barrel with a hand pump on it to serve gasoline, but most often it's sold in Coke or Johnny Walker bottles.

The buildings look like they've been abandoned for the last 20 years. To the right is the former School of Politics. We go down Kampuchea Vietnam Boulevard (now Kampuchea Krom), pass Santhor Mok School and turn right on Keo Mony Boulevard (now Mao Tse Tung). We go by the FNLPK headquarters building where we'd like to say hello to HE Son Sann who we had met at the camp. He's in a meeting. On the sidewalk, in the shade of a tamarind tree, a man is selling individually hand-rolled cigarettes, along with a few packs sporting a parakeet logo. Business is obviously retail. The sidewalks are in bad shape. Continuing along Keo Mony Avenue, we go by the large Damkor Market, then turn left. We weave around enormous craters. To the right is Toul Tompong Pagoda, the only building in the area to have been renovated, undoubtedly just given a coat of whitewash, then the Russian Market, a favorite hangout of Russians during the Vietnamese occupation.

Left of a station that might have been a Shell, we swing onto an unpaved street. Except for few streets on which there are remnants of asphalt between gaping holes, it seems that none of the streets are paved from one end to the other. A hundred meters down, the car stops in front of a house shrouded in trees. We effusively thank our impromptu driver. We've arrived at Sinath's cousins' place.

His uncle and aunt come out to meet him. I'm expecting an unending session of embraces, but not so. They greet one another and exchange smiles, as if Sinath had just left yesterday. Actually, they haven't seen each another for ten years. Neighbors also come over to greet him, but cautiously. Along comes a cousin, impeccably dressed, carrying some books. He had formerly studied in the USSR. He speaks Russian but, with the collapse of the Soviet Union, he doesn't use it. He's studying Khmer literature and has just come from an English lesson. He dreams of going abroad. At mealtime, another brother joins us. He's very familiar with NGO circles and is working nearby, with CRAH (*Comité de réception de l'aide humanitaraire* / Humanitarian Assistance

Reception Committee), a humanitarian supplies clearance agency. He has a brand new motorbike, a luxury. He offers to take us over to the house of another of Sinath's aunts where we are to be accommodated.

I go on a walking tour of the neighborhood. At the end of the street, a small bridge crosses an open sewer in which putrid, black water is moving sluggishly along. In Phnom Penh, the underground sewage mains haven't been maintained and are now clogged, so run off is out in the open. The neighbors are surprised to see a *barang* on their street, but no one dares approach me.

Shortly after a siesta, our bags tucked between Sinath's cousin's knees, the three of us get on the motorbike. We go by the Russian embassy, with its grey buildings behind high walls topped with barbed wire. Further on, public housing units seem to date from another century, standing in the midst of a giant squatter community, home to hundreds of families. The moss-caked concrete has never been cleaned. Balconies overflow with junk. Cardboard, plastic, scrap metal, bricks, anything is reused to split the apartments into smaller spaces. Huge tangles of electrical wiring complete the scene.

A few hundred meters further, what a change! It's the Cambodiana Hotel, an impressive building surrounded by landscaped grounds and flowering trees. The ornate Khmer-style architecture with sculptured roofing may not be a masterpiece, but it breathes luxury in comparison to the surrounding buildings. A number of UN vehicles and a platoon of cyclos are parked out front.

Almost opposite, at a coffee shop on the corner, one of Sinath's uncles is taking his siesta in a dilapidated folding chair, bare chested, a red checkered *krama* tied around his waist, flip-flops on his feet. The grimy concrete floor is littered with paper and gnawed-off pork and chicken bones. As in all restaurants, refuse is just thrown on the floor. On small wood-fired stoves, large pots are bubbling. A woman with a lovely smile, wearing her *krama* turban-style, serves customers at the tables. She gives Sinath an emotional hug and wakes up the old man who pulls himself together with a grumble, gets up, cracks his vertebrae, and puts on a smile when he recognizes his nephew. No body contact, just a few words of greeting. He has us sit down on tiny stacking stools and offers us something to drink. *Café teuk kor teuk dor ko* and *café kmao*, i.e. an iced coffee with milk for Sinath and a black coffee for me.

The old woman gives two dirty glasses picked up from the ground a quick rinse and places them on the coffee table. A boy fetches some ice from the neighbor lady, extracted from a rough-looking chest of sawdust. A chunk is sawed off and tied with string. The old lady hatchets it into smaller pieces and tosses a few into Sinath's glass. She adds a generous dash of concentrated sweet milk. Out of an earthenware jug sitting in a container of hot water, she pours enough coffee into the filter bag to fill the two glasses.

Given the dubious hygiene of the ice and utensils I'm not sorry I didn't get iced coffee. But with the heat, I'll have to get used to it. The Vietnamese coffee is very strong. Robusta to the 15th power. You can feel it go down and it keeps you cranked up for the day. There's no way to order tea, as Khmer hospitality has it that tea is available free of charge on the table. As for soft drinks, between Sarsi, a ghastly substitute for Coca Cola, and fluorescent orange or green Fanta, no thank you! I eventually get hold of a soda water, and this becomes my preferred drink.

At the top of the stairway, another aunt takes us in and gets us settled. The door opens into a dimly lit living room, next to a large bedroom with one large bed. The epitome of kitsch, the pillows are pink, the lights fluorescent, the photographs decorated with plastic beads, the mosquito net fuchsia, the bedcovers in large flower print… the place has it all. On the wall are full-length portraits of a policeman in full dress. She's proud of this son wearing an olive green uniform not unlike that of the Vietnamese soldiers… Every family has supporters of every political stripe, so it's hard to understand why they fought for so many years.

In need of money, she agrees to rent us her room for two weeks. She'll sleep on a folding cot that she'll put out at night. I'm going to have to share the bed with Sinath but, given our budget, I've no choice. On the plus side, we are next to the Ministry of Foreign Affairs, not far from the Royal Palace.

A windowless cubbyhole serves as a bathroom, with nothing more than a bucket of water and a squat toilet that hasn't been scrubbed since the war. Even in the capital city's downtown, the off-and-on power supply reflects the state the country is in. A stub of a candle replaces the weak glow of a grime-covered light bulb. The flickering flame imparts an eerie golden glow to the large cockroaches probing their way up the wall with their long antennae.

It's disgusting. How will I survive two weeks in this hole? The family is so kind and my gentlemanly instincts keep me from dropping Sinath and taking refuge somewhere nicer. Anyway, it's too late.

At nightfall, around 6 p.m., the streets close up. The remaining cyclos take their last customers home on unlit streets. What else can I do but turn in at 7 p.m., while Sinath chats with his aunt in the nearby entranceway? But at 4:30 the next morning, insistent chanting brings me into a half-sleep in which I waver between reality and nightmare. Actually, every day before dawn, the old lady religiously has her radio on to listen to the monks' chanting prayer. And this will go on throughout my stay. My relief when the broadcast finishes is short-lived because it's already time to get up.

In Cambodia, the day starts early. After a quick breakfast of a bowl of *hu tieu* soup and a couple of Chinese fritters, we gather our files and business cards and head over to the Ministry of Foreign Affairs. The offices open at 7:30 a.m.

But, aside from the guards on duty outside, the ministry seems asleep. We wait. About 8:15, a woman wearing a long *sampot* and carrying a school notebook under her arm, takes her place at reception. A black plastic telephone sits prominently on her desk—purely for decoration. She invites us to wait on a threadbare settee. The coffee table is bedecked with a bouquet of yellow and red plastic flowers.

We're invited in at 9 o'clock. The person receiving us speaks excellent French. We explain that the purpose of our visit is to prepare for the repatriation of Cambodian orphans from the border camps. Judging by his smile alone, we might conclude that we are warmly welcomed, but I feel the politeness might be just for show and fear an unpleasant surprise awaits us. Procedurally, the line ministry has to give its approval prior to that of the Ministry of Foreign Affairs. We go back to the line ministry to have a technical agreement signed allowing us to work with the local authorities. We could do without this time-consuming going back and forth, given the low level of activity we witnessed. But I remain hopeful that we'll get a lot done during this first trip.

At 9:30, we go from the Ministry of Foreign Affairs to the Ministry of Social Affairs, on Tou Samouth Boulevard (now Norodom Boulevard). The man in charge of foreign relations is away. Nobody knows when he'll be back. We have to come another time. Sinath contacts one of his cousins who lets us rent a motorbike. Everywhere we go, we have the uncomfortable feeling of being followed.

After lunch, I go over to SIPAR's office on Street 222. This organization publishes handbooks for teachers and has just undertaken a program for teacher training. The guard informs us that the expatriate woman looking after the place has gone to Kompong Speu. I will return by myself in the late afternoon. Katell, a woman of character, gives me a hearty welcome. We immediately see eye to eye and go out for dinner together. About 8 p.m. I start out for my temporary accommodation. I catch a late-working cyclo that takes me down the street alongside the Royal Palace. Suddenly, just after the Ministry of Foreign Affairs, we are startled by the click of an AK-47 and an order to stop. The cyclo driver rams on the brakes, tugging on the rod behind his seat, all but tipping us over. The night is pitch black; the cyclo has no lights. But his passenger is a *barang*. My face is given a scan by a flashlight and after an exchange in Khmer, the soldier lets us go. The curfew is back in force. Students have started demonstrating against the government and security has been beefed up.

The next morning, we go back to the Ministry of Social Affairs. Still not a word from the man in charge of foreign relations and without him, no appointment is possible. We decide on a city tour, with a focus on orphanages. They all have the name *Kolap*, rose flower: Kolap I, Kolap II, Kolap III, and Kolap IV. Run by the government's social affairs department, two of them are supported by the NGO Caritas. One of them is in the former French embassy. Totally abandoned, surrounded by a beautiful stand of trees, it's a concrete building of geometric form. The Caritas officer tells me that his organization doesn't look after this center, which is soon to be relocated to make way for the return of the French.

Almost directly opposite, at the foot of the Chruoy Changvar Bridge, another center is home to a large number of orphans. It's also in pitiful condition. The charges seem to be left on their own. No group living; the orphans survive as best they can. Another orphanage down the peninsula has been set up in a former convent. But a Khmer Rouge attack blew out the center span of the capital's east-west connecting bridge in 1973 to cut off the city's supply line. A ferryboat has taken over.

We don't know what to say after this orphanage tour. True, there's a desperate shortage of resources, but the shocking thing is the obvious indifference of the managerial staff of these centers. You don't need much to do a lot; where there's a will there's a way. Get the kids out playing, involved in sports, help them blossom, keep the place properly cleaned… That requires motivation and effort. Both seem to be lacking.

Later, when the Ministry of Social Affairs suggests that the orphans on Site II be taken in by the government orphanages, my reply is a categorical no. I think that integration is good, maybe necessary, but in the current state of affairs, it would amount to abandonment. This realization will have significant consequences down the line, because I will come up against a new problem, setting up sustainable shelters for repatriated children.

We survey the outskirts of Phnom Penh in search of sites for the reintegration. I like Ta Khmau. Chbar Ampov too. Russey Keo is too noisy and uncomfortably close to red light establishments.

I had tossed around the idea of going back to work for ACCOR and having heard that Cambodiana Hotel was looking for a financial manager, I arrange to meet the director. For me, it would be ideal to go back to work while taking care of the two centers. But it doesn't work out. The director knows that I would be living in Cambodia to do humanitarian work and offers me a ridiculously low salary. When you're familiar with the long hours of work in the hotel business, without a good salary, it's not worth the trouble. I wouldn't mind a low salary and caring for my own room and board, provided that I can stay free for the ongoing projects.

My sabbatical year is ending. I find myself caught up in a pursuit that will take much longer...

Meanwhile, the political situation looks very grim. Khieu Samphan was assaulted, which compromises the Khmer Rouge's engagement in the peace process. In Phnom Penh, student movements are growing. At noon, I have an appointment with Thomas, a photographer friend who's covering the region for the Gamma photo agency. He's staying in Cambodia at the Sukhalay Hotel on Achar Mean Avenue (now Monivong Boulevard). I go there alone by motorbike. Now certain that I'm being followed, I charge down smaller streets and make abrupt turns onto other streets. Because I'd been met at the airport by an FNLPK official, I'm cast into the opposition. And Sinath's passport that he obtained through the tripartite opposition apparatus, was signed by a Khmer Rouge official. So we are viewed with distrust. After a few minutes of maniacal driving, I've thrown them off my trail.

Over the noise of my small motorbike I hear gunshots in the distance. Near Central Market, the sound picks up. I'm stuck in the middle of a demonstration that the army is trying to disperse. They're shooting in the air, but some shots go in the direction of students hanging banners on top of buildings on Achar Mean Boulevard. Passers-by are running in panic. The army is coming from the north of the city toward the Faculty of Medicine. Sukhalay Hotel is between the army and me. I try to move forward, thinking that there's been a lull. A tank is stationed just out front of Monorom Hotel. Calm returns for a few minutes and the gnarled traffic heading towards downtown Phnom Penh loosens up. I try to slip through. The Chinese stores ahead of me have all lowered their metal shutters. But the shooting resumes and forces me to wait for another respite. After nearly an hour of starts and stops, I make it to my destination.

I push on the glass door. It's locked. Fearing a possible invasion by students dispersed by the army, the guards have blocked off the access points. Inside, a crowd of foreigners and Khmers in a state of panic are laying low in the lobby. Thomas sees me and waves. The guards open the door and let me in. Thomas is amazed to see me walk in and invite him out for lunch while the conflict is still raging on. He had a ringside seat for the demonstration and senses the danger. I had come on the scene when things were winding down, so hadn't seen the violence of the soldier-student clashes. Many had been arrested; apparently some had been killed, others injured. Things have now calmed down.

Over the next few days, between appointments at the Ministry of Social Affairs where our contact person has still not shown up and waiting at the Ministry of Foreign Affairs, my initial optimism vanishes. I'm asked to submit a detailed report and plan. I get to work on this. Given my precarious lodging arrangements, Katell says I can stay in the SIPAR house guestroom, but I dare not abandon Sinath. However, I agree to come over for a noon nap and to write up my report.

One evening, Sinath tells me that his cousin working at CRAH wants to have us over. I think that it's for a drink at a café. Wrong. We follow him to Boeung Kak Lake, in the center of Phnom Penh, and stop in front of a large dance hall. We're frisked outside the smoked glass doors and ushered into a huge dingy hall with Khmer music blaring away. Girls dressed in beer brand colors crowd around us extolling the virtues of their respective brew. Imported Carlsberg and Heineken are the in thing. Further on, short-skirted girls in gaudy makeup are dancing the Khmer *roam vong* with customers. The dancers make their way counterclockwise around some imaginary central point. I'm flabbergasted, to the great amusement of Sinath. The dancing hall of gigantic proportions is actually a brothel. Its customers are respectable civil servants with modest salaries, but with varied and considerable subsidiary incomes… This cycle of corruption easily convinces me to refuse any and all requests for envelopes or little gifts to move a file along. Ironically, years later, this space was reclaimed and became the site of Phnom Penh's biggest mosque!

I'm awakened each day by the chanting of the monks. I now shower at Katell's, where the bathroom is impeccable. She's most often out in Kompong Speu and I can relax in the calm of her house. I spend my days writing up the report. Without a typewriter, I use a little battery-operated Casio. I no sooner finish the report and turn it in, when I'm told that it's wanted in Khmer. Reports are submitted to the government in French administrative style. A skilled translator is required. Time is running out and I can't find anyone to do it. Sinath's level of English and Khmer are not good enough for such a report. Sutheany, Katell Benoît's assistant, a woman with a charming smile, has more work than she can handle. And I realize that even after the document is translated, I won't be able to get it typed up.

Transindo, now Indosuisse, provides a number of services for NGOs. In additional to a postal and goods importing service, it does document translation and typing, but at $15 a page, it's more than we can afford. Computers don't yet have Khmer fonts and the typewriters made in East Germany are clumsy to use. Khmer is written from left to right, but some letters are typed above or below other letters. If even the slightest mistake is made, the whole page has to be retyped. Few people are able to use one. I realize that it'll be impossible to get the file in this time, but I promise to get it to my contact on my next time through.

I've a few days left and dream of visiting the Angkor temples, but it's impossible right now. The eastern route is closed at Chikreng and frequent Khmer Rouge attacks make it impassable. The western route via Battambang takes several days. And a laissez-passer is needed to get through each province. All movements are under surveillance and require permits, especially for a foreigner. Even Kompong Speu, where Katell is working, 45 km out of Phnom Penh, requires a permit. The only recourse is to apply through the official tourism agency Apsara, and it charges several hundred dollars for the flight and temple tour. Out of the question. So I stay in Phnom Penh and put finishing touches on the file.

One afternoon, Sinath arrives, distraught. The ward police showed up at his aunt's place and told us we can't stay there. The police keep his passport and summon me. I go with him to the station, opposite the grounds of Wat Botum, but not without leaving word with Katell in case something goes wrong. The police tell me that I've broken the law that prohibits foreigners from staying with Khmers. The regulation is still in effect, although it has been less strictly enforced since the peace agreements were signed. Back in the days of hardline communism, Cambodians were not to have anything to do with foreigners. Those who worked for foreigners had to report regularly on their every move to the Ministry of Interior.

The discussions drag on. The officers also take my passport and now refuse to give either of them back. They want money. I refuse and threaten to go to the embassy of France. I haven't yet met the new ambassador but I bluff my way through. Seeing my determination, they give back my passport but not Sinath's, realizing they can be tougher on a Cambodian. I continue bluffing. I tell them that my colleague also enjoys the protection of the French embassy and that I'll waste no time in lodging a complaint with it. I play a tight game, because it's Friday afternoon and we're leaving on Monday morning. Sinath, who was planning to stay longer, is now afraid to stay and decides to go back with me. They drop their demands down to a pack of cigarettes as a tip, but I continue to stubbornly refuse, much to their annoyance.

As this is taking place, Katell suddenly pulls up in her old Toyota Corolla. She found my note and thought that two heads would be better than one in dealing with the police. Her arrival results in the immediate capitulation of the police officers, who hand me the second passport. His enthusiasm dampened by this event, Sinath decides to go stay at his cousins' place and I happily accept Katell's proposal that I lodge at her place. But I am left wondering what on earth I'm getting mixed up in.

Getting back to Bangkok, then Ta Phraya, is a deliverance. It's great to be back home, to enjoy uninterrupted electricity, the luxury of a refrigerator to keep things cool, a clean shower, and unlimited water. I call France and talk at length with my family about my impressions of Cambodia. I see that the repatriation process will take more time and energy out of me than I thought. Will I be up to it?

At camp the next day, I am delighted to be back with the old gang. The joy of the children is almost enough to drown my worries. They bombard us with questions about our trip, about Cambodia, about Phnom Penh. The Dangkrek orphans bubble over with excitement. Cambodia becomes something they dream about. Unlike many children, they're not really apprehensive about the return. They know they're being supported and that I'll not let them down. If they only knew of the difficulties I have yet to resolve, they would no doubt be less optimistic. I try to conceal my fears from them and keep my mind filled with their joy at the prospect of returning.

What's more, I started the process of buying an initial piece of property for the repatriation. Sameath, one of my students, just returned to Cambodia. Many of his family members, including his sister, still live in Siem Reap. He also has connections with the O'Bok center where other family members are working in the local government or at the hospitality school. In order to facilitate things and beat the anticipated inflation of land prices, I entrust him before witnesses with money to buy a piece of land. If we're to be prepared for the repatriation, no time can be lost. We determine possible locations on the map. Having suffered so much from the lack of water on Site II, we ask him to look for property along the river, not too close to town to avoid being bothered by the throngs of tourists that will soon be invading the Angkor temples, but close enough to enable the children to attend primary and secondary school. I buy the land without seeing it for 200,000 baht, or about $7,000, a good deal at the time. Without Cambodian citizenship, I agree to put the title in the name of Sameath's brother-in-law.

In January, with the agreement of Magali, chairwoman of SIPAR, I terminate my teaching job after my student exams. I thus shorten my contract by a month and a half. I need time to finalize preparations for the exhibition. Despite the great work done by my first volunteer, I also have to work on the financing end of things.

In late January 1992, Jean-Marie Le Guay joins me in Ta Phraya accompanied by Savang. It's very hard for Jean-Marie. The last time he came to Thailand was to repatriate the remains of Alain, his son and my closest friend, who drowned while diving at Koh Tao. It's also a grand return for Savang who had never been back to the camps. He had been interned there after fleeing Cambodia where his parents, brothers, and sisters died before his eyes. He let Jean-Marie convince him that this would be good for him psychologically. After suffering so much, it's quite a traumatic experience to go back to one's country and people.

Savang also came to help us in the final phase leading up to the exhibition, especially translating and writing material in Khmer, since the presentation will be in French and Khmer. A couple dozen thematic panels will illustrate Cambodia's agricultural resources and its heritage. Many photos, drawings, and paintings will showcase the country yesterday and today, its culture and ethnic diversity, the variety of its flora and fauna, its geographical, human, and religious foundations, etc. We even had rice samples planted in large trays at regular intervals to show the steps from seeding to maturity. Many traditional objects and items of clothing are also on exhibit: rice sickles, baskets, fish traps, wedding *popils*—little metal objects to ward against evil spirits, etc.

Jean-Marie brought an inflatable globe and maps of the world. Rathanak, a young fellow from the Dangrek orphanage, with the help of other young ones and a group of disabled persons, painted dozens of posters for the exhibition: gorgeous water color paintings of Cambodian rice fields. Several Cambodians were hired and trained to work as guides for the children. In the end, almost a dozen adults helped coach the school visits. The show is ready in all respects.

Opening day is February 3, 1992 in the presence of leading DPPU officials and as well as many representatives of both the UN and the Khmer administration. Father Pierre is also on hand. The meeting of Jean-Marie and Father Pierre is priceless, two brilliant men who shine side by side. The ceremony opens with a piece by the orphanage *chayam* drum group and continues with dances by students of the fine arts school. All of our charges were given something to do and are proud to be associated with this impressive reception.

The following days, according to a schedule coordinated by the education authorities, the various schools in the camp come by turn. After waiting patiently in rows, groups of 20 or so children are guided through the exhibition. Everything goes off without a hitch. An average of 200 children go through every 45 minutes. A meeting was held to prepare the teachers to put together a short write-up after the visit. This gets the little ones to listen attentively and take notes. After the visit, they're asked to come up to large tables and make a drawing of what they learned from the panels. It runs very smoothly. After a few days with one of us on hand to supervise, the Khmer teams are totally independent. On my 26th birthday, we get all of the exhibition participants together for a picnic on the edge of a new reservoir near Ta Phraya. We're channeling all our energy into the long-awaited, yet much-dreaded, repatriation process. The volatile camp security is a genuine concern. The future is uncertain. Mine is too. How will I be able to go on? With Enfants du Mékong? With another organization? Alone?

My relationship with Enfants du Mékong is starting to frazzle. Some sponsors write letters that are out of sync with the reality of the child they are sponsoring. Explain as I may, some are puzzled that my priority is the land, the children, not the sponsors. I'm having a hard time accepting the proselytism of some sponsors. I tried to explain my position in an article for the magazine, but it was censored out. I pointed out the problems that I see in some of their programs, mentioning the sponsorship I undertook, but I didn't get anywhere. In sum, I am finding it difficult to partner with them, in as much as I now realize my commitment is going to go far beyond my sabbatical year.

In Ta Phraya, we're looking for a name for our organization that covers all we do. Various names are casually tossed around. The concept must embody both the Khmer specificity and the family aspect. One volunteer comes up with *Krousar Khmer*, meaning Khmer family. It appeals to me and I want to bounce it off Marie-Claude, but she's off to the market. When I see her come back, I utter "Krousar Khmer." My Khmer is only so-so and my pronunciation off, so Marie-Claude hears me say "Krousar Thmey," or new family. Wow! The name's perfect. It covers exactly what we're doing, giving a new family to children without one. My wrong word became the right word, allowing Marie-Claude to come up with the tag I needed. A nice birthday present. We drop the word orphanage for good, calling it a "child welfare center," thus avoiding segregation. Moreover, we often take in children for a limited time. Once, a judge gave a mother a six-month term in the Site II prison and ordered that her child be placed in our center. He's not an orphan, but needs to be looked after while his mother is in jail, after which he'll go back to her.

After a viewing at the Nong Chan sub-camp, the exhibition migrates to Ampil, Rythissen, Samlor, and finally to Dangrek. Virtually all of the school children on Site II are able to visit it. On days when there's no school, the exhibition opens for adults and children not in school, as well as for repeat visits. In five weeks, the exhibition gives over 50,000 children the opportunity to discover entire segments of their country and culture.

Requests for the exhibition then come in from Site B camp representatives (under FUNCINPEC, with support from the SIPAR teams in Surin), followed by Khao I Dang (under the HCR). To my great surprise, prompted by Christophe Peschoux, in charge of the HCR on the Site 8 Khmer Rouge camp, the camp administration itself asks for the exhibition. It goes as smoothly there as in the camps run by the other factions, in fact, even better with regard to organization and timing.

A total of some 80,000 refugee camp children, all political factions combined, enjoy this first exhibition *Rizières: deux cultures à découvrir*. We never dreamed it would do so well. It put me on the radar of the UN people. Up to this point, I was tolerated without official recognition, and now I enjoy a good relationship with the camp administration, the DPPU, and UNBRO.

The time has come to try a road trip to Cambodia instead of going by plane via Bangkok, which is too much of a drain on my meager budget. A special permit from the Thai forces is needed to get across the border. In the next few days, I appeal to the border coordination forces as recommended by DPPU officers. I'm met by a very friendly colonel who tells me to go see the commander-in-chief in Bangkok. I go to Bangkok by train. It takes longer than by bus, but is much more scenic. The train leaves at about 12:30 p.m. and barely hits 40 km/h, halting at occasional rural whistle-stops. Sellers are incessantly coming and going with sticky rice, beef jerky, pineapple, and cold drinks. We arrive at Hua Lampong Station. At 6 p.m. sharp, the speakers reawaken. I'm always taken with this people who become immobile, everyone holding their breath while the national anthem plays, something especially impressive at the main train station of such a megalopolis.

The next morning I plead my cause with the commander-in-chief. I strike a sympathetic chord when he hears me speak a little Thai. He'd already been informed of what I want to do and gives me a laissez-passer. It's certainly not every day he sees a young bushy-haired, bespectacled foreigner address him with such a request.

I use the opportunity to handle some administrative issues. Stanislas Rollin lets me use his office where a telephone, fax machine, and computer come in handy, in fact, really handy, because of my ever-increasing communication needs. The repatriation process is underway and I absolutely have to get my funding applications in to the HCR and otherwise raise funds.

In late February, I make a last visit to Lard'hyao Prison. I've no regrets whatsoever about the time and resources I devoted to that cause, but I think my energy is better used with the refugee children than with European prisoners. A simple matter of priorities.

Upon returning to Site II, I learn that I just missed out on something big. Prince Sihanouk had traveled to Banteay Chmar, a Mecca for the resistance and home to the ruins of a temple built by Jayavarman VII. At the last minute, many carloads of volunteers got permits to attend the ceremony. For me, Banteay Chmar will have to wait.

On March 4, 1992, clutching my permits to cross the border, I leave on my second trip to Phnom Penh, overland this time. In Aran, I look for a local *tuk tuk* to take me to Klong Luk, the last Thai village. A shiny motorbike pulling a comfortable hooded carriage conveys me to the border. The road is blocked by soldiers. I have to continue on foot. I show my passport and the permits. They let me go through. I go on. Another check. I can continue and go over a wooden bridge. It's the Cambodian side. Finally! A few meters further, I leave the asphalt for an atrociously rutted stretch of road. I go through a crowd in utter bedlam. People dressed in rags are creeping along the ditches to sneak across the border. No concrete buildings, save a grungy health care center in ruins. One-legged persons are begging. Ten-year-old kids with babies on their hips are out panhandling. I find myself in a slum area of shacks made of salvaged cardboard boxes and tarpaulins. Destitution and desolation are everywhere.

I am attacked by touts trying to fill up a few taxis going as far as Sisophon. One of them is nearly full. Another one is full, but waiting to leave with a convoy. There is one seat left, half of the front left passenger side in a Toyota Corolla, the 4x4 of Cambodia, as it's jokingly called by the taxi drivers. If I don't take that seat, the option is to buy up two seats, but wait until two more taxis are filled before we can leave, so I accept. I have my bag stuffed in the already chock-full trunk. It holds two spare tires under a thick layer of red dust. The space is otherwise crammed with goods from Thailand, mainly fruit. Why on earth are they importing fruit? The trunk can no longer click shut. The lock must have been broken from being slammed down, so a strap does the job. The second passenger politely lets me get in first… which has me stuck against the gear shift and the emergency brake. To get the door closed, I have to shove over again. I'm down to one quarter of the seat.

The driver hoists himself into his seat, but a passenger slips in beside him, forcing him to grasp the steering wheel at an angle. The windshield has a long crack running across it. Here, traffic is right hand, but the steering wheel is also right hand, which is typical of vehicles imported or stolen from Thailand, where traffic is on the left.

We get going. The first concrete building is the Poipet train station, 200 m down the road. It hasn't been used in 20 years. Its walls are full of bullet holes; one side was knocked out by mortar fire. A number of families live in it, stretching a piece of tarpaulin over the remnants of the wall. Two hundred meters further on, a military checkpoint. The driver who has successfully gotten through three already, stops and tosses the officers a few cigarettes. Seeing my bewildered look, he guffaws from behind his sunglasses with a Ray-Ban label slapped across them, authenticating the fakes! I'm not sure how he can see past it. He starts off again without downshifting. The motor sputters and the pistons bang. Another 200 meters and another checkpoint. More cigarettes. We follow the other car, weaving around potholes. No, not potholes, craters. And along both sides of the road wretched shacks, shelters that defy description.

A few kilometers further, another roadblock. This time, a log placed across the road forces vehicles to stop. The AK-47 is cocked. Cigarettes are not on order; money is. The driver, taking it in stride, pulls out a wad of bills and produces the magic sum. "Open sesame." We move on. The driver pulls a cassette player out from above the sun visor and shoves a cassette into it. The device plays Khmer music with obvious quality issues. The rotation speed varies considerably, but it doesn't bother anyone. The air conditioning is set on high and I, thrust against the gear shift, catch the blizzard right in the face. At the checkpoints, I rejoice when the door opens and the air warms up a little. I need a checkpoint every ten minutes to avoid getting frozen. It's obviously just not my day with the a/c. It's missing a discharge hose, so my feet are getting a washing drop by drop. There's every indication that the trip will be a long one. It'll definitely take more than a day and we'll have to spend the night in Battambang. But I wasn't quite prepared for this experience.

Two hours down the road and we stop in a village heralded by two small badly damaged statues of elephants, painted white but splotched with red clay. Kon Damrey, literally "baby elephant," is the name of the village. I go to stretch my legs while the drivers have a chin-wag and I observe a number of drivers in the shade of a tamarind tree stretched out over motorbikes while waiting for customers. They doze with the precariousness of tightrope walkers. One *moto dop* driver is cleaning his nose with a pair of tweezers, verifying the operation in his rearview mirror. *Moto dop* is from the French *moto double*, because in principle a motorbike is built for two. Never mind. You often see one carrying as many as four or even five persons.

A few minutes go by and the two vehicles resume their infernal dance among the potholes. With the bouncing around, squeezing, and crushing, our bodies seem to be but one. Despite his acrobatic position, the driver is nothing less than a virtuoso of steering wheel techniques. Rare are the shocks that are violent enough to take the absorbers to the limit. We meet three UN vehicles—two white Land Rovers in combat formation cover a bulky UNAMIC Land Cruiser. The soldiers are on alert, wearing bullet-proof vests; their weapons are slung across their chests. There's a machine gun secured to the vehicle and a long retracted radio antenna, as disconcerting as those of a cockroach. The region remains unstable. The Khmer Rouge take no notice of the ceasefire. The UN soldiers, as yet few in this preparatory phase, realize they are vulnerable.

It'll be some weeks before UNTAC deploys its forces. There is talk of over 20,000 peacekeepers to be positioned throughout the country.

The eight of us in our little Toyota Corolla look small beside them. The other car going with us has ten people in it, four in the front, four in the back, and two children on laps. We cross several more money-extorting checkpoints—which they really are—and enter a part of the country featuring low mountains, not unlike the Alpilles. Sisophon is near. We cross an iron bridge that dates back to the French era. Its frame has sustained some smashing. Tanks that shot off mark. Further down the river is a railway bridge that hasn't been used in over 20 years. Some farmers wave us down. Landmine blasts have ripped off enough metal to prevent us from going over. I figure out what they are up to: no money, no planks, no crossing. The driver makes another payment. We just get over the bridge and a noise like a drum roll announces... a flat tire. The driver understands immediately. Everyone out. He empties the trunk of all the goods, now covered in thick red dust. My blue bag has gotten a sunburn. A spare tire, worn completely bald, is pulled out. We arrive in Sisophon around noon.

The city seems deserted. The central square is bordered by Chinese shop houses, buildings that are 4 m wide by 15 m to 20 m deep, most of them converted into provincial government offices. Small blue signs in Khmer and French designate the departments. Crumbling in ruins, all of them are closed. Sisophon is at the hub of the road to Poipet and Thailand, the road north to Thma Puok and Banteay Chmar, the eastbound road to Siem Reap, and the one we are going to take south to Battambang and Phnom Penh.

Some passengers get off and we stop at a restaurant just off the traffic circle. On a large table covered with oil cloth is an alignment of aluminum pots. Behind the table, a woman shoos flies away with the back of her hand. A swarm of the insects rises from the covers. She takes the covers off one by one to display the contents—soup, a curry dish, beef stew with vegetables—not exactly mouthwatering. I cautiously choose a dish that seems to have undergone the most cooking. Small pieces of pork bathe in a pot of water morning glory. The soft drink can seems to have seen a lot of miles, its paint worn off by too much buffeting while in transit over potholed roads. The famous red logo is unrecognizable and the tepid contents of the can undrinkable.

After lunch, we wait another hour for new passengers to fill the empty spaces in the car. It's about 2 p.m. More giant potholes and cash points make our progress appallingly slow. It takes us three hours to cover the 69 km to Battambang. Blasted out bridges are replaced by two palm tree trunks. Each time, the locals ask for money to lay planks, without which the car would tip over. When a vehicle goes off the rails, traffic is stopped in both directions until further negotiations prompt the villagers to lift the vehicle back on the road. No joining in to help one another. Everything has its price. The only one bothered by these shenanigans is me.

About 5:30 in the afternoon, Battambang shows us its happy face. The first travelers get off near Psar Nath, along a river bordered by flamboyant trees in blossom. The Chinese shop houses along the riverfront date back to colonial times. Even in their rickety state, they have lost none of their charm. We pass by a towering, badly damaged statue, a kneeling giant holding a type of sword, actually a stick. The name Battambang comes from the legend of a lost stick that was found by a giant. At Psar Thmey, touts offer beds for the night. I decide on a recently built house. The cost of a *pahi*, something like a camp bed, goes for a thousand riels… less than half a dollar. Many travelers have already staked their claim in the spacious hall where 20 or so of these beds are lined up. They are made of two crosspieces secured to a double wooden crossbar, over which blue or green canvas is stretched. Four poles hold up a mosquito net.

I pick an empty bed, but one of the female staff shows me upstairs where I'm welcomed by the owners. They saw a *barang* get off and don't want to leave me with the common travelers. They want to pamper me. A small mattress placed right on the red and white tile floor, common throughout Indochina, a pink polyester satin pillow, and my bed for the night is ready. The main thing is that, thanks to a breeze, it is not nearly so hot up here. I am offered a Battambang specialty—green, but yes, quite ripe oranges. Feeling fairly secure, I set my bag down, take my *krama*, and head to the outdoor shower. From a large gas barrel filled with murky water, I use a plastic container to draw what I need to clean off the thick dust caked on during the trip. The Lux soap bar is truly worthy of its name here.

In the middle of the night I am awakened not by the chanting of the monks, but by a strange psalmody: "Phnom Penh, Phnom Penh, Phnom Penh, Phnom Penh..." Like fireflies, tiny oil lamps in the street indicate the movement of people. It is just 4:30 a.m. and touts are already vying for travelers. A little later I approach them and two of them harpoon me, pulling me apart, each one trying to drag me to his vehicle. The strongest one wins and I am sardined in like the day before, only this time in the back, on a totally worn-out seat with only the springs and frame left. Four cars make up the convoy and are subjected to the gamut of checkpoints, first every 200 m, then dwindling down. Half an hour goes by and we approach a bridge. A soldier with bloodshot eyes, obviously drunk, threatens us with his AK-47. His price must be prohibitive, because the driver refuses. The staggering soldier responds by firing into the air. We choke back our fear. With little chance of having the last word, the driver pays up and crosses the bridge. Tensions ease and everyone expresses disgruntlement about the corruption in this country that opened up too quickly after years of glacial communism.

About 8 o'clock, we have breakfast at Moung Russey. Turned off by the *bobor*, or rice porridge, I decide on some donut-like fritters. Dipped in sugar, they help the coffee go down.

Then the same nagging story of bridges wiped out, unpaved roads, and flat tires. After Pursat, we get to Krakor at noon. Small slaughtered animals are hanging in stalls along the road. I think it's dog, served by some restaurants in Phnom Penh. But they are actually small fallow deer from the forest, a local specialty. I'm tempted to try it. The kitchen is an immense room at the back of the restaurant, where an army of girls is preparing the food right on the floor. Heaps of dirty dishes are waiting their turn in large aluminum basins. The toilets are simple open-air structures behind the house, a few boards nailed together over a stinking pool. The frail stilts shake with each step. I push open the door and grasp how it works. The toilet is a hole in the floor. A piece of board has been cut out to allow direct elimination! Big green flies are enjoying what's left of the previous user's poor aim... Ya gotta get used to it. Happily, the quality of the meal is not to be judged by the poor hygiene of the premises. The venison is succulent.

As we pass through the next towns, I note traces of the French occupation. Beautiful colonial buildings with vast grounds along tree-lined avenues. Kompong Chnnang, at the edge of Tonle Sap Lake, means something like "clay pot wharf." Kompong, resembling the Malay word for "village," means "town at the water's edge" in Khmer. Chnnang designates the regional specialty, clay cooking pots. Less than 50 km further, we come to Udong, the old capital of the kingdom before it was relocated to Phnom Penh by the French under the reign of Norodom I. Stupas can be seen on the hills in the distance. The beauty of the countryside is enthralling, despite the fact that my aesthetic sense has been greatly dulled by the arduous, bone-crunching trip.

The road starts to improve as we go through Udong, but checkpoints increase. Cigarettes? No deal. These are cash points and they want real riels. We go along the top of a dike under exquisite late-afternoon lighting. Dwellings perched on high stilts seem to barely cling to the road. Straw stacks here and there. Zebu cattle, those white animals that have a food reserve in their humps, graze on the sparse grass in the ditches. Ponds swarm with fish. Suddenly we see it, on the left, the Tonle Sap River flowing down from the lake toward the capital. Immense stretches of water covered with water hyacinths. I find the scenery delightful.

We see a couple of mosques. North of Phnom Penh are Cham settlements. Originating from Kompong Cham to the east, and more generally from Champa, an ancient kingdom east of the Khmer empire, the Cham were traditionally Hindu. Those who settled in Cambodia became Moslem in the 16th century under the influence of Arabian, Indian, Persian, and Chinese merchants.

As we approach Phnom Penh, I recognize Russey Keo, the noisy, insalubrious suburb that I rejected because of its concentration of prostitutes, not an ideal place for children to grow up in. We go by some apparently abandoned factories and huge unused gasoline tanks. Traffic has gotten heavier, with cyclos and motorbike-towed trailers on which dozens of passengers crowd. As we follow the Tonle Sap, I try to recognize places I'd seen before. Not far past Chruoy Changvar Bridge, recognizable due to its missing center span, we go by the former

French embassy, Calmette Hospital, and the Faculty of Medicine before reaching Psar Thmey. At 5:30 p.m. I'm finally here. Two full days to cover 420 km... But at one twentieth of the cost of flying.

I flop on the bed in the SIPAR house where Katell has invited me to stay. I dream, staring up at the ceiling, like an immaculately white sheet of paper. It's so quiet after hours and hours of tinny speakers, hissing air conditioning, the squeaks and screeches of the car, and the like. Now what? My mind completely at rest in this haven of peace and kindness, I have a week of fierce negotiations ahead of me. In eight days, I'll be back on the road. What will I have to show for it?

Than, my former translator, is still my right-hand man. He's short, businesslike, has a sharp-featured face, is always immaculately dressed, always on time, always even-tempered, and always available. He was a great help to me as a translator in the camps and will prove to be even more valuable in the setup phase in Cambodia. Rather than just diddling around anticipating repatriation, not even waiting for the exhibition to conclude, he left to join his sister who lives on a small street near Wat Langka, thinking he could find work with a UN program. But it's too early. UNTAC won't get underway until mid-March 1992. He therefore agrees to work with me. We get along well and he knows that a job with me will outlast the UN mandate. Having him on hand for meetings reassures me. His French is impeccable thanks to a stint in France with Citroën. Life was hard there and he couldn't get French citizenship, so he decided to return to his home country and settle in Phnom Penh. He's just the man I need.

The next morning, the Ministry of Foreign Affairs allows me to submit my re-updated files, translated and typed in Khmer on our spanking new letterhead bearing the Dangrek center logo. The whole project will come under Krousar Thmey. Everything is in order. At least, the way I see it. *Krousar Thmey*, New Family, the name causes my contact person to laugh. He asks where we're registered and what my title is. "In France!" I confidently reply. Actually, Krousar Thmey only exists because of the projects developed on Site II. The association is Cambodian because it came into being in the camp under Khmer control, but it has no legal structure. No document shows my position.

The law does not allow any association outside of the Communist Party, so I have no choice but to get registered as the representative of a foreign NGO. One that doesn't yet exist. So let's make one! My contact person has difficulty grasping the procedure, so I don't insist. However, there's always some new document needed or some translation that has to be corrected. Let's get back to work. Don't let tempers fray. Always, always stay calm.

In the evening, even though it costs over $7 a minute, I put through an emergency telephone call to my friend Marie-Caroline. A top student in my school, she gets things done fast and efficiently. Loyal to the nth degree, she's familiar with the project and has been sponsoring a child since its inception. The bottom line is that I need a legal entity. Can she call a general meeting of friends and put one together, appoint a chairperson, a secretary general, and a treasurer? As soon as I get back to Thailand, I fax her a draft set of statutes. That's it! The rest—fundraising, handling the sponsorship paperwork—I'll look after that. I just need to have the notice published in the official gazette.

While waiting for the new version to be typed out, I see representatives of UNICEF and submit a funding request to the HRC. The first repatriation convoy will soon be leaving the camps, and things will pick up speed.

With help from the Caritas staff, Father Émile Destombes in particular, a secretary agrees to type up my report. Their office is near Orussey Market. They've just gotten a computer with the newly created Khmer fonts. And, luckily, they have a generator, so they can work without waiting on the very unpredictable city power grid. The next morning, pleased with successfully getting the file corrected, translated, and typed in such a short time, I take Than along with me to meet my contact person in the ministry. Without even looking up at me or even touching the file that I'm handing him, he says that he doesn't need the report any more. He needs a different one.

What's wrong? What needs to be changed? No answer, just that he needs a different report. Than discreetly intimates to me that the report is not the issue. In fact, the man did not even take it. He wants an under-the-counter payment. I feel like bashing him in the head, but I succeed in maintaining a semblance of calm. Yes, an envelope might facilitate things and avoid these needless waits, these ongoing humiliations, these repeated frustrations. But I refuse to play the game, as I know it'll never end. I don't give him anything and won't give anything. Ever. I repeat that I am not involved in making money but in helping orphaned children grow up to be good Khmers. Totally insensitive to this cause, he answers: "But why are you looking after these parasites?"

Parasites? I lose it. "They are children just like any others, like yours. They did not choose to be born in the refugee camps and are just as entitled to live normally in Cambodia as any other children." Our meeting comes to an abrupt end and we make an appointment for two weeks later. I can't stand it. It's pathetic. What the hell am I doing with these civil servants that go out of their way to mess things up? I'm struggling as it is to raise funds, now I'm fighting a battle in government circles… I go back to Katell's place exhausted, disgusted, totally depressed. I lie down. The pallid ceiling I'm staring at is no longer a clean page to be written on, but the sky falling on my head. Over the next few days, I'm listless, incapacitated, but I can still think. I study the integration problems that the refugees will be confronted with. The NGOs in Phnom Penh go on and on about the conflicts between domestic Khmers and returnees. How can this antagonism be overcome? How can they be helped to work in harmony? How can I set up my own teams in Cambodia?

Even though I realize that I have to go back home on the same atrocious road, I'm relieved to go back, to get a break from this current dead-end proposition. I return to Ta Phraya the way I came. The same two-day aggravation. Only worse. It takes over two hours to fill the taxi. How I hate the tinny shrill of the cassette deck! The last person gets on and we go in the opposite direction to gas up. I'm at the end of my tether. What the hell! Couldn't he have filled up before? As if nothing can be foreseen here. We travel on from one disaster to the next, just like before. In the late afternoon, a torrential downpour pounds down. Mango rains, say the Cambodians of these April showers that make the fruit flesh out. The road becomes as slippery as an ice rink. The driver does a brilliant job, but the tires slide, the wheels skid, and the vehicle slews sideways, irresistibly drawn to the shoulders. After 11 hours of slalom and skating, I fall into the arms of my family in Battambang, a veritable hospice, a place to take a shower.

I leave very early the next morning for Poipet because the soldiers close the border at 5 p.m. Yesterday's rains have turned the road into an indescribable quagmire. The car goes in all directions. Twice, in a curve and in an attempt to avoid a rut, we almost slam into another vehicle. The pedestrians and motorbike riders must curse us when we spray them copiously with muddy water. When you know how hard it is to get those red blotches out…

The rain has cooled down the air, but the heat wastes no time in coming back. The last several weeks, the temperature has steadily risen to 40 °C in the shade. I'm thirsty. I dream of a freshly squeezed lemonade with a dash of sugar… knowing that I won't get any such thing until I'm on Thai soil. Faster than I expected, I reach home base in Ta Phraya before nightfall. Beat, I sit up against the wall on my mattress and listen to an entire rendition of Scarlatti's sonatas. After a good night's sleep, I already have to start planning my next trip. Happily, getting back to the camp, meeting the children again, sensing their enthusiasm and impatience to discover their country helps recharge my batteries. I've good reason to hang in there.

Ten days later, here we go again. I sleep in Aran so I can cross the border as soon as it opens. On the other side, surprise. A huge archway with a bamboo model of Angkor spans the road to welcome visitors to Cambodia. And what a welcome they get! Dust, potholes, plastic bags, scrap heaps… They find themselves in a dump. Cripples and beggars, it seems to be a meeting place of all the down-and-outs of Cambodia. What a sad first impression of the country! In just a few meters, one steps 40 years into the past! Fortunately, as soon as you get out of Poipet, despite the presence of landmines making it impossible to grow anything in the fields for the first few kilometers, the countryside is beautiful, as are the smiles of the farmers. Their simplicity is so touching. It's another two awful days on the road. Cash points have become routine, the potholes and dust inseparable companions. This time, no flat tire, no incident, and I'm in Phnom Penh the next afternoon. I quickly let Than know I'm back and ask him to join me early the next morning.

We have an 8:30 appointment at the ministry. Arriving a little early, Than and I settle on our sofas at the entrance. Reception has not opened yet. We wait. Aside from a few doors opening and closing and one or two stray souls in the corridors, the offices seem to be at a standstill. We wait two hours and still nothing. The receptionist kindly tells us that she'll soon be closing and that we'll have to come back. Her little black plastic telephone on the little desk couldn't have rung more than three or four times all morning. We wait almost as long in the afternoon. She doesn't understand. Our contact person hasn't shown up all day. "Maybe he went to a wedding," she ventures. "Come back tomorrow." The next day, he's another no-show. We try to find out what's going on. Is the man perhaps sick? Rather, we get the feeling that he's avoiding us. That means for once I have a little time ahead of me. I can go to Siem Reap to check out the land Sameath purchased and finally get to see the famous Angkor temples.

An hour on the road after a pre-dawn departure gets us to Udong. Despite the recent lifting of restrictions on interprovincial travel, controls abound on provincial borders. There's a cavalcade of cars ahead and a cash point seems to be blocking the road. Drunk soldiers? Fee inflation? We wait patiently in the dark. Suddenly a burst of gunfire. The flame spit out by the firearm proves that soldiers are close. Our hearts are in our boots. The driver shuts off the engine and switches off the headlights. Not a sound from the five or six blocked cars. Voices are heard. Then a yell. No doubt a soldier warning the first driver. The headlights go back on and things start to move. The first car pulls away, the others follow. When our driver holds the money out the window, another yell from the soldier. The driver grumbles and holds out more bills. Okay, we can move on. The driver groans angrily that the rate has jumped. Better not argue, just get going.

We again spend the night in Battambang where the family renting out *pahis* is happy to see me again. We get back on the road and turn on to National Highway 6 at Sisophon. A small truck with Singaporean plates once used for transporting medicine is the only vehicle at the departure point. Benches have been put in sideways. It seems to take forever to fill. When we finally get going, it's immediately obvious why there are so few vehicles on the road. It's worse than the previous ones. The truck does not hold up well at all to the potholes and the way we are sitting is of no help. We are as if on the sea, in a lurch that throws us against the metal walls. The two makeshift windows in the box don't let in a breath of air. The sun is gleefully making our perspiration flow in rivulets. We then open the side sliding door. Dust immediately sweeps in. We drag along this way for several kilometers, then catch sight of something in the distance that looks like a mini-Site II. It's a camp of internally displaced persons, Cambodians who have had to flee their land because of unremitting attacks. Near a bridge, the driver has us get out. He lines his wheels up on the sugar palm tree trunks. We go over on foot, but stay to the edge of the road. The ditches have not yet been demined. On the other side, the road is one of the worst I have ever been on. Dozens of bridges are out. The countryside has been abandoned because of landmines. Nothing but drought and desolation all around.

We arrive in Kralanh at noon, a small town 50 km from our starting point. Whoopee! Half way there. By late afternoon we make it in to Siem Reap. In the shadow of tall trees stands the royal villa. Opposite is the Grand Hôtel that has billeted a few tourists despite its state of disrepair. We cross the stone bridge and come to Psar Leu. Then a short stretch by *moto dop* before arriving at Sameath's place. The traditional wooden house stands on the other side of a pond, no doubt dug to raise the level of the lot to avoid flooding.

Two signs, one for the Monorom Beauty Salon, another a tailor shop. Sameath's brother-in-law is a tailor. His wife and daughters run the beauty salon. One of the daughters is talkative, but our conversation is limited due to her rudimentary English. To prepare for our clean-up, a young boy taken in by the family as a servant is dispatched to draw water to fill a big jar. I'm ashamed of being served like that and try my hand… The result is disappointing. I just don't have the knack. Every time I drop the bucket down, I only get about a third of a pail. After washing up, I meet the boyfriend of one of Sameath's nieces. He's a medical student in Phnom Penh up to visit his fiancée while on a break before the Khmer New Year. He speaks a smattering of French and our projects interest him. I ask about the medical school curriculum and how the faculty is run. During the meal, we are only men. This bothers me and I insist that the women of the house join us. No dice. We eat by candlelight, seated on the floor. When we're finished, the women take over and eat what's left. For a matriarchal society, the women seem to occupy a very unassuming position.

Worn out, I'm ready to drop. The family insists I have a bedroom. However much I refuse, I end up sharing a room with Than. I'm uncomfortable, but I appreciate the Khmer hospitality.

Still without an agreement with the Ministry of Foreign Affairs, we feel it's better to avoid any contact with the officials. However, I'm anxious to see the land bought by proxy. With Sameath in the lead, we motorbike past the *École française d'Extrême-Orient*. Its commodious buildings and grounds seem abandoned. A little further on, at Enkosar Pagoda, hundreds of students in blue and white are in their classrooms. In Cambodia, pagodas are often venues for knowledge dissemination. This is a junior high school. Enkosey Pagoda, further on, is one of the oldest in the town, and has several hundred primary school pupils. Small brick temples from the 10th century are still standing in the pagoda enclosure.

The vegetation gradually gets heavier and we enter a thick forest growing right up to the river. There are fewer houses. After another kilometer, we emerge from the forest and pass by barely used military barracks. A few cattle are grazing in front of the entrance where a platoon is taking a siesta. We follow a dirt road that narrows down into a sandy stretch for about 2 km, following a river that can be glimpsed from time to time. The road goes on interminably and I'm apprehensive about Sameath's choice. But he finally stops in the middle of the bush. We must have arrived. Not a tree for shade, just a few yellowed shrubs. The sandy soil is reddish white, as hard as concrete, reflecting the heat. It's stifling. It's hard to imagine that the river is nearby. We stroll over the property measuring 50 m wide by 240 m deep. Roots and wild grass are everywhere. At the back, an earthen dike that once demarcated the city of Angkor bears recent signs of fighting. It's big, but so far! Too late to change. Delegating means you have to accept decisions made by others. We push on along the river and find ourselves directly in front of Angkor Wat. I've seen so many pictures and paintings of it, and finally here's the real thing in all its majesty.

We're alone save for a handful of tourists. We cross a long causeway over the western moat. Once through the entrance pavilion or *gopura,* we are stunned by the incredible view of the towers. We continue on over another causeway bordered by serpentine balustrades, with heads of nagas, mythical snakes, at each end. The causeway gives way to a set of entrance steps. We take the central staircase to access the second gopura, which in turn opens to innumerable galleries. A closer inspection reveals hints of an exchange of bullets here and there. The temples seem intact, as if preserved from the human atrocities by the protective genies of Angkor.

The inner walls of the galleries are decorated with giant bas-reliefs. Given a glossy patina by time, they are somewhat like a strip of educational cartoons. The hand-to-hand combats are fierce. Foot soldiers pierce the flanks of enemy elephants and horses with their lances. The Brahman priest with his hair coiled in a bun bends his bow. Further along, the king and his court are on parade, the princesses on their palanquins, his majesty towering over minor ministers. Another bas-relief depicts the judgment of souls. Heaven or hell? Let the viewer decide. I prefer to think that these elegant notables are heaven-bound. Things are very nasty in hell. Demons torture their victims gasping for breath who are then made prey for wild beasts. Some, hooks in their noses, are drawn along like cattle. Others have their bones shattered or their bodies pierced with long nails.

The silence is incredible. From time to time the chirping of a bird then, suddenly, the strident trilling of cicadas breaks the hush. We come back the next morning to tour the temples on the *petit circuit.* Ta Prohm overwhelms me with its towering silk cotton trees, huge trees with gigantic roots that embrace the stones in a silvery lava flow. The walls buckle. It's said that the trees keep the temple from collapsing, but Sameath disputes that. Seeds sprout shortly after being deposited by a bird. The roots of the silk cotton or *Celba pentandra* tree then grow towards the ground, making their way into the cracks and crevices. As they grow, they force apart the stones that they lock in a voluptuous but mortal embrace. When the tree dies or is swayed by violent winds, the entire temple trembles and stones tumble.

I would like to prolong this visit with virtually everything to ourselves, but we must be off the next morning for the first repatriation. On our way before the crack of dawn, we are stopped at a village with fortress-like protection. High bamboo gates block our passage. I'm about to get out of the car to open the gates, but the driver stops me. Seeing the headlights, a group of soldiers in the distance extricate themselves from their hammocks and walk slowly toward us, carefully examining the ground. The driver tells us that they're picking up the landmines they put out the evening before for protection. Recently, a taxi drove over a mine undoubtedly forgotten by a soldier after a night of carousing, which left a large gaping hole in his vehicle. All the same, the rest of the trip is uneventful.

The next day, I experience the same feeling of joy when I get back to the kids. They were waiting for me, anxious to hear about my trip and the visit to Angkor. They're enthralled. The O'Bok bunch know that they will soon be leaving for Siem Reap and will be able to see the temples first hand. The Dangrek orphans will go to Phnom Penh. There was no choice of places to go. The teams in the two centers worked with the HCR to determine the repatriation destinations under UN protection.

On March 30, 1992, excitement reins all over Site II. Khmer music is blasting over the loudspeakers. We all put on white shirts. Whitewash has been applied around the outer perimeter of the camps, giving a festive atmosphere to the place. Soldiers and UN vehicles are everywhere. On the esplanade in front of the huge Rhytissen meeting hall, buses are parked in perfect alignment. An official stage is set up. Under the chairmanship of Thai Prime Minister General Suchinda and in the presence of a large number of Cambodian officials, Sergio Vierra de Mello, special representative of the HCR, kicks off the huge repatriation operation. Thai and Cambodian flags ripple in the wind.

Banners in both languages are splashed over the buildings, vaunting Khmer-Thai friendship. Khmers from all of the camps and belonging to all of the political factions will be repatriated, and this marks the beginning of a historic event.

This time, 527 persons will be going home after years in the camp. With the civil war, the Khmer Rouge, and the Vietnamese invasion, some haven't seen their home villages since 1970. Their fear is palpable. Fear of landmines, of malaria, of the Khmer Rouge, of their returning empty-handed to a country where no one will be there to welcome them. The domestic Cambodians are cagey about their coming back. Nevertheless, they are happy to be the first to go back to their land on Khmer soil, so dear to their hearts. I grasp how very lucky I am to be with them and to witness this whirlwind of emotions. They are happy to get back to being normal Cambodians. After so many years of suffering from being nobodies. After so many years as displaced persons liable to being driven out of Thailand at any time. After so many years of inactivity and hopelessness. Feelings are at a fever pitch. A cross-section of families with children, young people, and elderly had been selected to symbolize unity. Disabled persons will be handled separately by the HCR and leave later.

But the country is not completely pacified. Despite the Paris peace agreements, fighting continues here and there. That very morning, armed conflicts were reported north of Phnom Penh. Put on buses chartered by the HCR, the 527 returnees are going to Sisophon where Prince Sihanouk, chairman of the Supreme National Council, is coming to meet them with a retinue of officials. Then, in keeping with procedure, they will be transferred to an intake center to rest, get registered, be informed of their rights, get their ID papers, and then be escorted onward to their chosen destination.

As the Buddhist New Year approaches, everything grinds to a halt. I use the time to do some shopping in northern Thailand. A raft of visitors has bought up all my stock and the coolness of the mountains will give me a welcome break before heading back to Phnom Penh. Damien flies up to join me, taking advantage of flights chartered by the United Nations. With UNTAC just getting started, flights are frequent and often empty, so a special permit allows us to get on them.

In Battambang, I meet NGO leaders and visit the HCR reception center that just opened, fenced off with barbed wire. To protect the refugees, I'm told. There, I see families from Site II that were repatriated a few days earlier. For the time being, the center is still operating in standby mode, but reintegration problems are already surfacing. The HRC is short of land to make available to the refugees.

In Phnom Penh, I stay in Katell's house again, although I promise her I will very quickly find another place. The application with the Ministry of Foreign Affairs hasn't moved an inch. There's always something not right. The real problem, of course, is my refusal to pay a bribe.

While waiting it out in Phnom Penh, I take a look at available property. I very much like a piece of land in Ta Khmau. The location is very peaceful, banana groves have been planted round about, and the soil is very good. The children will be able to grow vegetables and fruit trees on it. I find another lot on the Chbar Ampov side. After considerable hesitation, I take an option on both of them. I figure that we can easily handle it, as I'm expecting a large donation from Belgium pledged in the wake of a Barbara Hendricks concert. The figure of 1,200,000 Belgian francs was advanced, i.e. about $40,000, to arrive in a month.

I also look for a place for the Krousar Thmey offices and for me to live. Since September 1991, I've been trying to sell my studio apartment on Ménilmontant Street in Paris. I bought it when I graduated in 1989 with five student loans. I fixed it up while working as financial controller for ACCOR. In September, a sales agreement for 390,000 francs was signed, but the buyer suddenly backed out upon learning there were two attempted murders in the building! With the bottom going out of the real estate market, I'm forced to drop my price. The place eventually goes for 280,000 francs, which allows me to contemplate the purchase of a small house in Phnom Penh. In December, I could have bought something downtown, but now I can only look at a fixer-upper in a lower-class neighborhood.

Since mid-March 1992, with the arrival of the United Nations, rents have gone up tenfold, with nice villas going for $3,000 a month. Many foreigners are evicted from their homes with only two weeks' notice. The owners, often high-ranking officials, are charging premium prices, even if it means they have to live in a backyard shack. They use the deposit money to buy up other houses to rent out as well. Fortunes are being made in record time.

After looking around, I find a house in Teuk Laak 1, a working-class quarter somewhat off center. It's of 1950s architecture and quite sound structurally, just needs a bit of renovating. It has a small front yard. The second floor has three rooms and a large living area; the third has two rooms, a spacious open terrace, and a kitchen off to the side. Strangely, it has no bathroom. The ground floor is occupied by a family who uses the back door, which makes it feel like I own the whole building. Houses are paid for in gold. I eventually get it for 80 ounces of gold, or $33,000.

But the law doesn't allow foreigners to own property, so, like all other potential buyers, I need a straw-man. Impatient to take occupancy, the next few nights I sleep over in the house. After cleaning the well, I start doing some laundry. News of my moving in has spread like wildfire, and the astonished neighbors gather around this white man out washing clothes. It's unseemly for a man, especially white, to stoop to perform household chores. So everyone offers his sister, his cousin, or his neighbor lady in marriage, all in good fun. There's no fence, so they unabashedly come in to check out the place and see how I live. I get the renovation work going right away. But during this time when all of Phnom Penh is getting a facelift, the only workers available are Vietnamese. Traditionally, the Khmers are farmers, soldiers, or civil servants, the Chinese businesspeople; craftsmen are often of Vietnamese origin. The first job is to get a perimeter wall up.

In mid-May 1992, upon returning to Site II, the child welfare center is in turmoil. Kong, one of my assistants, is going to be repatriated against his will. He overlooked getting registered with the children and staff, and finds himself on the list of early departures. When the time comes to get on the bus, he is terrified at the idea of being "thrown to the Khmer Rouge." I try to reassure him but he is petrified. He makes me promise to come and get him as soon as he is repatriated and put him up safely in my house in Phnom Penh. Something promised, something due. I look after the matter in the next few days.

With every new trip, the country changes. Poipet is getting busier and trans-border trade is getting organized. I ask the taxi to stop 28 km from Battambang, at Thmor Kol, a small village where the Sisophon and Bavel roads meet. Kong was left there the week before. I look for an administration office and come across a police station where I explain the situation. The officer speaks French well and points to a nearby refugee camp. Sensing my quandary, he offers to guide me through the maze of rice fields. I leave my bag at the police station, jump on his motorbike, and we zigzag from dirt trails to small dikes. Everything seems heat-parched and barren, as if there hasn't been a drop of water in years. Spots of blue appear in the distance, the plastic tarps providing shelter for the dozens of families repatriated to this lunar landscape.

An HCR vehicle is on site. Surprise! Out steps Norah, who I know from Site II, an Irish lass of resilient character working as a field officer. She's equally surprised to see me out in the middle of nowhere. When I explain why I came, she laughs, adding in dismay that no one can be let out of the place; the people are all under the control of the local government. Moreover, the night before, the police would not let a refugee out to attend to his dying mother in Phnom Penh...

We have a bit of a conversation.

"Bénito, you know, if it's impossible for me, assigned by the UN to help refugees, you can't even think about it! You're a nobody and here you are out in the middle of the rice fields, on your own, no vehicle, to take a refugee away? Are you out of your mind?"

"No, I'm not out of my mind. I promised Kong I would come and get him. I'm here to pick him up and we're going on to Phnom Penh."

"How on earth did you get here?"

"By motorbike, with the police chief."

"The police chief? The one who wouldn't allow me to let a refugee out yesterday?"

"Could be. He drove me out here and I've no intention of leaving without Kong."

"No, you're not going to turn everything upside down!"

"Yes I am, if it's okay with the police chief."

"Where did you come from?"

"Ta Phraya."

"How did you get across the border? It's closed?"

"I walked across. I have a permit from the Thai army."

Norah can't believe her ears. The people at Aran have to drive over to Bangkok, fly to Phnom Penh, and drive up to Battambang, while I just walked over the border.

"And where's the guy you're looking for?"

"I don't know yet, but I'll look for him."

Norah goes back to her work while I go looking for Kong with the help of a photograph, because I'm quite sure that just the name 'Kong' isn't going to be enough. I'm immediately shown a group of refugees off in the distance. I wave like crazy. Kong catches sight of me and races over at lightning speed, his arms raised heavenward; I'm his savior. He cries with joy. He tells me about the lack of water, the lack of shade, the hostile environment, and the Khmer Rouge or bandits that prowl about at night. Terrified, he won't let go of me. I reassure him by promising to get him to my place in Phnom Penh.

Norah gets ready to return to Battambang.

"Can you take us?"

"You're out of your mind. I'm not taking a repatriated person without permission when just yesterday I couldn't even let a person out with a written application. Sorry! I can take you but not the other guy."

It couldn't be more ridiculous. Of course, I turn to the police chief to see if he could take Kong along. No problem. He even refuses the money that it would normally have cost to go by *moto dop*. A little nose thumbing at the United Nations? I get in with Norah, carrying Kong's bag that weighs a ton. It's holding books that Sinath kindly dumped on Kong, for fear that he might not get them through or that they would fall into the wrong hands. That night I didn't even have to spend the night with my *pahi* family, as Norah let me use a room with two single beds at the HCR office. I get in touch with some expatriates working in Battambang in order to prepare for our outreach into western Cambodia. Kong is very relieved to get to Phnom Penh the next day.

On Saturday, June 6, 1992, we have an appointment at the Ministry of Foreign Affairs. My application hasn't budged. On June 8, I land at the ministry again. I need to write a letter to request an appointment. At 2 p.m., I am informed that the appointment is for the next day. On June 9, after getting conflicting information every half hour, I realize that my contact person will not be coming. I was able to pay off the lot in Ta Khmau with funds received from friends. But the money from the Barbara Hendricks concert is not forthcoming, despite repeated promises and calls. I'm worried. I really like the property in Chbar Ampov, but we could lose the deposit. I succeed in reaching the contact person in Belgium, who is in a state of confusion. Instead of 1.2 million Belgian francs, we'll only be getting 120,000, i.e. less than $4,000, and he doesn't know when. I'm having serious cash flow problems. If I don't come up with the balance in two weeks I'll lose my down payment.

While in Phnom Penh briefly this time, I meet the director of Indosuisse, now a management company for NGOs in Cambodia. With UNTAC now up and running, the company is expanding rapidly and he's recruiting. He urgently needs five qualified employees. I immediately think of some of my students, an unhoped-for opportunity for them. He gives me a few days to brief them once I get back to the camps. I already have some picks among my students or Alain's. Young graduates of working age are in a real dilemma. The repatriation process has started. Despite the great fear of returning to an unfamiliar land, early repatriates have a better chance of getting jobs with United Nations agencies or companies. Those down on the list will have to wait. It'll be a year before things wrap up. For some, it's better to go now, even if it means missing out on the free issuance of ID papers and certain HCR benefits. The repatriation prospect is as disruptive mentally as it is physically.

A surprising message is awaiting me in Ta Phraya. I'm to call back a person in France who reportedly has some funds for me. The person I talk to tells me that his deceased son had some money in an account. The father doesn't want it. He'd heard about our work in the camps and asked if I could use the sum. It's a little more than I need. Random chance, good luck, providence, or coincidence, I don't know, but it couldn't have come at a better time.

That evening, a United Nations vehicle is sitting outside our usual bargain restaurant and two soldiers are enjoying a leisurely meal. For some days now, they've been there for lunch and sometimes dinner. One is from Algeria, the other Morocco. We hit it off right away and they come over for a drink. They are UN observers, based near Thma Puok, just on the other side of the border. They go back and forth through a military post that is out of bounds for me.

There are also some new faces. Groups of Buddhists and monks of various orders are working under the umbrella of the Coalition for Peace and Reconciliation (CPR). They're supporting Cambodians rallying to this theme. There's talk about support for civil society. Venerable Maha Gosananda will soon lead the first march for peace to Cambodia, the *Dharma Yatra*.

Nearly 2,000 participants are to march from Site II and cover the whole country of Cambodia, starting in the north, led by such admirable activists as Peter Gyallay-Pap, a stateless person. I thus learn that it's possible for a person to not be considered as a national by any State. He holds a passport issued by the United Nations.

This first *Dharma Yatra* is critically important as the repatriation process is encountering difficulties. The HCR proposes a number of options. The first is to grant pieces of farmland in the deep countryside, materials to build a simple house, tools, seed, and food rations for 400 days. The second includes the same provisions, less the land allotment. The last is a one-time payment of $50 per adult, $25 per child under 12, and food rations for 400 days. That's not much, given that inflation has been galloping since the arrival of the United Nations.

It takes no time for the first option to be dropped. The land allotted by the local authorities is often mined or inadequate. After seeing how long it takes the first beneficiaries to get clearance for a piece of land and the obstacles encountered, 87 percent of the people go for number 3, the money option. Some areas cannot be developed because of landmines or fighting, but sometimes simply because of the violent hostility of the local communities. Around Battambang, Rattanak Mondol district is particularly unsafe. Many Cambodians have had landmine accidents. One person out of 90 is an amputee, which is much higher than the national average. After years under UN protection, the refugees are facing the terrible reality of daily life in Cambodia. One has to eat every day, but what if you have no job, no land? Health care facilities are either non-existent or in total disrepair... and nothing is free. Some repatriates even leave the place to which they were sent and return to the camp.

Word gets around and anger brews at Site II. The amounts distributed are insufficient. Riots lead to the closure of the camp for several days. The demonstrators demand more money for repatriation. Public buildings and the United Nations supply stations are looted. The situation is tense, almost explosive. Repatriation is suspended for two weeks. That's unfortunate for me, because I want to meet the potential applicants. Or, rather, it's fortunate. Alain had made up a list of about 15 students who would like to get out early because they have lost faith in the repatriation process. My good relationship with the DPPU comes in handy. On June 11, I'm allowed to have them called up to the camp entrance. I choose five, including Nou, Sok, and Savouth, alias Mr. Rooster. I advance them money for the trip and give them my address in Phnom Penh, very happy to see them get jobs. After teaching them, what a pleasure to give them a leg up! Teaching tends to be frustrating when you rarely see the results. This time, I feel like I've done something useful. So my house is in the shambles of renovations, but at least it's a place for these individual refugees to stay until they can manage on their own. They'll find Kong already there.

I fear for the safety of the children if the situation should worsen. The children are unsettled. But those in the *chayam* group are all excited about their upcoming trip to perform in the Thai capital. They've been invited by the French school and the Belgian embassy in Bangkok. We get permission for all to make the trip. Sinath, Cham, and the dancing teachers are included. But tensions persist and the event is postponed. A few days later, calm returns. The children travel directly to Bangkok on a Site II minibus, where I join them after doing a round of fundraising conferences in Singapore. They had a terrible trip. Many got carsick despite taking anti-nausea medication.

The kids are totally flabbergasted. Billeted with French and Belgian families, they mix with the young pupils of the French school. We had repeatedly told them in advance that the way expatriate families live in

Bangkok is by no means typical of all Europeans. Some of the houses where they stayed have yards, even swimming pools. What we take for granted is special for them. Some walk straight into glass doors. They have difficulty navigating a staircase, ascending or descending. They love escalators and go up and down just for fun. They're fascinated by 40-story buildings. Elevators leave them awestruck. All along the way, they were already getting a foretaste just seeing the rows of concrete houses, they who know nothing but bamboo and thatch. They find the traffic mindboggling. They've come to put on a show, but they also attend one, that of a modern teeming, noisy city. They think I'm a magician who has transported them into a fantastic dream.

The *chayam* concert is a resounding success. The children are received at the residence of the Belgian ambassador, and are most impressed to be applauded by an audience of foreigners. Such ovations help them grow in self-confidence, something they desperately lack.

On June 25, 1992, I leave again for Phnom Penh. With summer, the rainy season moves in and makes travel much harder to the border and Cambodia. Between slip-sliding along and getting stuck in slimy sinkholes of mud requiring a tractor to pull us out, travel is a slow affair. But in return, there's a feast for the eyes. In just a few weeks, the countryside is covered with a green checkerboard. The yellowish fields have given way to an impressive palette of greens, the intense greens of the seedbeds, the light greens of newly transplanted seedlings. Nature makes sport of its nuances. Depending on their level of maturity and the amount of water they are growing in, rice plants have different colors and shimmer under the slightest breeze. Aeolus brings life to the carpets of green and the rice fields. The little boy in me makes me want to frolic about in them, nibble on the tender shoots.

Early in the rainy season, when only the lowest tracts of lands are flooded, which is often right along the roadside, the farmers plant seedbeds. Then they can be seen out in the rice fields, a knotted krama tied around their necks, containing a specific quantity of seeds. The seeds have been meticulously selected from the previous harvest. They sow them broadcast with the right hand. Several weeks later, when the rainy season is in full swing, the seedlings are uprooted by hand. I'm awed by the spectacle, these men and women identically garbed with broad-brimmed straw hats, under a scorching sun or in driving rain, barefoot and stooped over, going first to one side, then from front to back. Bent akimbo, they uproot the seedlings carefully and gather them in bunches with the left hand. When they have a handful, they deftly turn around and, balancing on the left foot, place the right foot on the left knee. They strike the bunch sharply against the sole of the foot to shake off the soil clinging to the roots and thus lighten its weight. The movement is precise, invariable. These meticulously calibrated bouquets are then taken out to the field for transplanting. On the plowed fields, the farmers in rigorous alignment take a few rice seedlings in their right hand and plant them five or six centimeters apart. The seedlings, very compact in the seedbed, can breathe here, prosper, and three or four months later, yield the plump golden heads of rice ready for harvest. Due to the lack of irrigation in these parts, unlike neighboring countries, it is very seldom possible to grow more than one crop a year. The yield is often poor because of a lack of technical advancements and fertilizer.

In Phnom Penh, the house renovations are winding up. A distant cousin arrives, interested in doing humanitarian work for an indefinite time. I'm not yet very busy in Cambodia, so I don't have much for her to do. She agrees to monitor the progress of the application at the Ministry of Foreign Affairs. Hope it goes well! They're specialists in wearing a person down, and wear her down they will. She may not have cherished memories of the Cambodian government apparatus, but she did a great job for us. Like a fuse, she got a jolt of adrenalin each time she met with the officials. But she was duly rewarded through the festive outings, especially with French soldiers, one of whom became... her husband.

Our funding applications filed with the HCR in Phnom Penh were approved. We had asked for and received $69,000 to buy land, build two welfare centers, and run them for a year. On the other hand, still no agreement in sight with the Ministry of Foreign Affairs. A new contact person comes right out with it, very suavely and with a naughty grin: "You know, your application isn't moving along... You have to understand us and help us. Our salaries are very low." At that point, I answer him tit for tat, all the while smiling: "True, your salaries are low, but your income is high! I have come only to help Cambodian children. I really don't have a salary. I don't see why I should pay yours." I anticipate a furious reaction. Quite the contrary, he mildly responds: "I see that you understand how things work in Cambodia. We'll see." I don't know what to think of this meeting.

I learn that the HCR has received a request from Austcare, one of its powerful financial supporters, to do a film on repatriation of the children. They do what they can to nudge along my application with the able assistance of Margie and Vada from UNICEF. They had agreed to fund a third welfare center to take in the last of the children abandoned in the camps. The HCR is also anticipating that the Cambodian welfare workers will jump the gun and leave before the repatriation operation is over in order to get jobs with UNTAC. So I come up with a working agreement that meets with their full approval. We will work together to put as many unaccompanied children as possible through the repatriation process, with priority on getting them back with their families. Once the repatriation effort concludes, the HCR's Cambodian teams will become Krousar Thmey teams. That way, the HCR can fulfill its responsibilities right to the end with a competent staff base, the Cambodians have a secure future, and Krousar Thmey takes over the contingent of trained workers.

These mutual arrangements in place and the happy atmosphere in the two small Site II centers lead the HCR to choose Krousar Thmey as its reference program for child repatriation and to recommend that our activities be featured in a film. An Australian television team comes to scout for locations on Site II.

United Nations soldiers and staff are swarming in. NGOs proliferate to such an extent that an "NGO land" comes into being in downtown Phnom Penh's Boeung Keng Kong ward. With every visit, I come across volunteers of all nationalities. This is a real shake-up for Cambodian society. The riel, the national currency, is supplanted by the American dollar. The first foreign bank, Cambodian Commercial Bank, a branch of a large Thai bank, materializes not far from Central Market, on Achar Mean Avenue. It's the bank chosen by the United Nations and the peacekeeping forces collect their salaries there. Out of affection for Cambodia, I go for the Foreign Trade Bank, a Cambodian government enterprise, which I later have second thoughts about. Every time a transfer is made, it's a struggle to see the money credited to our accounts. Everyone seems to have a different view about stagnant money.

United Nations vehicles are everywhere. At night, foreigners converge on No Problem Café on Street 178, in an immense colonial house. The city is changing fast. All kinds of establishments spring up to entertain the UN soldiers. New karaoke joints, massage parlors, and other places of ill repute open weekly. In one karaoke establishment, the drink menu comes with a list of girls, in descending order according to nationality. So much for a Russian girl, so much for a Thai, so much for a Vietnamese and, at the bottom of the list, so much for a local girl. Things are moving fast, very fast. Too fast?

On July 3, 1992, I get a yes from the government. The Ministry of Foreign Affairs invites me to sign the memorandum of understanding in August. I won! And without paying a penny!

Things now really pick up speed. I prepare an application for the Ministry of Social Affairs. First for the two centers in Siem Reap and Ta Khmau, then for the one in Sisophon. But Social Affairs has in mind that down the line the children will be integrated into government orphanages. Not a chance! Fortunately, an agreement with the HCR and UNICEF makes this impossible. Nevertheless, I understand their fears. There's great distrust between the camp orphanages and the domestic orphanages. They've been enemies for years and have a hard time working together. As a token of good faith and of my commitment to a non-political integration, I suggest that the ministry appoint a representative in each of our centers. They can thus keep an eye on what's happening there and it'll save me the bother of writing up reports, which in any case never meet with their approval. And I can get our values through to the ministry staff. At their working meetings, they can weigh the pros and cons between the huge State-run facilities and small private ones like ours.

In the government's eyes, caring for orphans has long been simply a matter of giving them something to eat. They do not tackle things like playing games, providing emotional support, helping the child develop humanly, socially, and culturally. They have neither the resources nor the training. Civil servants are neither better nor worse than anyone else. By working with us, the government staff will soon catch on to our mindset and grasp the essentially family type of concern for children that prevails in Krousar Thmey. By keeping the facilities small, of human dimension, better results are achieved than in the huge impersonal centers run by the government.

This leads me to suggest that government staff join my teams. They find this disconcerting, but their fears subside. We come to an agreement... My next job will be working with the teams at the provincial level. I waste no time getting in touch with the provincial authorities.

I then come to realize that in each of our centers for repatriated orphans, there are already excessive numbers of children of primary school age. To avoid giving the impression that the children from the camps are dislodging the others, it is imperative that extra classrooms be built as the centers go up. Our goal eventually is to mainstream the children into their new environment. They must not live as returnees without outside contact. In addition to including government workers on Krousar Thmey's teams, we need to start hiring local staff. That's a big order to begin with, as we are in the process of repatriating structures that are already operating; but it matters for the future. Similarly, the local structures already up and running must remain open so that the children from the camps are accepted by their peers as full-fledged Cambodian children.

The stage is thus set for us to start rebuilding three classrooms in Ta Khmau, putting up two classrooms at Enkosey Pagoda in Siem Reap, and five classrooms in Sisophon. This way, at each location, we make more seats available than we take. Than monitors the building work and agreements out of Phnom Penh while Sinath handles things on Site II.

In late August 1992, I head for France for about five weeks to work on files, meet corporate leaders—including ACCOR top management—in an attempt to garner their help to fund the building of primary schools. The projects are going full steam ahead and I need more people around me. I can't do everything; I have to delegate. My trip to the Hexagon proves to be fruitful.

I receive a call from the chairman of the Agir pour le Cambodge association. He knows that I need a chairperson to run Krousar Thmey in France, a strong leader who can find new donors and take on the commercial aspect of fundraising. One of his contacts has just returned after years abroad and is looking for something to do in his retirement years. Humanitarian work interests him, but the big organizations aren't comfortable with retiree volunteers and reject him out of hand.

Philippe Magnier retired after long years with Total Group, with whom he worked as a geologist, then as deputy chairman in the United States. We meet him along with Jean-Marie. He invites us for lunch in Montorgueil, near his home base in Paris. I'm immediately taken with his can-do attitude. White-haired and bearded, he's a Captain Haddock type, big hearted, doesn't beat around the bush, and sometimes sounds harsh. He agrees with our non-denominational approach, shares our zest for action and our stringent management. He's outraged with the large sums of donated money that big organizations waste in advance on advertising. Philippe puts down two conditions—that he be kept busy and that he be considered as a volunteer one hundred percent. Rightly, I had no intention of letting him stand idle and even less of putting him on a payroll. Right from the start, we pride ourselves in minimizing administrative expenditures and have always kept them under 4 percent of donations received.

I go by the Institut Européen des Affaires where I studied and give a presentation on Krousar Thmey's activities. It has two goals: appeal to this brood of students, generally from well-off families, and make them aware of our financial needs. When I finish, two students say they would like to spend a couple of months in Cambodia. That's too short, but I get their help to put together a second exhibition, a job that will take them at least six months.

The unqualified success of *Rizières: deux cultures à découvrir* convinced Jean-Marie and me to put on another exhibition. My travels in Cambodia reveal that children born and raised right in the country are no better aware of their rich heritage than those in the camps. Moreover, we believe in the strength of identity to help the younger generation to cleave together and become rooted in their culture. The two students do research work with Jean-Marie, then arrive in Cambodia in April 1993.

I am also looking for a young person to manage a restaurant soon to open. When I bought my house in April, I recalled a suggestion from a volunteer worker in Ta Phraya. I had told him about my high school business venture when I would make pizzas on Friday night to sell at the market on Saturday morning. He quipped that I should open a restaurant in Phnom Penh. When I saw the big house, its rooftop terrace, and huge kitchen, the restaurant project came back to mind. I mentioned this to my family and one of my sisters introduced me to the brother of a boyfriend who was interested in working with me. He is sort of adrift and looking for something to do. He isn't particularly qualified for anything in Krousar Thmey, but has energy to spare and the will to succeed. He loves cooking and has an eye for things smart and classy which makes him the right man to get the restaurant going.

A few weeks later, he lands in Phnom Penh. He didn't get a wink of sleep on his night flight, finds the weather stifling hot, and asks where he can take a shower. I show him the 8,000-liter tank that I had built to ensure I had enough water. In 1992, water is a rare commodity. More than a week can go by without a drop from the city supply. He calls out to me. He wants to know what he should do to rinse off. Puzzled, I go downstairs. Unbelievable! There he is splashing about in the middle of the tank in a froth of soap bubbles. The usual practice is to take a bath in one's undershorts, right out in the yard beside the tank, simply drawing water with a metal bowl. He didn't figure it out and just jumped in the water tank, liberally shampooing and lathering himself up. We burst out laughing. The water has to be emptied and a water truck called to refill the tank with clean water. This misunderstanding of customs and habits reminds me of the story of a Cambodian who stayed with some folks in Versailles. He filled up a bathtub from which he could draw water to pour over himself while he stood beside it, oblivious to the flood he was causing...

During the next few days, we design the tables and chairs and come up with a menu. I give him carte blanche for staff hiring and training. His business insight is more valuable than hospitality school training. I get Sok back again, who doesn't find Indosuisse very challenging, and he proves to be very helpful with the nuts and bolts. A short, stocky man,

Sok is very clever and good with his hands. He lost track of his parents during the evacuation of Phnom Penh in 1975 and grew up in the Khmer Rouge youth brigades. When the Vietnamese arrived, he was conscripted into the army, but deserted and fled to the refugee camps. Inquisitive by nature, and especially drawn to anything technical, he studied under Gilles and Alain at the Dangrek Technical School. Both thorough and trustworthy, he remains one of my right-hand men. He will go on to have a smashing time in Paris, rub shoulders with the French, enjoy our gastronomy, and become a French sausage foodie.

On every trip I make between the border and Phnom Penh, I'm loaded down like a donkey. I'm gradually transferring my things from my house in Ta Phraya and filling the one in Phnom Penh. But with the supplies needed for the restaurant, including white porcelain dishware from Thailand, it'll take months. I share this concern with our Maghrebian soldier friends who we see regularly at meals. They're going to Phnom Penh next week to have their vehicles serviced. One of the pair agrees to haul my dining room supplies to Phnom Penh. Given the condition the road is in, I fear that the dishes will end up in shards. He scoffs. I didn't get his point. They pile my stuff into the vehicles and cross the Cambodian border. There, an enormous MI 26 Soviet helicopter with the capacity to swallow both trucks takes them on board. On the ground in Phnom Penh, they casually drive up to my house and unload the goods. What a show off! remark my friends. Indeed, given the context, it's hard to imagine more seamless logistics.

It seems preposterous to me that the UN system could be so dysfunctional. True, it might be hard to get vehicles serviced out in the provinces, but move them by helicopter? There are good garages in Thailand… To top that, I learn that all of the military's water supply goes through Phnom Penh, Battambang, and Sisophon, with the help of a flotilla of Transall C-160s and helicopters, while the border is a mere 50 km away.

But when you say United Nations, you're saying standardization, centralization, and systemization. To preclude any misadventure, everything follows strict administrative procedures, regardless of the mission. Where safety is involved, okay, but what a waste!

My move is now over, so I can give attention to our long-term setup in Cambodia.

I am back in Thailand on October 18 and rush to Bangkok to pick up Jean-Marie, accompanied by a photographer who will cover our first repatriation. I make a lightning trip from Ta Phraya to Site II in order to oversee the preparations. Everything is ready. We will depart for Siem Reap on November 2. Completely run down by all the travelling, I need more than a week to get back on my feet. Since starting my forays into Cambodia, I've been sick constantly and just can't tip the scales over 54 kg for my 1.73 m frame. I'm done in by the air conditioning on the bus. I feel feverish, at the end of my tether. I decide to just stay home.

It's a no go. That very evening I get a message from Than in Phnom Penh informing me that the Siem Reap governor has refused to give us a permit. Officially, Krousar Thmey has no building in Siem Reap, because we started building as a private home… Everything's there, but with no permit, the HCR won't let the repatriation go through.

So I rush over to Siem Reap, leaving Jean-Marie behind, even though he would like to come along. I prefer he wait in Ta Phraya. I'm shivering with fever and can't stand up. Fortunately, I can sit in the car. The road has been improved. Truckloads of red dirt have been brought in and heavy machines are out grading. In Siem Reap, I don't have the strength to eat; I just flop off to sleep. The next morning, a zombie bearing my name shows up at the governor's office, makes a fast-track appointment for 3 p.m., is received by a bright, understanding deputy governor, who signs the repatriation agreements. For once I win the lottery jackpot on the whim of the deputy governor. It's over. The zombie gives you his kind regards and goes back to bed before heading on to the camps.

As November 1, 1992 unfolds, the children in the O'bok center, Vuthy, the director, and all the staff leave the center for the departure platform where they spend the night. The next day, we're at Site II just as it opens. The children have taken their anti-nausea pills and are all set. The week before, the HCR saddled us with a few additional cases:

Moth, a mentally handicapped boy who was being looked after in a specialized psychiatric center, and Nimith, a baby with TB abandoned in a Site II hospital. Nimith finds refuge throughout the whole trip in the arms of the cook. Marine, an intrepid volunteer, looks after Moth. He's a real handful. Despite the tranquilizers, he is prone to violent outbursts. He is extraordinarily strong and hits out here, there, and everywhere. But Marine, firm yet tactful, calms the boy down.

The boys and girls are nearly dead on their feet. For nights on end, the excitement of leaving has kept them from sleeping. We had T-shirts printed for them. The seamstresses made each of them a backpack. The rest of the effects will come by truck. The kids get onto the bus. I take my last pictures of Site II. I imagine the impressions of a child born in the camp, about to safely cross the border of the country of its dreams. I don't want to go by bus over these first few kilometers; there may be a long wait. Jean-Marie gets on the bus, cool as a cucumber. I'd like to know what he has on his mind. He takes a serene look at each of the children. He may look absent, but has never been so present.

I charge by motorbike to Ta Phraya and join the convoy at Aran. The buses park. Many children are already sick. The break is welcome. We wait to be escorted by the Thai authorities. The HCR chief wants to share the trip with us, so leaves her driver and air-conditioned car at the rear of the convoy and joins us on the bus.

A horn blast and the convoy is back on the road. Entering the town, we turn left, pass the train station, and head toward the border. The soldiers, accustomed to this exercise, lift the crossing gate and let the buses through, all numbered in series. On the Khmer side, no control. An HCR Land Cruiser takes the lead, with the blue UN flag flapping in the wind, its wheels sending up a thick red cloud that invades our bus, choking us. Each one puts a krama over his face to filter out the dust. The children cough. In a few minutes, the white T-shirts turn an ochre color. The children arrive at the center about 4 in the afternoon. The Red Cross makes an exception and allows us to bypass the formalities and head straight to the welfare center.

I want to create a sense of adventure in the children, but one step at a time. I ask that the truck stop at the bridge over the river. There's still another kilometer to go. The most curious ones hurry on, while those who are tired and the youngest ones hobble along around Jean-Marie. As they approach the center, the first ones break into a run. The sight of the two-story building gets them shouting for joy, which spurs the slower ones on. They burst with delight, hopping on the beds and touching the walls. It's magical, everything new in a house that's built to last. After a thorough exploration of the place, they wash up in the river running along the property. The water level is high. Those who don't know how to swim cling to branches and go in up to their knees. The girls modestly put on their sarongs before stepping into the water. Suddenly the shrill song of the cicadas breaks out, signaling a new life on Khmer soil.

The next afternoon, Jean-Marie takes a *coyoun* to visit the temples. The name is roughly translated "cow engine." It's a cross between a truck and a carriage, a type of truck box set up on wheels with a motor and steering at front. Foolproof simplicity. All jump up into it. The neighborhood children gape at us. We invite them to join us. The temples are nearby. The Angkor Wat central tower is visible from the second floor of the center, but we have to detour because of the river. A few kilometers on and we're in front of the sumptuous edifice. The kids dash across the entrance causeway. Their happiness is unbounded. The symbol of their identity and national pride is right there, in front of their enraptured eyes. Angkor—the word is magic, awe-inspiring. Angkor, they've seen it painted in every color, at sunrise, at sunset... Angkor, for which so many men have fought. Angkor, that will soon be drawing millions of tourists from all over the world.

The children scamper up the steps, two at a time. Despite their ungainly flip-flops, they agilely jump from stone to stone. In the first ground-floor gallery, they discover the bas-reliefs, hundreds of meters long. They stroke the contours, lean against the reliefs as if they want to imprint their shape upon themselves. They flatten their cheeks to the stone. They ascend to the highest level of the temple and search the horizon from the central tower, trying to catch sight of the center, their new home. The forest blocks our view, but it's only two or three kilometers away as the crow flies. Old bald-headed women in white dress offer to burn incense sticks for a few riels. Ceremoniously, the children start praying. To Buddha? To the good spirits? Certainly their thoughts turn to the end of a nightmare, at any rate, to the hope of a more dignified, more human life.

We break into the dense forest to the north. The strident song of the cicadas reaches a crescendo pitch. The road crosses the moats, the causeway of the giants. Huge *yeak thom* stone statues clutch a *naga* that leads up to the stone gateway topped by giant heads with four faces. We enter the city of Angkor Thom, built by King Jayavarman VII, whose reign in the 12th century yielded the most monuments and irrigation works. It is said that the pains of his people made him suffer more than his own. A little further on, like a forest of stone, stands the Bayon temple, majestically, with its 54 face towers said to represent Jayavarman VII himself or, more plausibly, Buddha. All the children want their picture taken in front of these smiling faces.

Tomorrow, the children will be registered by the Red Cross and go with Vuthy to meet the school principals. Enrolment is merely a formality. But we don't know if there is a difference in levels between the camp schools and those of Cambodia. Tests are held and the results are overall very encouraging.

Jean-Marie and I stay with the children for three days before heading to Phnom Penh. I'm fed up with the road, so with the lake water high, we take the slow boat down the Tonle Sap. It takes 36 hours, finally giving us some time… to take our time. At meal time, if it can be called such, because Asians eat at any time, women offer pork or chicken skewers and fried rice. We sleep on hammocks. There is a strong fish stench. It's from a cargo of *prahok*, a paste of fermented fish, a specialty of Siem Reap highly prized by Cambodians. Like a good French cheese, a good *prahok* has to have a strong smell. Personally, I haven't acquired the taste for it.

Phnom Penh is unusually crowded with people. The water festival, celebrating the reversal of the river's flow, draws huge crowds. Actually, the Mekong's headwaters are in the Himalayas. The river flows through Cambodia and is swelled by the water flow from Tonle Sap Lake as it heads to the sea. Come the rainy season, at the same time as the Himalaya snow melt, and the level of the Mekong rises 7 m, higher than the level of the lake. It's the principle of communicating vessels. Water from the Mekong is pushed back up the Tonle Sap River from June to October. The lake's surface area then jumps from 2,700 to 12,000 km^2, i.e. five to 20 times that of Lake Geneva. In late October, with the ebb in water, the river flow reverses, heading toward the sea. It is an occasion for celebrations featuring boat races. The inversion of the waters means the return of the mythical naga and its flooding the Angkor region with fertility.

As for me, I'm not sure in what direction my next trips will take me as I coach the repatriation operation, but on I must go!

I first go to check on the progress of the Ta Khmau welfare center building site. Things look good; the foundations are almost finished. In Phnom Penh, the house is full and preparation for the restaurant is moving ahead. The pace is again hectic. One day, accompanied by faithful Than, I bolt away on my motorbike to check on the furniture. I negotiate with the cabinetmaker to be sure that everything will be ready on time, then start to speed off:

"Thank you, see you soon. But where's Than?"

"But you came by yourself!"

"No! My assistant was on the back; I was talking to him all the way here!"

"Let me assure you, you came alone!"

When I get back to La Casa,* I find my Than, totally unperturbed. "I was on the back but when I got off to close the gate, you took off so fast that I couldn't get back on." Gales of laughter.

Starting in mid-November 1992, back and forth trips become easier because we're allowed to take UNTAC flights thanks to my working relationship with the HCR. Airplanes and helicopters operate regular flights. The Transall service between Phnom Penh and Battambang or Siem Reap and helicopter on to Sisophon enable me to save a lot of time and energy.

---

* Since our idea was to feature Mediterranean food on the menu, we called the restaurant La Casa. This name remains linked to the Krousar Thmey offices to the present.

On December 26, 1992, La Casa opens with David and a Khmer female chef in the kitchen: fresh pasta, wood-fired style pizza, Aussie steak, scalloped potatoes, chocolate mousse, but also *amok* and a few Khmer specialties popular with foreigners, both the NGO and UN crowd. Phnom Penh's restaurant scene is still bleak. La Casa ranks with No Problem and La Paillote as the most frequented addresses in Phnom Penh. French air force pilots make it their headquarters. We get along well with a number of them who let us in on unofficial visits to the cockpit… and even with a little copiloting thrown in if it's a volunteer's birthday.

To resolve our electricity problems and eliminate generator noise during operating hours, a French air force captain hooks us up to the generators of the *Mission d'Assistance militaire française,* located a few streets away. We buy 400 m of wire and add our contribution to the snarled mass strung along the row of concrete poles. The distance results in a major energy loss, leaving us with barely 170 volts. Enough for dim lighting, but not enough to keep the one computer running. Every day except Mondays, there are seven kitchen workers and five in the dining room serving an expatriate clientele, often by reservation only. We serve an average of 70 settings a day. In addition to the profits going to the association, La Casa becomes an ideal venue to talk about our work and thereby make acquaintance with many potential donors.

In early January 1993, prior to the second repatriation operation off Site II, I go look at the Ta Khmau building site. Everything has to be finished within three weeks. I leave reassured. The repatriation process is coming to an end. Entire sections of the camp have been emptied and it will soon be completely shut down. Repatriation of our Dangrek welfare center is also imminent. Eight days before the move, I'm called to the HCR office in Aran. Phnom Penh has advised that there's been a delay on the construction site and the repatriation is in jeopardy. But there's no way it can be postponed; the Australian film team is about to arrive.

I head back to Phnom Penh by car. Philippe Magnier and Savang are with me. The road has been graded by the United Nations, and with a very early start from Aran, we're at La Casa by late evening. The peacekeeping forces deployed throughout the country have greatly calmed the outlying regions. Although it remains impossible to make a night trip, a journey can be finished up after nightfall. The next day, the work site is a disappointment. Because of unusual rains in January, things have fallen seriously behind. They haven't finished the second floor, and the kids are supposed to show up in exactly six more days. I go ballistic. The work site trembles. I demand three eight-hour shifts that will work around the clock. A generator will provide power for lighting. Sameath feels very small. If everything's done in a week, I'll add a week's pay. If not, I won't pay the last week. The message is clear. Priority is to be given to anything visible. The television team is following the repatriation operation and we cannot serve them an unfinished building. I return to Site II and reassure the HCR. Everything is set. I promise that the building will be ready, but keep my fingers crossed.

On the way back, we stop at Battambang to allow Savang to visit the house where he was born. Savang is so expressive, his language so well chosen and so colorful that one has the impression of traveling in his memory. The new owner understandingly lets him soak up the place. Along the Sangker River, he's also reunited with some of his relatives. He's assailed by his cousins and bombarded with questions. But they also take it out on his suitcase that's searched, emptied, and the contents spirited away.

We stay overnight in town. Philippe complains of hunger, so we look for a small street restaurant, one with a few tables and metal stools, or better, pink or blue plastic chairs. The food looks good, the hygiene doesn't. As in Phnom Penh, you can't have a meal without bunches of street kids crowding around. I refuse to give them money, as the practice causes an exodus of children from the countryside and swells the networks of beggar children. As long as they don't get anything, they just stand there looking hangdog as we eat. For want of anything better, we treat them to a bowl of noodle soup or a plate of fried rice. The restaurant keepers really don't want them sitting with us at the table, so put their serving in a plastic bag and hustle them away. I don't let them. The price is the same, so they are entitled to sit at a table, with dignity.

Obviously, they're not just pretending to be hungry. They literally throw themselves on the food and gobble it down in a few minutes flat. They give us the traditional, so elegant *sampeah* to thank us warmly before leaving. Whenever we treat a child to a soup, other children appear out of nowhere and we have to leave if we don't want to spend the night there. This is something new. From Phnom Penh, it has spread like gangrene throughout the country. Obviously we will have to come up with something for street children.

Peter, our stateless friend, offers us very basic lodging for the night. I'm a little ashamed to have Philippe sleep on the floor. But he shames me in return by taking it very much in stride, using his shoes as a pillow.

February 3, 1993 is the grand departure. The children are beside themselves. Wanna, the blind boy, guitar slung over his shoulder, is carrying a box of carefully folded clothes and one of the backpacks made from Bangkok Chinatown cloth. His buddies guide him. To make it easier to manage the children and to issue family books, they are put into groups of five or six.

The Australian team is there, Savang, and my friend Thomas as well. Iconic Australian actor Jack Thompson, as the HCR's volunteer ambassador, comes with us. He radiates kindness and calm. At Sisophon, we get off the bus and muster again near the station. A whole train car has been reserved for us and has "children" written in chalk on it. The bigger children act as porters between the bus and the train. The *chayam* players coddle their drums. On the roof, Australian soldiers armed with machine guns see to security. An empty flatcar is secured to the front of the train as a buffer in case a landmine has been put on the track. There's no charge to ride on it because it's unsafe, but still poor farmers generally take it in droves.

The train fills and by mid-afternoon, it's the big getaway. It takes 20 hours to cover the 370 km separating us from the capital. The children's happiness is complete. The *chayam* team drums on unremittingly. No arguing, no animosity, but incredible rejoicing. Wanna won't let go of Jack Thompson and becomes his protégé. Jack takes out a harmonica and plays him a round of country tunes. Wanna listens solemnly, feels the instrument, and puts it to his lips. When it emits a sound, he brightens up and jumps for joy. Jack shows him how to breathe in and out, do harmonic glissandos, link the notes. He lets the boy manage on his own before giving him another lesson. Wanna won't be parted from the instrument and Jack ends up giving it to him. I have never forgotten this splendidly tender scene and was to see it again years later in the film *Australia* where Jack Thompson plays it out with an aboriginal boy.

Night falls and the exhausted children crash out on and under the wooden seats. The Australians attempt to string hammocks to the luggage racks. Twice, the hammocks yield to the weight of our giant friends. Peter Carette is about 2 m and Marcus is not much shorter. They fall and are half knocked out on the seats, almost crushing two of the sleeping children with their weight. It was close. It would have really taken the cake if newspaper headlines were to announce: "Film team follows HCR child repatriation effort, inadvertently crushing them en route." As is often the case in Cambodia, what starts tragically finishes hilariously. Laughter shakes the entire car. More afraid than hurt, just the same our giants leave the train with big bruises.

At Chom Chao, the point where the repatriated Phnom Penh-bound children get off, they are transferred for the night to the intake center. At La Casa, we voraciously down an Aussie steak with scalloped potatoes before crashing, crammed three or four to a room. Emotionally drained from all the excitement, we're instantly in dreamland.

At the break of dawn the next day, I check the construction site with Than. The roof is almost finished. The visible tiles have been set. The façade is painted. The back and interior are not what they should be, but everything the camera will cover is completed. The impossible has happened. And I'm spared being upbraided by Jennifer, in charge of the HCR in Phnom Penh.

Two hours later, the Care agency truck speeds onto the narrow road. The *chayam* drum team is going flat out. Cries of surprise ring out as the children catch sight of the building. The vehicle stops in front of the courtyard. All jump down and run helter-skelter. This buzz of excitement reminds me of the scene in Siem Reap, but more intensely here, as I am more familiar with these children that I saw come in to our Dangrek center and know their backgrounds. Mr. Mul Bun Hanh, a blind amputee, who we accepted at the request of the HCR, feeling his wheelchair tipping over, panics and reminds us of his presence. Disabled, with no family, he will live with us. Vasa, ever a tease, tells me, beaming and in fun: "It's only that big?" The kids quickly pick the beds they like. Sophea can't stop touching the blackboard. Everything is new, everything is for them. They can't believe it. A permanent building? For them?

The next morning we learn that that the repatriation of other refugees by train was suspended because of rocket fire on the tracks. A team is out repairing the damage.

The kids make their first visit to Phnom Penh, taking in the Royal Palace, Wat Phnom Pagoda, and Central Market. They just can't get over the three-story buildings in the city, modest as they may be. They've never seen such edifices before. At Wat Phnom, a stump of a hill in the middle of the city, they go to pray to Buddha and set birds free. Dozens of birds are held in cages until someone buys them and sets them free. It's a way to get good luck. An old woman negotiates the release at 500 riels a bird. The children each get a bird to wish themselves good luck on their new life on Khmer soil. They grip them very firmly in their hands. So firmly that Rong, aged 7, smothers his bird. Instead of flying off, it falls dead to the ground. Strangely, the incident doesn't cause a whimper of sadness, but a collective giggle. Back at the center, the children finally get a good rest. The Australians take their leave, camera and film packed away. For me, a phase has been completed.

I'm already on my way back west with the site team to start building a new center in Sisophon, funded by UNICEF. An unpleasant surprise, the land promised is no longer available. A house has just been built on it. I'm asked if I can wait a few days until the problem is solved. Back on Site II where the HCR is finalizing the last repatriations, I find some stray children from Site II and Site B in our Dangrek center. They will be included with the final repatriates. In Sisophon, one week later, a second house is beginning to rise from the ground. For a problem that was supposed to be solved, things are going the long way around. The Social Affairs Office assures me that it's just a misunderstanding. I threaten to file a complaint with the governor. I patiently wait another week, and a third house is taking shape. I no longer believe in promises and go straight to the governor who issues an order for a solution to be found. Another property is proposed, 300 m from the first. To avoid any further change, I have gravel, sand, rebar, and concrete delivered immediately to the site. Two separate teams start at the same time on the main building and three wooden houses for the staff. This will provide temporary housing for the last abandoned children in the camps.

The area is infested with thieves. At night, we have to sleep on the bags of cement so they won't be stolen. The foundations are poured in black, compact clay. The Thai battalion repairing the Poipet–Sisophon road lends us a mechanical shovel to dig a pond and put in a ditch all around the lot for flood prevention. The children already foresee a duck-raising venture.

While the construction work is going on, I make an increasing number of trips between the border, Siem Reap, Sisophon, and Phnom Penh, but frequently by air. When in the capital, I attend UNICEF's childhood welfare coordination meetings. The problem of street children is becoming acute. Except for one very modest project, nothing is being done for them. Than and I are thinking about it at the very time that the coordinator of Terre des Hommes Germany comes looking for us at La Casa. For years, Walter Skrobanek has been living in Asia, mainly in Bangkok, where he married a Thai women's rights activist. An exceptional personality, remarkably fluent in French, he's very interested in the cultural education that we are developing with dance and musical groups and with the exhibitions. He leaves me to understand that he will help us to fund certain projects. He's one of these very well-educated Germans who have dedicated their lives to their ideal of justice. Despite his lack of familiarity with the field and with the Buddhist religion, he nevertheless cannot stand being pushed around. Blond hair, a big mustache, and a ferocious appetite round out his Germanic self-confidence, and he has a great time putting the young French whippersnapper that I am in his place. Semantic arguments usually spice up our meals together.

We see Walter regularly. I share his concept of humanitarian aid and development problems. We address the danger of individual sponsorships. Like many organizations, Terre des Hommes Germany is being shaken by discord. On the one hand, people at headquarters with their focus on marketing and fundraising feel that individual sponsorships are practical. On the other hand, those in the field, upset by the drawbacks, burdened with the follow-up work, irritated by the sterility of an often awkward relationship, are advocating that individual sponsorships be discarded and a type of sponsorship be developed more in tune with the needs and more effective, in other words, program sponsorship. We see eye to eye on this option, because repatriation makes it hard to follow up sponsored children outside of the orphanage and in many cases spread all over the country. The language barrier, a different culture, and a deficient postal service compound the work, something that the sponsors often fail to grasp. They are disappointed with the few answers they receive. Moreover, with the repatriation over with, we have new costs to assume, notably staff salaries, so sponsorships now cover only a small part of the cost of a child. And with new programs being developed, we just don't have the time.

AN OVERVIEW
(April 1993–1998)

On April 30, 1993, Site II is closed for good. The HCR has the last abandoned children moved out on a truck, along with the staff of the welfare center. The camp will be bulldozed over, marking the end of Cambodian refugee camps in Thailand, except for those opened briefly in the wake of the 1997 conflicts. Once over the border, as we had agreed, the HCR's staff becomes Krousar Thmey's staff. A group of 16 children are housed in the just finished wooden houses, while work continues on the main building. Although a little bit like camping, the children thus help put up their own facility.

Early April marks the kickoff of the electoral campaign. In May, Cambodians countrywide will share in the first free legislative elections from which the new government will be formed. A long list of parties are campaigning, the big ones—the CPP, Cambodian People's Party, led by Hun Sen, Heng Samrin, and Chea Sim; FUNCINPEC, the royalist party with Prince Ranariddh and Sam Rainsy; the BLDP, an offshoot of Son Sann's nationalist party—and 20 or so smaller ones. The Khmer Rouge boycott the elections and launch sporadic attacks to stir up trouble.

It becomes difficult to source building materials. Sisophon's cement comes from Thailand, its bricks and tile from Siem Reap, wood from the northern part of the country, and steel from Phnom Penh. We sometimes have to borrow supplies from COERR who is putting up a training center behind Phnom Bach. Workers are locals or Vietnamese. Further compounding things, wood is paid for in gold, cement in Thai baht, wages in riels, and steel in dollars! And no time can be lost. The rainy season is fast approaching. We are 600 m off National Highway 6, on a dirt trail of black clay. When it rains, no vehicle can get through, only oxen. We have to leave our motorbikes, bikes, or any other powered vehicle at a neighbor's house out on the road. Going on foot, a person has to roll up his pant legs, then take off his shoes, and carry them; otherwise, they would be sucked off in the 30 cm deep mud.

If we don't get our supplies in before the rains hit, we won't be able to finish the buildings until after the dry season returns in November. Fortunately, the weather's on our side. This year, the rains come late, allowing us to move ahead with the structural work and to stockpile materials.

Negotiations with ACCOR bear fruit. The group agrees to fund two schools of three classrooms. To be politically correct, Alain Dupuis, the head of Eurest (ACCOR's worldwide institutional foodservice), and very involved in Cambodia, asks me to consult the two leading parties. He is married to Yary, a charming Cambodian woman with whom he is very much in love. This translates into building one school in Hun Sen's territory, the other in FUNCINPEC's. The Hun Sen people give me carte blanche, i.e. build it where it's needed. The FUNCINPEC crowd ask me to build in Ampil where the party's headquarters are located. Ampil is in Oddar Meanchey province, north of Sisophon, not far from the Thai border. I go on location with three of my key staff members in order to assess the need. I have a gut feeling that it's not a good area, as a lot of money has already been poured into it with little to show. I fear that this community of refugees and displaced persons has gotten into the habit of holding out their hand and of complaining rather than rolling up their sleeves. In fact, every time Prince Ranariddh visits, you'd think Santa Claus had come to town.

There are no taxis going through to Ampil. Drivers will go half way, as far as Thma Puok, a constituency belonging to the FNLPK, but no further. Why not? The peacekeeping forces say there's nothing out of the ordinary. Sometimes the Khmer rumor mill causes anxiety even though the situation is calm… We'll see. We therefore take a taxi to Thma Puok, knowing that we'll have to catch motorbike taxis to go on to Ampil. This trip can't be postponed because I'm expected in Siem Reap the next day for a meeting with the governor. A few kilometers after we start, our white Peugeot 504 shows its age. No more brakes. The hydraulic system has conked out and the driver wants to go back to Sisophon. He needs money to get the car repaired. We compromise. He agrees to take us as far as Ampil provided that I look after the cash points. If not, he won't make any money. To put him at ease, I jokingly say that I'm General Bénito and just the sight of me is enough to open the gates. The region is infested with gated checkpoints and armed soldiers. Unlike the rest of the country, a number of zones that we're crossing are still controlled by nationalist, royalist, or Khmer Rouge factions. The tension is palpable due to guerilla fighting. At the first checkpoint, I stick my head out the window and order the guard to open up. The driver slows, gears down, and prepares to pull on the emergency break if needed. As if by magic, at the last second, the soldier on duty opens the gate and clicks his heels. My road companions chortle. The driver gives me a dumbfounded look. He can't understand what happened. The others laugh until they cry. They can't get over my nerve. At the next checkpoint, the same scenario. Sameath comments: "No bills here, just salute General Bénito!"

The driver stares at me, not knowing who to take me for. Am I really a general or a complete loony? Better not let him think too much about the latter. Each checkpoint goes the same way. We don't meet or overtake anyone except for a few military convoys loaded with uniformed men. Strange. This road is usually very busy. But we merrily keep right on going as far as Ampil. When we get there, we go to the market for a coffee. The place is deserted, closed. We look for the district chief who gives us a stunned look and asks where we've come from. Actually, maneuvers started this morning against the Khmer Rouge guerilla. With no idea how we got this far, he advises us to leave right away. Given my determined look, the soldiers must have taken me for a military adviser. Wasting no time, I ask him for statistics on the number of children that need schooling. Unaware of the nature of my mission, he gives me all the data by age group and grade. I take note and check the figures against the number of seats in the existing classrooms. There are more seats available than needed. Conclusion: no school needed in Ampil.

He belatedly regrets giving me the actual figures, as he won't be getting his brand new school. We head back the way we came. The driver, unsettled, speeds on to Sisophon. The road had been fixed for the umpteenth time with American assistance, mainly through USAID, despite the fact that it served the Khmer Rouge. It is now in pitiful condition. Having no brakes does nothing to facilitate the slalom movement and we often slam straight into ruts, not an ideal treatment for the back. But the atmosphere is joyful and we chant our new motto: "It's the Khmer *roam* dance on the road!"

We limit our travel in the provinces because of increasing disquiet in the upswing to the elections. In May, the weather is hot and so are tempers. These are the first free elections and the stakes are crucial. Some expect a societal change. Others are afraid of losing their privileges. And the Khmer Rouge are out to sabotage the elections.

The top priorities of the United Nations were demobilization and disarmament of the factions, but given the obstacles, these goals are very quickly abandoned. John Sanderson, lieutenant general of the UN forces in Cambodia, prefers a pacifist approach. Unlike the French, Americans, and Dutch, he fears that confrontations will break out if he pushes for disarmament and demobilization. This leaves large numbers of weapons out in the hands of unpaid armed soldiers who make ends meet by extorting the people.

This brings together all the ingredients for an explosive situation, despite the presence of 22,000 UN personnel, soldiers and civilians combined. Some are committed and campaign to explain what casting votes and democracy are all about. They explain that secret ballot means that no party has any way of finding out how individuals vote. Ever superstitious, the Cambodians think that the party in power sees everything and knows everything, as in the days of the Khmer Rouge. And isn't the CPP's logo a *tevoda*, a type of Khmer angel? "It has pineapple eyes," goes the Khmer saying, i.e. eyes that see in all directions.

Many foreigners have accepted jobs in the provinces despite the dangers and pressures and do outstanding work. Some even lose their lives there. The people are afraid. Since the Khmer Rouge regime and the Vietnamese occupation, they've learned to say nothing, know nothing, think nothing. Become a silk cotton tree, kapok in Khmer, which also means deaf. The people have had the Khmer Rouge slogan drummed into them: "If we keep you, nothing gained; if we do away with you, nothing lost." They've learned to avoid talking politics. But how can you organize elections and get people to debate if no one talks politics? The task is indeed daunting.

The image of these volunteers is unfortunately tarnished by a number of kinks in the UN system. Discrepancies and blunders multiply. When the United Nations arrives, it needs buildings—for the police, army, polling stations, the list goes on. Peace in Cambodia had been in gestation for years, but it seems that nothing was thought out. Instead of building permanent structures that could be used afterward by the Cambodian administration, Algeco mobile offices are brought in from Australia, costing as much as putting up their equivalent in concrete in Cambodia. After just two rainy seasons, they're shot, leaving basically nothing for Cambodia. In this way, a big chunk of the $3-billion peacemaking budget, rather than contributing to development, is funneled back overseas. Leaves one wondering if the international community isn't serving itself at the expense of the people. A substantial amount of French aid goes toward expert fees and per diems for the French soldiers. Australian aid focuses on the purchase of prefabricated buildings and diverse Australian equipment. Part of Japan's aid is used to buy Toyota or Nissan vehicles. Each country finds that all or part of its money is generously handed out. Some countries even make a profit. The people in charge of the Bangladeshi contingents reportedly did not distribute the per diems meant for the soldiers. Soldiers from one of the Balkan countries were said to be ex-convicts, promised a reduced sentence for serving in Cambodia. Under such circumstances, how can one but be surprised by the excesses and the execrable image of the UN in this vast, cacophonous operation?

The most offensive thing is the attitude of many UN workers with regard to Cambodian government officials. True, many of the latter are not the most zealous, but given their salaries and working conditions, that too comes as no surprise. The UN administrators have an impressive arsenal of computers, while the Cambodians type things out on their antiquated East German typewriters... when they have paper. How often we see ridiculous scenes of a uniformed but uneducated UN person leaping from his car with driver and shouting orders in broken

English to educated Cambodians that speak not only Khmer, but excellent French and English? Humiliation is daily fare. A uniform or a title often shields abuses of power.

In Sisophon, the Dutch troops build a veritable fortified camp behind barbwire fences and sand bags. They're prepared for only one thing, a fight with guerilla soldiers. In Kompong Thom, the Indonesian troops don't even speak English. In Phnom Penh, the Africans assigned to teach traffic management to police officers end up causing traffic jams.

In Siem Reap, the Bangladeshi battalion assigned security duty is headquartered less than 500 m from the Krousar Thmey center on the same road. One of my friends is looking for us and asks them for directions. Totally oblivious to our location, the receptionist calls over an officer, who calls another one, then another. Along comes a soldier who introduces himself as the social affairs officer. He asserts that there's no such facility in the neighborhood, even though we're only a stone's throw away. Four times a day the children parade by their base on bicycle or on foot, but the soldiers are unaware of our existence. He concludes by saying: "I'd better get to finding those orphans!" In 1993, during a Khmer Rouge attack against Siem Reap, the Bangladeshi battalion goes into hiding instead of providing protection.

A few months earlier, cars were few and far between. When the UN arrives, the traffic situation changes dramatically with thousands of white Land Cruisers, pickup trucks, and minibuses, a big "UN" splashed on the sides and hood. And that doesn't include the flotilla of imported machinery. A lot of aid is pledged for the pacification of Cambodia and various schemes are devised to siphon off as much of the donated funds as possible. Then there are a few colored vehicles privately owned by small NGOs or Cambodians. Some vehicles have no license plates. Could they be UN or other vehicles stolen and repainted? It's not a stretch to wonder. The police and army rival factions make a killing because of legal loopholes and of the Wild West atmosphere that has prevailed since the sudden opening of the country.

One night, two different police units clash in front of the UNDP offices as they steal brand new, neatly parked vehicles belonging to the agency. Car theft is so widespread that whenever drivers park, they put a lock on their steering wheel or gearshift. Katell Benoît taunts this armada of spanking new UN vehicles, seldom seen out of town but often seen parked in front of restaurants and dance halls. To set herself completely apart, she paints a big DEUX (French for "two") on her car as opposed to UN (French for "one").

Although it's an exaggeration, one sometimes finds oneself thinking that, in order to repair the Khmer porcelain, the UN elephant is blithely stomping on it. Yet, despite so many abuses, the electoral process moves forward and the elections are held from May 23 to 28, 1993. Aside from small skirmishes, the Khmer Rouge cause no disorder; there's no attack. Overall, it's a success.

On June 10, Yasushi Akashi, the United Nations representative for Cambodia, announces that the elections were free and fair. The results: FUNCINPEC, 45.2 percent; CPP, 38.7 percent; BLDP, 3.7 percent. Contrary to expectations, Son Sann's party that managed Site II, the largest refugee camp, suffers a dismal fiasco. FUNCINPEC wins the elections because of the image of the highly esteemed Prince Sihanouk. The CPP dismisses the results.

Sin Song and Prince Chakrapong, a son of King Sihanouk and brother of Prince Ranariddh, cook up a secession of six eastern provinces, which terribly embarrasses the UN whose efforts come to naught. Prince Sihanouk intervenes, making it possible to find a compromise, Cambodian-style. Cambodia will have two prime ministers. Prince Ranariddh, the first prime minister, won the elections but has no say in the administration, the army, or the police that remain in the hands of the CPP. Hun Sen, the second prime minister, lost the elections but retains power. A coalition government is formed with co-ministers from each party for all the leading ministries. This system is doomed because of their mutual hatred. To reduce the friction, minister and secretary of State appointments are liberally distributed. The army becomes the Mexican army, with hundreds of generals and non-commissioned officers and few troops, except on paper. People would like to see government funds used for other purposes, such as social affairs and education. For the most part, the latter are left with the NGOs.

The departure of the United Nations is an opportunity for us. NGOs can buy some of their vehicles. We put in a bid for a Nissan pickup truck and two motorbikes. And the HCR donates a Toyota pickup to us. Those are our very first vehicles, with which we travel faster and more conveniently, especially in the provinces. The roads are potholed and driving is fatiguing, but we are more independent.

In early June 1993, I'm back in France to do some fundraising. As before, a conference tour takes me to Chambéry, Marseille, Lyon, Grenoble, and Versailles. My network of family and friends is going all out. I am introduced to two applicants, Nelly and Guillaume, who would like to give us a year. They want to go together. They have a yen for Asia, but Cambodia in particular. They were turned down by a number of organizations because they are neither married nor engaged. Personally, that doesn't bother me; it's none of my business. To me, the important thing is that they do good work and that they come as volunteers, because I've no budget for them. No plane ticket, no allowances. They agree and help me out greatly in moving exhibition preparations along.

Administrative obstacles with Enfants du Mékong and the difficulty of finding out the exact amount of donations lead me to have it out with Yves Meaudre, the charity's director. Our philosophies differ. I appreciate their sincerity and kindness, but don't agree with their management. A former Site II volunteer offered me his very first paycheck. He's surprised when he doesn't get a thank you from me. The Enfants du Mékong administration earmarked it for another program without telling me. We decide to go our separate ways. Everyone can now choose the agency he would like to contribute to.

But we fear the loss of sponsors, and therefore of funds, at a time when we're going full steam ahead with projects opening up everywhere, including three primary schools under construction, three welfare centers operating, a center for street children, an exhibition being prepared, and lots of ventures on the drawing board. After having teams go out into the province to update the children's files, after nights at the computer and sending files, we forego our vacations. By September, we're relieved. Nearly all of the sponsors have stayed with us. We now make the decision to maintain existing sponsorships but discontinue individual sponsorships.

Likewise in summer 1993, new donors raise our spirits. Krousar Thmey will henceforth focus on Phnom Penh and western Cambodia with three pillars: child welfare, education of handicapped children, and culture.

Exchanges with Walter Skrobanek, coordinator of Terre des Hommes Germany, yield tangible results. He agrees to fund the opening of the first home for street children. Than and I immediately start working on the project. We spend evenings scouring the streets to find street children, mainly boys aged 9 to 14, who are on their own. Some sniff glue from the bottom of a plastic bag. They cinch the neck with their hand and inhale the fumes, snorting deeply. The bag inflates and deflates. With every breath, more solvent is inhaled with the already permeated air. The kids' eyes are bloodshot and they're stoned out of their minds.

We tell them that the glue is frying their brain, but they draw in more heavily, as if to scoff at us. I'm tempted to make my house available to them, but realize that that's not the solution. We have to find out where they're from, why they're out roaming, how they can be rehabilitated. Some patterns emerge. They are often children of a first marriage and rejected by the new spouse, so they leave a family in which they are unwelcome stepchildren. Some leave overly large families that are having a hard time feeding them or have been sent out to beg. Others are enslaved, forced to do domestic chores, sometimes beaten or even raped, so take flight. Glue sniffing helps them forget their hunger and sorrowful condition. The arrival of the UN crowd fosters their multiplication, because holding out the hand becomes profitable at a time when inflation and dollarization are making life in the countryside untenable. Adding to that, many refugee children flock to the cities, drawn like moths to the bright lights of the karaoke bars and restaurants.

The children soon locate places where they can arouse the sympathy of rich foreigners, some of whom receive a per diem as high as the monthly salary of a Cambodian civil servant. They make more at begging than their parents do at work. Bands are formed with their little leaders. Violence takes hold and its victims are many.

Our priority is to offer a way out to the most vulnerable, a structure wherein they can find security, food, care, and comfort. Such a foster home has to be managed by two teams, the first to spot children recently arrived in the city, give them medical care, talk to them, calm them down; the second to look after them by providing them protection, care, and a basic education. Once we win a child's trust, we can find out its past and work with it to offer an alternative to the street. Our experience in the camps leads us to try hard to get them back in a family. Some of our workers will be provided with a motorbike to look up the families in the provinces. To make a long story short, the project takes shape in just a few weeks. Terre des Hommes gives us funding for the purchase of land, the building, and the first year of operation. An audit will determine what follows.

Many NGOs are working on the street children problem. There is an attempt to work together, but it's precarious. Some NGOs proselytize, and we don't agree with that. We're opposed to giving aid in exchange for religious membership, a sort of commercialism that disparages both the country and the child alike. At our coordination meetings, we therefore divide the city into sectors to avoid stepping on each other's toes. Our budget is too low to afford a location in downtown Phnom Penh, so we set up in Psar Depot, a working-class neighborhood.

In just a few days, we find a small lot with a wooden shelter on it. We buy the property and enlarge the building. Than is the center's first director. I am impressed with the courage he displays in agreeing to work in such conditions. At meetings with other NGOs, we have always advocated a basic setup in order to keep the children from getting used to a level of comfort that they won't find when they get back to their families... But we've really gone out on a limb! How could any children, let alone street children, agree to stay in this barely upgraded hovel?

Yet, Than's patience and vigilance bear fruit. In a few weeks, about 20 boys aged 9 to 15 are staying there. The atmosphere is cheerful. We sometimes take in a girl or two. Actually, girls seldom last very long on the street. They are immediately the prey of traffickers. When Than and his team spot one, she must be quickly put under protection, as young virgins are highly valued by soldiers, as well as by nouveau riche Cambodians who have done well for themselves financially from the peace program.

Given the scope of the problem, the first center for street children is soon swamped. With support from the French Ministry of Foreign Affairs, we double its capacity a few years later when a second center is opened in Phnom Penh and two more in the provinces. To coordinate all these programs, I recruit a man formerly in charge of a medical team on Site II. Phanna has the ability to lead a team while keeping in tune with the children. A man of profoundly human qualities, he has a winning way. The first thing that he generally does is provide treatment for minor medical issues while speaking reassuringly to the child. The next step is tricky and decisive. Does the child want to go with him? Phanna speaks French and English fluently, which facilitates our working meetings. It's one thing to provide support, but it's another to raise public awareness regarding the dangers faced by the children.

Meetings are held among NGOs with a child welfare outreach, while UNICEF initiates contacts with other organizations in Thailand. In June 1994, a week-long study trip is held in Bangkok and in northern Thailand regarding child prostitution. Three NGOs are invited to attend: Redd Barna, World Vision, and Krousar Thmey. We are joined by a representative from the Ministry of Interior, one from the Ministry of Social Affairs, and two delegates from UNICEF. A serious warning is sounded by the End Child Prostitution, Abuse And Trafficking (ECPAT) office. After touring various child welfare programs, we come back to Cambodia with the desire to do something specific to fight child prostitution.

Thailand, up till now a paradise for foreign pedophiles, is starting to tighten up its legislation and fight corruption-related impunity. Inevitably, the problem migrates to Cambodia where the sexual abuse of minors is already very prevalent in the population at large. It's not uncommon for children to be raped by a family member, a new mate, or a neighbor. With the spread of AIDS, the demand for young virgins is booming. A number of Chinese or Cambodians of Chinese descent "consume" girls whose virginity is thought to be an elixir of youth. We realize that it's perilous to go after the rich Cambodians and the officials—military officers or policemen—who protect these networks, but that's no reason to do nothing about it.

Rather than creating a specialized organization, we initially manage with what we've got. It seems good to have an NGO coalition with a view to making ourselves less vulnerable. This results in the establishment of ECPAT Cambodia in October 1994. I share the vice-chairmanship with the Redd Barna director. We change the name to "End Child Prostitution, Abuse And Trafficking." The member organizations of ECPAT decide to focus on limiting the spread of child prostitution and trafficking and to raise public awareness, especially among foreigners.

In liaison with human rights advocacy organizations such as LICADHO, we conduct a number of direct intervention and preventive operations. By 1995, Krousar Thmey has an investigative team working out of our Psar Depot center. They listen to the stories of the street children, collect information from hotels and guesthouses, compile testimonies, and monitor pedophiles, either to bolster a case and file civil action or to get the police to intervene. We are strapped by a judicial system that does not always take well to an organization's filing a civil suit. It's also difficult to get the families involved, either because they're getting money from the children or are ashamed and clam up. And getting the police to do something is often problematic, even though it's the logical thing to do.

After weeks of investigations and shadowing, we can sometimes provide complete information to the police for an immediate raid. But instead of coming back with a person caught in the act, the officers often return smiling but empty-handed, saying they didn't find anything… but no doubt with their pockets overflowing. Corruption is our number one enemy. Without a specialized police force, duly trained and properly salaried so they don't succumb to corruption, working with them takes a lot out of us, even though it's necessary. True, NGOs have a lot of clout, but our interventions must remain incidental. Our role is to provide a referral and to urge the government's departments to work transparently and effectively.

The emergence of too much media hype about an NGO or a person can also be a great danger, as is illustrated by the case of a well-known NGO director who claimed to be saving children from prostitution but who ended up being charged with embezzlement. Unhappily, although he was justly sentenced, the optimism and goodwill of thousands of donors were jeopardized by his misconduct. I feel that it's suspect and dangerous to have an organization founded on the ambitions of an individual.

Initially, ECPAT Cambodia's initiatives are spectacular. But they involve painstaking effort, are costly in time and resources, and often have no lasting effect. We're novices in the field, no doubt overly idealistic. The differing viewpoints between NGOs and the need to get together to make decisions are inconsistent with emergency management. We believe that the government can mete out justice, but the reality leaves us disappointed.

One of the first cases we handle is that of an expatriate pedophile living in Phnom Penh; it results in a media disaster. Wanting to let the judicial process take its course and thereby support it, rather than just using the press as a lever, we raise the ire of western journalists who take up the cause of the defendant who claims to be a victim of homophobia. Despite undeniable evidence and the testimony of several minors, we have a real fight to keep him behind bars. He has all kinds of support. His lawyer submits numerous applications to have him released on bail which, most happily, are turned down. At the trial, despite his plea of innocence, he is sentenced to 24 months in jail, five of them immutable. When released, he holds a press conference in which he rails that he was denied justice. However, he is unmasked by LICADHO who got hold of information on his expulsion from Myanmar. He had worked there for a company that fired him for the sexual abuse of children of local employees. His guilt is finally brought out into the open.

But even though we eventually win both in the courts and with the media, it must be conceded that this case alone cost us tremendously in effort and funds and we got very little for it. Once out of prison, the pedophile continues living in Cambodia. The child victims, for whom we got damages in the form of a financial plan for their education, tried everything to get their hands directly on the money. We had to put up uncompromisingly with the incessant insults of their families who would have preferred to spend the reparation money on consumer goods. It felt as if everyone was against us.

The decision was subsequently made that Krousar Thmey would no longer take direct action, but would focus on prevention with a poster campaign on the theme of fighting child prostitution and trafficking. A theater troupe puts on dialogue sketches highlighting the problem. Over 200,000 posters and billboards are produced on the subject. Hundreds of shows are put on in the villages, particularly in western Cambodia where trafficking and prostitution are endemic. We are also giving particular attention to the issue of trafficking children to Thailand.

When the border opens in 1991, Poipet is but a small town of a few thousand inhabitants. The border is under military guard. A few merchants and porters smuggle goods to and from Thailand, nothing more. There are only two concrete buildings, a small health care center of about 40 m^2 and an abandoned train station. The health center rarely opens its doors, save to admit its incompetence and a total lack of medication. The station building is nothing more than bullet-riddled walls protecting a track from which the rails were filched and sold long ago. The bridge between Cambodia and Thailand is still of wood. Traffic has increased, so some of the planks need to be replaced. Most dwellings are makeshift shelters of salvaged materials—plastic tarpaulins, cardboard, and old gas cans cut open and flattened into metal sheets... The shantytowns are concentrated around National Highway 6. The land round about is strewn with landmines.

With the opening of the country and repatriation, the town starts to grow. Farmers move in and increase the mass of destitute people. They hope they can make a living from begging or as day workers, hiring themselves out to haul goods from one side to the other. Many soldiers, policemen, and customs officers are assigned to control the surge in cross-border trafficking. Businesses open. Storage sheds go up, not to mention places of pleasure. Buildings spring up in total anarchy along the national highway. The slums move back but expand exogenously, with new shelters gradually appended on the outer rim, despite the risk of landmine explosions. Accidents happen and few escape alive, as the only decent hospital is in Mongkol Borei, 65 km away over a road in a gross state of disrepair. A lack of drainage turns the town into a foul-smelling swamp. The traveler leaves Thailand with its manicured thoroughfares, its road signs, and properly aligned electrical power poles and finds on the Cambodian side a putrid quagmire, with garbage heaps and plastic bags rotting under the sun.

In 1993, a Thai civil engineering team rebuilds the road from Poipet to Sisophon. For a few months, a road as smooth as a pool table makes it possible to get to Sisophon in 35 to 40 minutes instead of the usual four hours. But trucks and tanks quickly cause a return of the ruts.

Aware of the problems caused by the proliferation of street children and to support single-parent families headed by widows, I put before the Ministry of Social Affairs a relocation plan for dozens of families, including the building of a temporary intake center for street children. In 1994, I sign a contract with that ministry that sees Krousar Thmey granted 8 ha of land, complete with landmines. With the support of demining organizations, the property is gradually made safe. We encounter endless hassles with the local government and especially a few soldiers who are after this land right along the border. We plant boundary stakes every 20 m around the lot, only to find out that we barely escaped disaster. New landmines had been laid to keep us from getting on it. Eventually, with help from the Air France Foundation, we get 20 small wooden houses and two buildings up for the temporary housing of street children. This way, we manage to occupy 25,000 m^2 of the 80,000 m^2 lot.

Quite naturally, as a result of our work with agencies in Thailand, our Poipet center will be a transit point for women and children released from Thai prisons.

Opposite Poipet, on the Thai side of the border crossing, is Khlong Luek. Five loaded buses have just arrived from Bangkok. A vehicle belonging to the prison authorities accompanies them. The soldiers have all the Khmers get off, men first, of all ages, often very dark skinned. Most of them went to work on the docks or on construction sites in the Thai capital, lured by people smugglers promising an El Dorado. Caught by the Thai police as illegal aliens and thrown for a time into the Suan Plu immigration detention center in Bangkok, they are repatriated by the International Organization for Migration (IOM). They weren't there long, as they were able to come up with the 200-baht fine, equivalent to three days of work. Those with no money will not get back home for a while. On the list of people judicially accused of being illegal aliens, they will be ground in the jaws of the Thai legal system and prison world for months, sometimes even years.

The pattern is dreadfully repetitive. They pay someone to guarantee safe haven in Bangkok and a job on a construction site or on the docks. A couple of months' salary goes to the smuggler. They work there for four to six months, under the watch of the local police who turn a blind eye in return for a few bills. They end up getting arrested, often reported by their bosses in exchange for the silence of corrupt officers or caught during raids subsequent to political promises to clamp down on illegal immigrants. The luckiest or the best informed have successfully gotten a good part of their wages home through Khmer networks. These costly transfers enable them to feed their families. The men come home with empty pockets, but the exhausting work and humiliation have not been in vain. Novices return to the country bone-weary and empty-handed, robbed by the police, prison guards, and Khmer soldiers, while spouses, children, families have stayed behind begging or working in Poipet, patiently awaiting the return of a husband or brother and the lifesaving money.

Despair then sets in. The illegal foreigners seek to hide their failure. They break away again to new ventures that they hope will be less humiliating. Some never come back, convinced that the infernal cycle will never end. Their older children in turn try to survive as waste pickers, selling junk they find in the garbage. Their wives, with no strength left, fall into prostitution or rent out one of the younger children to begging or prostitution rings. What hell! The machine is well lubricated. Every cog in the wheel of authority gets its share of this wringing out of the wretched. Despite repeated fiascoes, every day, dozens of farmers take to the road. They've lost their land to pay back money borrowed for medical care and they think they can succeed where others have failed.

In Poipet, there they are, heads bowed, hunched up in single file, at the mercy of a kick or a wallop from the disdainful border guards, who restrain themselves for a moment when we are present. Further on are colorful lines of women, among them prostitutes swept from dens of vice and elsewhere. They are easily recognizable by their gaudy makeup. Some are barely 15 years old. Still further down, groups of children and toothless old women lay prostrate, victims of begging rings. The traffickers run less risk and make just as much money. They rent children in Poipet or kidnap them and take them to Bangkok. Forced to beg at shopping mall exits, Khmer children are easy to spot. Darker skinned, clothed in rags, they speak a bit of rough Thai. Those not so clever only last a few days in Bangkok. The shrewd hang in there for months before being caught, jailed, and expelled. We're there for the latter ones.

For some months now, Krousar Thmey has been working with a program for the repatriation of jailed children in Bangkok. We liaise with other Thai organizations that monitor child inmates of the IOM detention center to meet them when they arrive, sometimes with accompanying adults. The danger is to mistakenly take in an adult, generally a woman claiming to be the aunt of a child, but actually a member of the trafficking ring. Women are more successful in convincing children to go with them and can slip through the net if arrested. If they are allowed to get into our center, they often leave with children in tow. The facility is open, as are all those of Krousar Thmey. Therefore, vigilance is the byword.

We start conducting interviews and investigations to identify the real families and help get the children reunited with them. Sometimes, the families are in cahoots and the child is again exploited by the networks. Persons claiming to be relatives and who may try to make off with a child are generally known to the minors. They are perhaps distant family members, adults they've been with in Bangkok, who have often mistreated or threatened them. The children daren't resist them for fear of reprisals. Our workers have the sensitive job of finding out who the real parents are. The children have no address, no ID papers, and no reliable register of civil status. With such a nebulous background, it sometimes becomes impossible to sort out their problems.

They are often overwhelmed by what has happened to them. Manipulated, abused, rented out, sold like merchandise, that's all they've ever known. For them, there's nothing abnormal about being exploited by the adult world. They don't trust us any more than the traffickers. True, our people speak more kindly, but couldn't that just be a strategy for further abuse? They feel they're simply an unlucky lot. Even if they want a better life, they feel it's an impossible dream, that they're victims of a curse.

I get the feeling someone is watching me. A little girl in a pink tracksuit is looking mischievously at me, amused. Unlike the others, she is not cowered by the soldiers; in fact, she just ignores them. Squatting on both feet as Asians commonly do, propping her little head up with her hand, she's taking it all in. She watches me negotiate. She quickly understands that we're accepting her in the center. Channa is 10 years old. She has never known her father or mother. She's very light-skinned, no doubt the child of a Khmer-Vietnamese relationship. For years now she has been used by traffickers to beg in Thailand. She's familiar with the shopping malls, the central train station, and the Chatuchak Market street maze. Despite the police presence, the flow of foreigners willing to part with a few baht of alms makes the ordeal worthwhile. Although she speaks Thai very well, Channa has been arrested several times. It's become a routine. Expelled again, she knows she'll soon be back on the sidewalks of Bangkok, then on to Suan Plu Prison.

Somehow she remembers that she saw me there. I had asked to visit the prison. I saw dozens of Cambodians there awaiting deportation, and had spoken with some of the women and children. At one point, the prison director, overhearing me speaking Khmer, butted in, apologizing for the "intolerable" situations I might have heard the women tell me about. He asserted that the "contribution toward prison expenses required of each prisoner at the time of deportation was waived for children." Fearing that someone might have told me that the usual 200-

baht payment had been exacted from all of them, he quickly added that it was the fault of a female prisoner. He pointed to a large Black French-speaking woman in white pajamas. Understanding what she was being accused of, she broke into a rage and shouted in French that the director forced her to collect the money from everyone, babies included, and give it to the guards. Seeing her all worked up, I had no trouble understanding why the director chose her to do the dirty work, in as much as Asians are often afraid of Blacks.

To our surprise, Channa makes herself at home in our center. She's always asking after the *barang* with big glasses. She weakly attempts two runaways, and then opts for stability in exchange for the illusion of freedom on the streets. In order to protect her from bad influences, we transfer her to Ta Khmau where she is given sewing lessons. At the same time, she takes traditional Khmer dance classes, which give her self-confidence.

The children repatriated from Bangkok prisons and abuse victims bring a structural problem to light. The centers have a ceiling of 35 children. Any more than that and it's impossible to properly care for a child needing support. We're unsuccessful in reintegrating children from the Bangkok prisons; they feel lost in the welfare center where the other children have not had the same traumatic experiences. This leads me to envision a smaller, more family-like facility. Starting in 1996, we develop a new support concept, the family shelter, wherein each child feels closer, is given a greater hearing ear, and finds things more lively.

Noy looks like an innocent little girl of seven. Smiling, playful, full of life, she skips about in the yard of the Kpop Veng house, enjoying games with her new brothers and sisters. Other children like her come here from Poipet after being helped out of prison and repatriated by the IOM. Noy, as is the case for most of these children, was the victim of a lucrative trafficking scheme. She left with her mother to beg in Bangkok and knew no other world than a spot on the sidewalk outside one of the big shopping malls where she was plunked by the traffickers. When she was five, an empty soda can was put in front of her to catch the coins. She whimpered constantly because of the ear disease her exploiters kept her infected with to more readily arouse the pity of the Thais and stir their generosity. When she arrived at the family shelter, she was suffering from skin problems and an ear infection, but especially from the emotional trauma of the years of abuse. Rythy and Srey Vy, the couple acting as parents in the Kpop Veng family shelter, had to show extra attention and affection toward Noy to help her smile again. Two years later, like most of these children taken in, it's hard to imagine the hell that she went through. Kpop Veng is one of our family shelters that offers a warm environment for children suffering from deep emotional wounds.

The family shelter operates on a simple principle. We put up a house and look for a couple to act as parents. The husband has an outside job; the couple has one or two children of their own. We train them and put them in charge of as many as ten additional children. Of course, we provide financial support for the children and give the couple a salary. It's just one more big family among those from the countryside. The children placed in it are of varying ages so they can help one another.

The outcome of the first shelter is so encouraging that we quickly decide to put up more. Always two in one province, close enough to each other so that the two couples acting as parents can be mutually supportive, but far enough away so that the children don't mix at the same schools. The name Krousar Thmey doesn't appear on the buildings. Only those familiar with the association can recognize the style and colors. Things are purposely kept low-key in this manner and the number of children (relatively) small to avoid stigmatization. They're not problem children taken in by an organization. They have a family like everyone else that fits in with its environment.

Given their success and the satisfactory outcome for the children taken in, these homes rapidly increase in number, three around Phnom Penh, two in Sihanoukville, two in Kompong Cham, two in Battambang, and two in Siem Reap. But when a dispute between two children ends in the fatal knifing of one of them, the first home is considered haunted by evil spirits and is closed. Currently there are ten of them.

Poipet is the entry point for all Cambodians who, after losing everything, scrape together the few baht needed to pay for last week's food. Thousands of them haul goods legally or illegally across the no man's land. Thailand supplies the western zone with large quantities of fruit and vegetables, along with an impressive amount of manufactured goods for the whole country—plastic utensils, fashionable clothing, building materials—nearly everything goes through Poipet. Stocks of used clothing from Europe, and even more from Korea and Japan, are sold in Cambodia and smuggled the other way into Thailand. Vehicles are not allowed over the border, so everything is packed on men's backs or heaped to overflowing on hand carts. There are unbelievably ingenious ways in which a few kilos of fruit can be hidden. From a wheelchair laden with several bags and ridden by a disabled person to double-bottomed carts, anything goes if a little money can be earned. Little kids puff up like the Michelin Man with several layers of clothing packed on before crossing the border.

In mid-January 1997, we're in Poipet. We're having lunch at a market stall. Thary is chatting with Dana, the director of our single-mother support village. I'm busing finalizing a report, but overhear a few things. My report finished, I ask Thary, if I understood correctly, why somebody wants me to go looking for some children in Thailand. Beggar and waste picker children take the official bridge daily across to Thailand. Or they sometimes take the side road under military control, or another passageway through the mine-strewn ditches. Policemen and customs officials have paid tens of thousands of dollars for a posting in Poipet that they recoup after a few months of racketeering. For a long time now, the customs people don't care about hunting down children or small-time smugglers. There are way too many of them and the take is too lean. So why am I expected to drive around looking for children who are much better than I at crossing the border?

Great is my shock when Thary tells me that some children have been killed by Thai soldiers and the families want to recover their remains for burial. I'm stunned by the news and by the fact that Thary, my assistant, chairman of the Cambodian Committee for Children's Rights, did not react immediately upon hearing the news. No reaction, no questions asked, no desire to investigate, understand, or take action. As if the murder of little waste pickers was a routine affair.

He then realizes his error and we go off together. It's obviously too late, but I want to get to the bottom of it. I also refuse any manipulation by the Thai media. I want to put a stop to these unpunished crimes. Asking around, we find ourselves in the middle of a slum with soggy heaps of decaying garbage nearby. Families live there in a bewilderment of shelters made of cardboard and recycled materials. A tarpaulin is hung over four bamboo poles to provide a little shade. Some monks and women are chanting in prayer. A few women wish us welcome.

As was their habit every day, five friends crossed over to the Thai side to look for empty drink cans where the pickings are much better and where there isn't so much competition from other waste pickers. They get one baht for every three cans, so once they collect 45 cans, they can buy a bowl of noodle soup. On their way back, the children came across a group of adult Cambodians who invited them to have some chicken. They followed them to a farm. The adults stole some chickens and a bicycle and were making a quick exit over the border. But the border patrol were alerted by the famers and caught up with the culprits.

The night shift is well-known for their brutality. Without warning, they opened fire on the group. The adults got away safe. Four of the children were wounded, three of them seriously. Gnep suffered a light wound to his hand and was able to hide behind a thicket. He witnessed the scene. The soldiers thrashed the three injured children to get them to say where the adults had gone. The children had no idea, so the soldiers gave chase as far as the border. Then, to avoid a diplomatic incident, they retraced their steps. Rather than help out the groaning children, they finished them off in cold blood with a burst of gunfire on each of them.

Gnep, paralyzed with fear, spent the night there after the soldiers retreated. In the morning, the day shift soldiers spotted him, took him to the hospital, interrogated him, then turned him over to the Khmer police. I want to find this child. We head to the police station but are stopped by a man who informs us that the child had been released the day before and that he knows where to find him.

We cross National Highway 6 and enter another shantytown. We catch sight of Gnep. He says nothing. His hand and forearm are badly swollen. The wound is open and flies are feasting on it. Somehow I think

I know him and ask him. Yes, he remembers me very well. Yes, he was filmed by the Serge Moati team in 1996 when a story was being shot for the 50th anniversary of UNICEF. Yes, he had come to the Poipet center for street children, but preferred to go back to the streets. He chafed under the center's rules and wanted to remain free. His parents? His father died, his mother is begging in Thailand. Who's looking after him? Nobody. From time to time, neighbors give him a handout of rice. For a long while now, he's just fended for himself. We can't just leave him there. If he doesn't get treatment, he'll surely get an infection. I can barely hold back my tears, but I do, at least in front of him. Is there absolutely no end to misery?

We invite him to go with us to the hospital in Sisophon. He hesitates, but finally agrees. In Sisophon, the hospital is empty. There is no staff around, just a few beds in the larger rooms that have no doubt never seen a broom. Patients lie on straw mats right on the metal bed frames. A small wobbly pole allows a sugar solution drip to be administered, slowly, interminably. Everything seems to be happening in slow motion. Even those who are there to bring food for a sick relative seem lifeless. The hospital smells of death and oozes with despair. The state of neglect and pallid atmosphere of the place make us decide to move on to Battambang. Gnep agrees. That night, a doctor friend associated with MSF redoes the bandaging and advises us to have the boy hospitalized at Kantha Bopha Hospital in Phnom Penh, belonging to Beat Richner.

Richner is a Swiss one-man show, a little batty, and very virulent against all humanitarian organizations… that he's never met. In Switzerland, we've often been invited to share in debates with him, but he refuses if he's not the only guest. True, his system is a bit of a white elephant and wouldn't keep going without the millions of dollars that he collects, mainly in Switzerland. But it must be admitted that without him, many children would have died long ago. He's doing an outstanding job. He was present before the war and returned to Phnom Penh on November 2, 1992, the date of our first repatriation to Siem Reap. Since that time, several hundred medical assistants have received rigorous, competent training under him.

In an impeccably tiled waiting room, patients wait, squatting on their haunches. A take-a-number system keeps the intake orderly. Gnep is taken right in. I assign a Krousar Thmey staff member to watch over him and bring him food while he's in the hospital. He is very well looked after.

When he is released, we invite him to visit Krousar Thmey's offices and give him a wooden train, a gift from students of the French high school in Singapore. For the first time in his life he has his own toy and has fun playing with it like a child of his age. A brief Agence France-Presse report on the incident appears in Cambodia's papers: "Thai soldiers bring down a dangerous gang of Khmer bandits armed with AK-47s out to steal motorbikes in Thailand. The gang leader was wounded, treated, then interrogated by Thai secret service officers before being turned over to the Cambodian authorities. He acknowledged the facts." That's how history is made. The gang leader is in front of me. A scrawny 11-year-old waste picker who witnessed the cold-blooded execution of his three buddies…

I am writing up the *Lettre de famille*, a quarterly newsletter for Krousar Thmey's supporters, and I have a terrible time relating the whole story about Gnep. How can children be victims of such great injustice?

We receive a visit from Madam Bun Rany, wife of Prime Minister Hun Sen, and the ambassador of Japan to our first school for deaf children going up in Chbar Ampov, not far from the first school for blind children. I attempt to raise the issue by introducing Gnep. A female assistant rushes over, shoves him 70,000 riels, and orders him not to bother the First Lady. She doesn't want a diplomatic incident… and, what's more, he's just a little waste picker. "Dust of life," as they are called by the Poussières de Vie organization in Vietnam. I'm absolutely disgusted. After his wound heals, Gnep chooses not to go back to Poipet and lives at the Ta Khmau welfare center.

I'm haunted by this story. At night, I often think about this child, what he went through, and feel so powerless. As the years have gone by, I've come to feel relatively at home here, but the more things go on, the more I have my doubts. I find it quite difficult to share my feelings with my Cambodian friends. I can't understand their reaction or lack of reaction. I'm unable to come to grips with the fatalism of karma.

The construction team isn't free to work on the primary school site in Poipet, so I ask our Sisophon director to supervise it. Though a man of many human qualities, accounting is not his strong suit and he always turns the books in late. There are no banks in Cambodia's provinces and all purchases are paid for in cash. We have staff go out to the provinces regularly to take funds to the different centers. The accounting records are collected and brought down to Phnom Penh to be collated, the data entered and analyzed. Large additional amounts of cash have to be delivered to our building projects. It's challenging to sort it all out because of the currency exchanges needed to buy various materials.

Tremendous mental gymnastics are required to convert everything into dollars, the currency of our accounting system. Although invoices are useless here—because the merchant always asks the buyer how much he wants to be shown on the receipt—they are a necessary first step in the accounting paper trail. But they are not used as a basis for audits. Having sat down and sketched many a building, I have learned to calculate the amounts needed, the working time, how much rebar the concrete will require, etc. My training as an auditor and business instinct come in very handy. My Khmer remains basic, but I have learned many of the terms used on a construction site.

For the Poipet building, all the bills have been collected and the amounts verified, but the figures are way off the estimates. We have overspent, notably on bricks and tile. I have some digging done to see if the foundations are of the proper depth and factor in a possible loss of tiles during transit and setting. Did the tiles and bricks grow wings and fly off to Poipet? To get to the bottom of the abnormally high bills, I ask the director to come and see me in Phnom Penh. I hope he will understand that this control is in his best interests. Feeling trapped, he bolts. I warn his friends of the consequences and give him an ultimatum to show up. The ultimatum comes and goes; I have no other choice.

We're bound by friendship, having worked for a long time together and spending many a night discussing things over a beer at his place, but I can't just let this go. Otherwise, the hemorrhage will spread throughout the organization. With a lump in my throat, I file a complaint with the police. A clue from an employee leads us to his hideout. Driving a pickup truck, I collect three policemen at an intersection, promising them a Krousar Thmey Tshirt, and the man is arrested. If I'd waited for the police to do their work, nothing would have happened. My man offers no resistance and we end up at the central police headquarters where he spends the night. He translates the details of his case himself. I know that with a little money, he can evade the net.

I offer to make an arrangement with him. We'll go through with the court case and I'll see to it that he gets only six months in jail, during which time I'll look after his family. When he gets out, he'll work for us for two years without pay in order to make good his debt, at which time he can either stay with us or leave. I'm sickened by this situation. Today, I'm losing a friend for whom I have much affection. How I would like to be able to turn a blind eye. But it's not my money. My decision is not as a friend, but as the director of Krousar Thmey. As unpleasant as the decision is, it's in the interests of the children.

On a number of occasions I go visit him at T3 Prison, a colonial establishment erected in downtown Phnom Penh. The place hasn't been maintained since. After going through the outer enclosure wall topped by a high fence, there's a small iron door. Prisoners work in vegetable gardens under the supervision of guards. A second door lets me into a small courtyard. The walls are slick with moisture and exude a musty smell. There's saltpeter everywhere. I introduce myself and explain why I've come. I'm asked to wait. There's already a crowd on hand. As in all prisons in Cambodia, family members have to bring the food necessary for the survival of the inmates. To get food to a prisoner, one also has to pay a little bribe. No one dares ask me for anything. This time, I'm dressed as a delivery boy with pizzas from La Casa. I'm very uncomfortable doing this because this man used to be a close friend.

During this troubled time when many an NGO has seen a cashier or financial officer take off with money or materials, when theft has become run-of-the-mill, it's very hard to chart a steady course. Instability prevails at the government level, at the United Nations, among neighbors, and even among family members. Theft is becoming a national pastime. There is seldom any effort made to look for the perpetrators and even less to arrest them. The police, when not implicated, sometimes refuse to act unless they get a share of the booty retrieved. When a motorbike thief is caught by the police, the latter sometimes turn the villain over to the enraged populace; there's nothing like a public lynching as fodder for the tabloids.

Stolen vehicles are only recovered for half of what they're worth. Civil servants receiving but a pittance of a salary, corruption remains the only expedient to feed their families. Amid these circumstances, there are frequent incongruities, and it's important to let others know that one is keeping a watchful eye. The prison sentence is a warning. The name "T3" will be used years later by a very trendy hip-hop discotheque built on the old prison site.

Meanwhile, every time I pay a visit to the Ta Khmau center, Wanna, the young blind boy, asks me insistently why he can't go to school. There's no special school for the blind in Cambodia and there never was one. As is true of other disabled persons, the blind have always been kept in the background, neglected, abandoned. The only available statistics, compiled by the American Red Cross in 1993, show that there are a large number of blind people, proportionately six times as many in Cambodia as in Europe, mainly due to measles. When a child gets sick with the measles and is suffering a vitamin deficiency at the same time, the disease can result in blindness. And contrary to what is commonly thought in Europe, we've never met a child blinded by a landmine accident. If a child detonates a landmine, it's usually fatal. Moreover, statistics show that some 60 percent of blind children die within two years after becoming blind simply for want of care. The handicap is considered bad luck caused by evil deeds committed in a previous life, so the victim has to atone for his errors.

When Wanna hears his friends leave for school every morning, he wants to go with them. While in camp, he used to attend a small special school project sponsored by the International Rescue Committee for disabled children. It was not carried over into Cambodia. Wanna, bright and full of energy, is hurt by such discrimination and harasses me. When he hears me arrive at the center, he finds out where I'm at and won't let go of me. I made an enquiry at the Ministry of Education; it has better things to do. UNICEF likewise has other priorities. There's a shortage of primary schools, even though schools double their classrooms by having morning and afternoon classes. So… the blind…

One day I give in to Wanna's unrelenting barrage and promise him a school. I've got to keep my word… But I already have more than enough to do. I know nothing of the issues facing the blind. I vaguely heard about the small program on Site II, but I don't know where to start. I take on the role of a detective looking for a Neang Phalla, director of the Site II special school. I'm told to go looking in Psar Touch (Little Market), a very crowded neighborhood in Phnom Penh. Of course, no one knows Neang Phalla. I somehow find out that she's working on voter registration for the United Nations… A real breakthrough. Might as well try picking out one soccer fan in a crowded stadium.

Like almost everyone in the run-up to the elections, many returnees are working in voter registration. I go from station to station and finally meet an Australian woman who remembers talking about disabled children with a short lady who'd been in the camps. She isn't sure where the person is working, maybe Chamkarmon district. I carry on my quest. I get lucky; Phalla does work here, but has just left. I return the next day and find her expecting me, as her colleagues had told her about my query. This wisp of a woman, 40 kg at the outside, may look frail but she's got a firm hand. Her English is a little weak, her smiles ingratiating, and she's very self-effacing, but she's very determined. I don't know her, but she knows me, the barang with the big motorbike who founded Krousar Thmey where Wanna lives. I get straight to the point. We want to open the first school for blind children and need her long term. She still has some time on her contract with the UN, but to my surprise she accepts on the spot my offer of just $100 a month, while she's getting $170 with the United Nations. And she's going to have to go it alone, something most Cambodians don't like to do.

She starts the very next week. Her first job is to get statistics on blind children and find out where they're living. She needs a means of transportation. Buy a motorbike in Phnom Penh? Nothing to it. Everything is neighborhood oriented. I go to Psar Orussey (bamboo brook market). I happen to catch sight of a blind child in one of the ground-floor stalls. I enter. The boy is curled up in his chair, unattended. I ask his parents if he goes out to play with others. "No! He just stays here because he bumps into something every time he takes a step. He'd break a leg if he goes out on the sidewalk. He's very frail." And it's true. Vissal is like a plant deprived of water and sunlight. So, an outing on the street… It must be admitted that Phnom Penh's sidewalks, encumbered with goods on display, are not pedestrian-friendly. In this neighborhood, if it's not the motorbikes and other two-wheelers, it's the open manholes or potholes that can trip the unwary. It's best to keep one's eyes fixed on the ground. This makes me realize the exceptional ability of Wanna who even gets on a bicycle with his friends.

Actually, young Vissal never receives any motor stimulation and is kept in a nearly autistic state. When he hears my voice, he starts talking unstoppably. A real chatterbox. Since we are just starting, I tell the family that he can go to school in a few more months if he wants. He is indeed among the first enrollees.

Phalla is disheartened by her findings of the first weeks. She has some statistics. District or ward chiefs tell her of this or that family with a blind child, but families rarely come out and say they have a child that's blind. They keep it hidden as if it was something shameful for the entire family. No one wants to admit the curse of having a blind child. So the child wouldn't be sent to school, unless it's an opportunity to get rid of it. Some families even ask us to just take the child for good. Out of the question! These attitudes will have a major impact on the approach that we take to get families involved and explain why we're reticent to take in child boarders. Phalla gets assistance and encouragement from a female volunteer.

To understand how these challenges are dealt with in Thailand, I get in touch with a Thai woman who worked on problems involving disabled children in the camps. She works with the Thai Foundation for the Blind. The Thai people have a similar attitude toward the disabled, so her expertise proves invaluable. Moreover, although of different origins, the Thai and Cambodian languages are related and borrow words from each other, although they are pronounced differently, something like English and French. The way the two languages are written is similar, although Cambodian is more complex. Two consonants placed one after the other change how the second one is written. But more so than any overseas expert, human resources from the neighboring country are really the best.

We have an ideal piece of land in Chbar Ampov. I earlier had a real problem getting this property because the benefits from the Barbara Hendricks concert turned out to be ten times less than pledged. It's ready to have a building put on it. Just have to find the money, get the permits, but, most importantly, develop a curriculum.

The beginnings of Khmer Braille had been devised on Site II, based on Thai Braille. This rough model did not allow school textbooks to be transcribed. Every country standardizes the Braille it uses, so it's important that one Braille system be developed in Cambodia, once and for all.

To achieve this means getting all the stakeholders involved in a broad consultation process. Without a consensus, we can't move forward. So we use La Casa's dining rooms before and after working hours to hold a number of meetings with experts from organizations specializing in blindness, NGOs devoted to helping the handicapped, linguists from the Ministry of Education, and an authority from UNICEF.

I'm no specialist in linguistics and education, but express the desire that the system make it possible for blind children to be fully integrated into the Cambodian educational system. I rule out developing a special form of education for special individuals. In light of my meetings with numerous professionals in France, Switzerland, and Thailand, I firmly believe that blind children should be mainstreamed in the schools. Writing is the key to passing on culture and our blind children must be able to understand the specificity of their language and how it is written. That is central to the debate.

The UNICEF linguist feels that the way Khmer is written is already too complex. Each of the 33 consonants changes when preceded by another consonant. To the 23 vowels several extensions must be added, and some vowels are pronounced differently depending on the group of associated consonants. When it comes to writing, things really get complicated, with many vowels assigned a place above or below the consonant. For a word as simple as "I" (or "me"), pronounced *khniom*, four separate signs are superposed, thus giving the word four levels of letters. How can all that be transcribed into Braille? A blind reader cannot feel up and down looking for signs. He has to be able to read from left to right, sliding the index figure on the paper. The traditional system has only six raised dots, making 63 combinations possible for reading. It therefore doesn't fit the bill.

To transcribe all of the letters into Braille, two or three of the six points have to be used to show the position of each letter. The blind child has to memorize all of these possibilities, frontwards and backwards. When he writes, he puts a sheet of paper into a reglet and presses on an embossing device to form raised dots. He therefore writes from right to left before turning the sheet over to read from left to right. He has to learn to think backwards to read where he's at.

What a nightmare! Transcribing all the letters is like building a gasworks, and the linguist contends that it would be more logical to develop an abbreviated system like some in Europe. That may look obvious, but the blind would be confined to a specific system, thus ruling out integration. So I go for what a number of European experts propose—the most complicated system in which all letters are transcribed. It's a huge wager on the future, as this system is very demanding of the young blind students, taking a long time to learn and requiring a tremendous ability to memorize.

To start with, all writing is done using a reglet and stylus. But the Maryknoll Association very quickly gets some Perkins for us, special typewriters that use only six keys to make the raised dot letters.

While this is going on, work starts on the school for blind children. If everything goes well, it will open in the first few months of 1994. We start with 12 pupils, soon joined by more. The first classes focus on mobility and orientation. These children who have up to now been stuck prostrate in a corner and have never been stimulated need to learn how to control their bodies and manage space. At first, they lose their balance. Wanna is an Olympic champion compared to the others. The clumsiest simply want to stay hunched up against the wall. With patience and encouragement, they improve. In a few weeks, they're no longer the children they were. Even the school has changed. Like luxuriantly growing flowers or plants, the blind children overcome their inhibitions and move about almost normally. Some use the canes that were donated to us, but most go from one classroom to another almost naturally. They have learned to hold their right arm up in front of their face to protect themselves from obstacles. Nothing was built specifically to adapt the external environment to their disability.

They gradually learn to anticipate hazards and nothing surprises them anymore. They flourish. Some have even started learning Braille and how to use an abacus, a small Chinese calculating tool constructed of a wood frame with beads slid along wires. The first primary school textbook was transcribed and a few copies typed up, one sheet at a time using a Perkins. We want the children to have the same textbooks as their peers. They're so happy that when vacation time comes, they don't want to leave. They just want to keep on studying Braille and enjoying the mobility and orientation sessions that are bringing them to life.

Now that the school has gotten off to a good start, I want to raise awareness. We need to gain the confidence of families with deaf children that were located. Indeed, shame keeps too many families from sending their child to school. We want to get the message out that blind children can now go to school too. We think a big grand opening ceremony will be helpful. I write my first letter to His Majesty King Norodom Sihanouk, explaining what we are doing for blind children. Actually, he had already heard about it and expresses how touched he is and how much he admires our initiative. He sends me a beautiful congratulatory letter, adding that he regrets being unable to preside at the ceremony, but will delegate his wife, Queen Monineath, for the occasion.

The Royal Palace sets the date for November 30, 1994. News of it spreads like wildfire. After the initial jubilation over the good news, we're panic-stricken. How will we pull it off? How does one address the queen? What should we wear? Who should be invited? We get advice from the elders, start building a wooden tribune, and receive numerous inspection visits during the week from Phnom Penh city hall and Royal

Palace officials. Many say that the neighborhood isn't up to a royal visit. Others feel that it will be too much work to get the road fixed. And, to top it off, city hall lets us know that we can forget about the tribune because the grand opening won't take place at the school. In pictures? At the Royal Palace? Where are we to take the children? I take it as a bad joke. And, in fact, all current road work in the neighborhood suddenly grinds to a halt. Like everyone else at Krousar Thmey, I'm desperate. Scalding hot one minute and chilled to the bone the next.

We look for a solution. A picture inauguration is meaningless. The school won't get the media hype that a ceremony would. If we are to change the attitude of Cambodians toward disabled children, demonstrate that they can go to school like anyone else, we need the support of the country's senior leaders. We need an event covered by the print and broadcast media. While awaiting a solution, we go on with the preparatory work.

Happily, we're present at a working breakfast held at the French embassy. Christiane Le Lidec, the ambassador's wife, in charge of humanitarian affairs, is very active in interorganizational cooperation. Her big thing is to get French NGO leaders to foster responsibility among Cambodians and thus get Khmers out front in the NGO community. She had visited several of our programs and recognizes the value of our approach. I tell her about the sensitive matter of our inauguration. In a flash, I see that she will get something done. That very afternoon, she's attending a ceremony with Her Majesty the Queen and tells her about the school. Late in the afternoon, the Royal Palace calls to confirm that the queen will be at the Chbar Ampov school on November 30. Thank you, Christiane.

The next morning, city hall casually asks what we think about the photo inauguration. Apparently its officials haven't been informed. We let them know about the Royal Palace's decision. A ripple of panic. The ceremony is 24 hours away and, since they stopped everything, nothing is ready on their side. That day, we see that Cambodians, sometimes so laidback, really have what it takes to respond to orders with alacrity and effectiveness. Less than an hour later, truckfuls of dirt are unloaded, bulldozers are grading, and officials fan out through the neighborhood to inform the public. No work is allowed the next day. The plant growth is dense, so all are pressed into working with the army to make the zone secure. Workers whitewash the tree trunks to a height of 1 m. That evening, the place isn't recognizable. It looks like new.

On November 30, 1994, at 7 a.m., we're out and at it. Starting at Monivong Bridge, thousands of children in blue and white are lined up on either side of the road, ready to wave the little paper Cambodian flags and portraits of the king and queen that were distributed to them. It's a non-stop 3 km chain from the bridge to the school.

At 8 o'clock, the first officials take the seats assigned to them by the protocol department. Many of them are already sporting the first cellular telephones and are preoccupied with their gadgets. At 8:30, the sirens wail. Walky-talkies crackle everywhere. Motorcycle drivers in immaculate white open the way. Her Majesty the Queen steps out of the car with her lady attendants. With Phalla, we bow to her. She's delightful. Totally natural class and elegance. HE Kong Som Ol, minister of the Royal Palace, does some last minute fine-tuning. Everyone is there—the wife of the prime minister, the minister of education, the minister of social affairs, the governor of Phnom Penh... The tribune can't hold any more. Hopefully it doesn't collapse! The blind children out in the yard face the tribune. Wanna and a few others accompany the *pin piet* orchestra.

After the chanting of the monks who bless Her Majesty the Queen then the rest of the assembly, the young Ta Khmau dancing girls begin their elegant sway for the dance of the benediction. Hands and feet twist gracefully in a way that only Cambodians can master. A spray of jasmine flowers rains upon the distinguished guests. May they all be blessed! Her Majesty the Queen is so moved to see the young orphan girls dance to the music played by the blind musicians that she stands to applaud them. The other invitees take a self-conscious look at one another and follow suit in this impromptu gesture before the speeches start. The statements proceed, followed by the giving of gifts and a tour of the school. The children and persons on hand for the event bow to the queen, who smiles at them and touches hands, besprinkling one and all with her grace. The contingent of North Korean bodyguards see to her safety and, sometimes a little roughly, keep in check the overly demonstrative surges of those so happy to meet Her Majesty.

The ceremony ends at 11 a.m. The officials depart. We can get out of our suits that are soaking wet. We're exhausted but happy. The event is aired over and over by all of Cambodia's TV stations. It lands page one in all the Khmer newspapers. The following days, many families visit the school and enroll their blind children. The wager has been won. We are beginning to see a change of behavior with regard to a disability. A mother, in tears, comes with her child. She saw the news story several times. When her son was born and she realized that he would be permanently blind, she thought of doing away with him and then killing herself to escape the shame she brought on her family. Now she knows that he will have a future. With the staunch support of Their Majesties the King and Queen, and with that of Prime Minister Hun Sen, what we are doing becomes meaningful. Handicapped children can enjoy a normal childhood.

Sophat, one of our first blind students, tells us that he has many brothers and sisters and, thirsting for knowledge, would go to school with them every day. The teacher left him outside, so he would listen from the window. When the teacher asked questions, Sophat would answer out loud before anyone else, which annoyed the teacher. With the Krousar Thmey school now open, Sophat is proud to walk right into the classroom and sit at his own desk.

My intention is to speed up the involvement of the government and of families in the development of education for blind children. In 1996, when we need to build a second school for blind children, we appeal to the generosity of the government. But its budget is yet too tight for it to contribute to the building. We ask only for some land. Thanks to the intervention of His Majesty King Norodom Sihanouk, we are offered a lot in downtown Battambang, right along the river. It looks great, but local rivalries weren't factored in. In fact, the land is coveted by some soldiers. We expend a lot of energy to assert our rights. Moreover, squatter families are living on it. We get them to agree to leave.

Once the land is clear, it looks like we can go ahead with the building.

The perimeter wall, sacrosanct in Cambodia to mark off the boundary of one's property, causes a ruckus with our next-door neighbor, who also happens to be a soldier. He challenges the layout and attempts to do us out of many square meters. A beautiful banyan tree is growing in the disputed section. Many meetings and letters later, a Solomonic compromise is eventually reached with the provincial governor. The perimeter wall will start at the middle of the trunk of the banyan tree. Building work gets underway with Sameath's team. As the foundations are dug, we discover a mass grave, undoubtedly from the Khmer Rouge era. We ask the monks from a nearby pagoda to conduct the ceremony to bring repose to the wandering souls of these genocide victims. So tradition has it. The bones are moved to the stupa of a city pagoda and the work continues.

It's one of our bigger construction projects. Jean-Luc, our Sisophon-based coordinator, and I often travel there to check on the work and bring the necessary money. We still have to carry large amounts of cash. Our many ongoing projects keep us on the road constantly. I never sleep more than three nights in a row at the same location. We save money by using our own construction teams, but we've run out of manpower. We therefore have to trust the site assistant. There's no more cement left in the region, so I entrust $15,000 to Sameath, who's been working with us problem free for four years now. He's to go pay for the cement ordered at the Thai border. A number of days go by with no news from him. We first think he's met with an accident, but then realize he's vanished with the cash. Searches and complaints with the police are in vain. He's never seen again. We've just suffered our greatest loss.

A bitter lesson learned, we turn supervision over to a French architect living locally. He costs us dearly. From the beginning, it's a real dilemma. Should we build on our own at very competitive prices, but with heavy supervision to preclude the risk of fraud, or turn everything over to contractors whose profit margins jack up the costs significantly?

For our next building projects, we arrange an invitation for bids and award contracts to local companies. They take responsibility. It's more convenient and more orthodox from the accounting standpoint, but after tough negotiations, it costs only a little more than doing everything ourselves, provided there's no theft. But it's too much for me to wear the hat of cost cutter and bargain hunter. Just the same, compared to what other organizations are paying, we're doing very well in keeping our costs down.

Despite the obstacles, we're very proud when this new school opens. First, it's gorgeous. Designed for blind children, it will also be used for many deaf students for a long time after. Distance makes it necessary for us to take in some students as boarders during the week. But to keep families from shifting them onto us and getting used to not having their children around, we require that they go home on the weekend and for all vacation periods.

Like she did in Chbar Ampov, Her Majesty the Queen confirms her support for the education of blind children. She comes to inaugurate the school. This time, at the request of His Majesty the King, I am made Commander of the Royal Order of Sahametrei, one of the highest distinctions conferred upon a foreigner. Before a very select audience, from the minister of interior to the minister of education, from the provincial governor to the most senior military officers, the presence of all confirms a change in the government's attitude toward educating young blind people.

This change is even clearer when Prime Minister Hun Sen, after spending half a day visiting the Chbar Ampov school some months earlier, also gives us his blessing by arranging to make a personal financial contribution each month. Having lost an eye himself in battle, he's very sensitive to our cause. He'll often be at our side to cut through red tape. He helps us get land for the later schools, in Siem Reap in 2000 and Kompong Cham in 2002, then in Phnom Penh Thmey in 2008 for a new school to replace the first one in Chbar Ampov.

The first school for blind children was built 480 m from the Tonle Bassac, a branch of the Mekong River flowing south. It became unusable due to erosion and sand extraction. When Koh Pich Island was developed by speculators, sand was extracted from the riverbed, which caused the banks on the other side to crumble. The school had to be evacuated in 2008. After lengthy haggling with the government, Prime Minister Hun Sen was prompted by His Majesty the King to find us a piece of land in Phnom Penh Thmey. The Enfants d'Asie association, with which we have cooperated on some projects in recent years, agreed to the request from the Ministry of Social Affairs to let go the unoccupied half of its property.

This new school rounds out the education apparatus for blind children—a network of four specialized establishments spread out in a balanced way over Cambodia to provide the first three years of schooling for blind pupils, who are then streamlined parttime into the classrooms of nearby public schools. These schools also provide training for primary school teachers at the national Ministry of Education level who care for the 45 integrated classes opened in remote districts. Some of the teachers are blind themselves. These human resource successes are a jewel in our crown.

In 1996, an NGO referred Srey Neth to Krousar Thmey and she began attending the Chbar Ampov school. She was born in 1976 to a farming family in Kandal Province. She is a docile little thing, glowing with inner joy despite her disability. Blind from birth, she was not admitted to primary school in her village. Although we pick up the children and take them home before and after school each day, transporting the children of faraway families is a real problem. We keep this to a radius of about 15 km around the school. So Srey Neth is taken in by a nearby family working with us. Despite being homesick and afraid of being alone, Srey Neth is delighted to find a warm environment in which she can satisfy her thirst for knowledge. Her life has changed. She is a high achiever and is accepted in the nearby public school, guided by her sighted schoolmates. This integration is contributing to changing the mindset with regard to disabilities.

In 2007, in the footsteps of our first three blind students, Srey Neth in turn receives her high school diploma along with two other blind classmates. I am always taken by her radiance. She speaks English so well that at official events, I use her as my interpreter. Srey Neth reads in Khmer my speeches transcribed for her in Braille. Her concern for the future of the blind leads her to choose a career in teaching at the Krousar Thmey school. She works in the provinces when we have awareness-raising campaigns on integrating disabled persons in society.

Wherever a dozen or so blind or deaf children are found in a district, we train a teacher from a school in that district and request that an integrated class be opened. To begin with, this was done without official approval from the education ministry's people in charge of disabled youth, who are quite inflexible and go by the letter of the law that requires at least 50 students before opening a class. How would 50 deaf or blind pupils ever be found in a district? But of greater concern is the fact that 50 disabled persons in a class is an unmanageable number. Happily, with the support of HE Im Sethy, secretary of State for education, we are able to open classes out in the provinces, with varying results. The process is long and hard in this Buddhist country, yet we are moving along in leaps and bounds.

Due to the success of this venture and at the request of numerous stakeholders in the field of disabilities, we look into the problem of the deaf in Cambodia. A superficial investigation shows that even greater numbers suffer from this disability and they too are not getting an education.

To the sound of music played by a blind group, a troupe of boys and girls are doing the peacock dance, a traditional Khmer dance. The green-costumed girls and boys meet and cross in tune with the music. As they step from one foot to the other, the peacock plumes they're wearing on their heads undulate like stalks of wheat in the wind. Mirrors on each side of the hall reflect this harmonious swaying. Other than their gaze focused on a point to the right front side, there's not the slightest hint that the performers are deaf.

Actually, they follow the rhythm of the instruments as they pick up the vibrations transmitted through the wooden floor. But they also need direction from their music teacher who, like a good orchestra leader, keeps the tempo with gracious movements of the hands. The *pin peat* orchestra is made up of seven young blind children playing drums, cymbals, xylophones, and flutes.

Lookalike twins Sophey and Sothea create an effect of perfect symmetry when the dancers advance simultaneously in two lines. When they move sideways toward the mirror, suddenly four identical faces appear to the audience. When the show is over, the visitors break out in rapturous applause. They are surprised to see the deaf students wave their hands vigorously aloft on either side of the head, their way of applauding. Sophey and Sothea were born deaf and very soon invented and expanded upon their own signs known only to them. Communication with the rest of the family was rare and often little was understood. They lost no time in feeling at home in the classroom when the school opened.

Whether deaf or hearing impaired, the causes of the disability are many, from a lack of hygiene to taking fake medicine. For a number of reasons, we built this school in 1997 a few hundred meters from the first school for blind children. The choice of teaching methods is just as crucial. After consulting various groups both locally and in Europe, I opt for American Sign Language with an eye to consistency in a region where English is widely used. The World Deaf Federation urges us to create a strictly Cambodian sign language and to open a boarding school for the deaf.

But I'm unwavering in my position. I categorically refuse to put them off by themselves. I don't want to separate the children from their families and their environment and do everything possible so as not to have young deaf as boarders. If, because of distance, we have no other choice but to accept them as such, I see to it that they go home to their families on the weekend. I want to promote their integration into the real world. But we share the view of this federation on the need to Khmerize instruction for the deaf. We therefore invite a sign language committee to coach the school as it grows and to come up with specific signs for Khmer cultural concepts. Using this approach, we develop the first school textbook for the deaf.

These schools take off like wildfire. After one school opens in September 1997, a second follows in 1998, a third in 2000, a fourth in late 2002, and a fifth and final one in 2009. For the deaf students, we adapt the Ministry of Education's curriculum to the degree of deafness of the individual student. To enable a measure of oralism, European volunteers come to train Khmer speech therapists to learn words and sounds that the auditory prosthetic makes possible. This opens up new prospects for young deaf persons.

Those who are able to do so attend public school, but find it more difficult than the blind. We have a hard time introducing a teaching assistant to interpret the course in sign language because it is viewed as distracting to the other students, something that the public schools reject. But students succeed just the same and qualify for high school diplomas in 2009.

This doesn't go unnoticed. In 2010, following a visit from his wife Bun Rany, Prime Minister Hun Sen agrees to have our teachers listed with the staff of the Ministry of Education. This is a tremendous step forward in integrating our programs into the national education plan and the highest accolade for our efforts spanning nearly 20 years. Things are now much more promising for the deaf. As has been true since 1993, we put culture at the heart of our programs.

In November 1993, the exhibition *Cambodge, un peuple, une culture* (Cambodia—One People, One Culture) opens at Enkosei Pagoda in Siem Reap, in the presence of Nouth Narang, minister of culture. The ceremony is opened by a trot dance group. The pagoda's venerable and community of monks are present. Children from the neighboring schools have been brought in. It's our first time opening on Khmer soil and we're proud to have a minister with us. On some 30 large panels featuring photographs with captions, drawings, paintings, costumes, and traditional objects, the exhibition gives an overview of the country's beliefs, handicrafts, architecture, communities, flora, and fauna. The country's fabulous natural and cultural heritage is presented in greater depth. It doesn't depict any Khmers that are red, pink, blue, or another color, but centers on one people made up of diverse ethnic groups with a duty to preserve its variety, its environment, and its heritage.

Dr. My Samedi, chairman of the Cambodian Red Cross, sees the value of what we're doing. He lets us use a Red Cross truck that we drive for a year to transport the new exhibition from town to town and to pick up children attending school in remote locations. For many, the exhibition is their first school outing. For all, a real event.

As in the camps, a team of seven Cambodian guides were trained to welcome the visitors and give a commentary on the exhibition themes.

Before each new showing, two coordinators go to the next province to handle the logistics, finalize the schedule, and promote the exhibition with the local people. We work closely with the education department of each province to invite the teachers and have them prepare their students for the event. They are even invited to write essays. And over 125,000 children are exposed to the message conveyed by the exhibition.

The exhibition is then opened up to the general public. *Cambodge, un peuple, une culture* will be presented in Cambodia's main provinces. Pagodas, traditional venues for the dissemination of knowledge, are chosen for the exhibition, in order to ensure a non-political continuity and to promote the spirit of reconciliation among Cambodians.

Salas, large halls used for worship on Buddhist holidays, prove to be ideal venues for the exhibition. Simple beds, *pahis*, are hauled on the Red Cross truck to enable the team to stay overnight on location. Nelly and Guillaume are thus able to experience the way Cambodians live, the elders and especially the monks who reside in pagodas. Some young monks unabashedly flirt with Nelly or ask the men on the team to show X-rated movies! Many Cambodians find that some monks these days are the product of a poor upbringing and choose to live in a pagoda as an easy way out. And it's true; the genocide tragedy has dug a wide gap between the older venerables and the younger monks. The former reflect wisdom and serenity, while the latter are seen smoking or fiddling with their cell phones while ceremonies are being conducted.

In France, the Espace Albert-Kahn in Boulogne-Billancourt kindly let us use copies of old photographs of Cambodia. Given the success of the exhibition *Cambodge, un peuple, une culture*, Jeanne Beausoleil, curator of the museum, suggests a follow-up. Early in the 20th century, Albert Kahn, a millionaire banker and philanthropist, dispatched photographers all over the world. Around 1900, one such photographer captured for posterity farmers, dignitaries, and rural scenes of Cambodia through photos. Stored on glass plates, they are high-quality color autochromes (a process invented by the Lumière brothers, an additive color photography that uses a layer of minute grains of starch dyed red, green, and blue coated with a panchromatic emulsion). They are printed and put on display in our exhibition. This enables Cambodians to see that life in the countryside has changed very little. The exhibition *Albert Kahn, Cambodge, mémoire vive* transforms traces of the past into a living memory for a country experiencing a rebirth.

On billing from April to October 1996, the exhibition also aims to raise the awareness of the French public regarding the reality of Cambodia and the work done by Krousar Thmey. It was opened by the Cambodian ambassador to France, HE Hor Nam Hong, which gives Krousar Thmey increased visibility with Cambodian officials, but more importantly with the Khmer community in France. This success and our acknowledged ability in the field lead us to getting UNESCO's patronage for another Krousar Thmey exhibition in Cambodia: *Tonle Sap, source de vies,* highlighting the ecological and heritage resources of the Great Lake, with a view to its preservation.

In October 1995, a new program opens that we are fully behind, sponsored by Terre des Hommes Holland. Holland is a center of arts and culture. Phnom Penh is a major crossroads, a transit city, and the people living there tend to not be really rooted down. Social programs are having a difficult time fighting cross-border human trafficking. Further, there are few activities that help children find anchorage in their own culture. Among the arts that children can learn, shadow puppetry, an art form that's all but disappeared, has the potential to bring tradition and modernity together. "Traditions pour demain" (Traditions for Tomorrow) is the right name for this project. Resurrecting shadow puppet theater would not only preserve a traditional art form, but also provide a medium to disseminate modern messages against trafficking and prostitution, and about AIDS prevention.

A new volunteer, Élise, is put in charge of the project. She's petite, resilient, and saucy—very Parisienne. She'll sometimes look at you askance while sizing you up from head to foot. But she's awesomely efficient.

On my way back from Europe, I make a detour to Jogjakarta to meet some shadow theater masters in Indonesia who have kept the tradition alive. My idea is to set up a cooperation arrangement with them. Unfortunately, it doesn't work out. I find the artists quite self-seeking, interested only in putting on shows for tourists, more concerned about making money than working with a little group in Cambodia.

Fortunately, Élise hits pay dirt in Cambodia. She comes across a former shadow theater teacher and succeeds in eliciting his help. He's a short, wiry, loose-jointed man, wrinkled and wizened. His shorts are tailored from cloth remnants; his eyes are veiled by coke bottle glasses. He hisses when he laughs and whines constantly. He and his wife make a pair like something straight out of Dubout. Under the Khmer Rouge, he cached over a hundred leather puppets, burying them in a wooden crate in the ground. He moves to downtown Sisophon and teaches the class to make leather puppets and manipulate them.

Meanwhile, we ask students at the Phnom Penh University of Fine Arts to design a small center in traditional architectural style for us. The Banteay Meanchey provincial governor agrees to let us have a piece of land in the middle of town. I would like passersby to stop in and see the classes being taught and attend performances.

Having such a central location on the way to and from the market will help people get familiar with a lost traditional art now being revived. Our building team does a brilliant job. For the finishing, we ask a local artist to paint the gables and pediments. The result is splendid. But far from being satisfied, the young fine arts students use *Reasmey Kampuchea*, Cambodia's leading daily, to accuse me of disfiguring the building with drawings that they claim are of Thai origin, calling me an enemy of Khmer culture. I'm flabbergasted.

But I then recall a remark made by Walter Skrobanek, a respected authority on Asia: "When you dabble in elements of national identity, especially in the culture of a country that has let it go by the wayside, one awakens extreme passions. One dabbles with pride and nationalist sentiment, and this upsets people. Rather than thanking you, the very ones who have done nothing to preserve their own culture prove to be the most aggressive and will stab you in the back."

I photograph the paintings and consult eminent Khmer specialists. They brush off these student attacks, attributing them to a cultural misunderstanding characteristic of the younger generation. In fact, these drawings are of Khmer origin and were picked up by the Thai when they occupied the western provinces of Cambodia. When these provinces were liberated, Cambodians stopped using such motifs, wrongly thinking they were Thai. Eventually the same daily published a correction written by the experts, one of whom is the national museum director.

After the center opens, the performances are an unqualified success. The *pin peat* group provides musical accompaniment. The shadow puppet theater puts on scenes from the Ramayana as well as shows on such modern themes as child welfare. To expand the project, we hire a Cambodian from France. We feel it would be good to help a young Khmer return from abroad to work in Cambodia. His familiarity with the two cultures would be a bridge between France and Cambodia. But disappointingly, he riles up all the teams of the centers, volunteer workers included. He has an individualistic streak and bucks authority, so I have to let him go. But using his French contacts, he dangles the prospect of high salaries and lures our drawing and music teachers away. Only our old master remains. It's a hard blow. After several weeks of looking around, Thary recruits new teachers and to top it all a woman director. The center gets a new start and a fruitful partnership is started with the Khmer Art and Culture School. Its curriculum includes dance, music, drawing, sculpture, puppets, and Khmer literature. Since then, the school has never had an empty seat, taking in over a thousand students each year.

On Saturday morning, July 5, 1997, I'm on the boat back to Phnom Penh. After crossing the lake and starting down the river, we're stopped by an army boat, checked, and searched. It's the first time. In Phnom Penh, I rush to La Casa, only to hear gunshots and rocket fire in the distance. My teams tell me that fighting has broken out to the west. Rockets from Chom Chao were reportedly fired by soldiers into the first prime minister's camp, which started the fighting between the troops of the two prime ministers. The shots come closer. The French embassy has an order broadcast over Radio France International for everyone to stay home. By mid-afternoon, the first of the wounded are brought into Calmette Hospital. A tank takes position at our street corner, which becomes the last open street in the neighborhood. Access is cut off to the west. People start fleeing to the east, some with a bundle hoisted on their heads, others lugging a television set in their arms. Panic reigns.

Fear is written on everyone's face. Everybody is fleeing, thinking that war has returned.

My neighbors are paralyzed. They watch me, wondering what I'm going to do. Ever since one of them had the gall to ask a waiter to find him a young orphan girl for one of his customers while another had been taking advantage of young country boys for years, we have little to say to one another. They're wondering if I'm going to do like the other neighbors and head east. It's out of the question. I don't want to abandon my house and Krousar Thmey's property to looters. When night falls around 6 p.m., the shooting dies down, as if the soldiers don't like the dark. There are about 20 of us at La Casa—a few volunteers, some Cambodian staff and a neighbor woman who's taken refuge with us. Astrid is missing. She's our communications agent and didn't make it back to Phnom Penh. She was flying in from Bangkok and was supposed to land at 12:30 p.m. The plane turned back after just missing a blast of machine-gun fire. We watch as TV5 broadcasts again and again the message to stay away from the French embassy, located at the heart of the fighting—it's right next to FUNCINPEC's headquarters—and to remain at home. How long will it go on? Even with our stockpile of food for the restaurant, we can only last a few days. It's impossible to go to and from the provinces. We're not sure what's going on out there. I try to keep the most flighty on an even keel.

Around 5 the next morning, Sunday, July 6, 1997, I go with Sok to get rice from our Chamkarmon street children center. There are a few stray vehicles on the streets. Some businesses have opened and are selling Mama noodles, sugar, and other staples for a small fortune. We gas up the vehicles in case we have to leave for Thailand.

At La Casa, the day goes by like the one before. A lot of noise. Gunshots can be heard from afar. When they draw closer, I cluster everyone in the bookkeeping office, the safest place in the house. Just the same, everyone is in good spirits. Keeping our cool, we calm down the Khmers who are extremely uneasy. At lunch, not knowing whether to make a run for it or barricade the doors, we decide to enjoy a good meal. We uncork the best bottles. About 12:30 p.m., an embassy security guard, probably a secret agent, raps on the door. Since our street is the last one open, he wants up on La Casa's roof to get a bird's eye view of the situation. When he comes back down, we invite him to join us for lunch. We enjoy ourselves, pretending that the restaurant is open, true to its tradition of being "the" number one in Phnom Penh. With no cooks, we fix him up an Aussie steak and scalloped potatoes au gratin, followed by chocolate mousse. Uncouth perhaps, but merriment is an excellent antidote for stress. In the afternoon, the shooting becomes more sporadic. Khmer radio announces that Ranariddh's troops are retreating and that his supporters are on the run. The end of the fighting is near. Sunday night is calm, only an occasional shot heard here and there.

Come Monday and tension is still running high. Soldiers are loading tanks, pickup trucks, and other army vehicles with anything they can get their hands on—motorbikes, mattresses, TVs… It looks like the whole city is on a moving spree. The CPP soldiers have won. They're making off with the spoils of victory, looting the houses of the opponents and of any who had fled. Neighbors steal from one another. At the end of the street, motorbikes are stacked unbelievably high on army trucks. Thousands of motorbikes are thus appropriated. Then come the private pickup trucks of the soldiers, who likewise grab as many two-wheelers as they can load up. I see something strange that looks like a low flying helicopter. A motorbike driver has just swiped a fan and its blades are rotating like mad. Finally come the infantrymen pushing scrapped vehicles that won't start or carting off spare parts. The neighbor across the way, who holed up during the fighting, puts on his soldier's uniform to join in the fray.

On Tuesday morning, I join a reporter friend working for *The Cambodia Daily* to take some pictures and size up the damage. Aside from a few bullet scars and a gaping mortar bomb hole in Preah Kossamak Hospital on the dike off Pochentong Road, there's not much apparent damage. Many shots were apparently blanks. A lot of noise was made to scare people, but not a lot of damage was caused. However, the looting wreaks horrendous devastation. On the national highway out to the airport, tanks continue to protect stacks of furniture, mattresses, or tires... No business is spared. A company executive tells me that when he arrived with a guard, he had to fire shots to stop the looting. His vehicles, equipment, and the spare parts in his garage had disappeared, the washroom sinks were torn out, and the electrical wiring wrenched away. Thieves astride his roof where trying their hardest to saw away the metal structure to get at the steel girders.

Telephone service is restored. The French ambassador, away for a meeting, comes back on the first flight from Bangkok, furious that he had been delayed. His office overlooking the FUNCINPEC grounds was hit by a mortar shell. Christiane, his wife, had spent her time reassuring the Cambodian staff cringing in the embassy buildings. The place had previously experienced one of the most dramatic events of Cambodian history and many feared a return of extreme violence. The airport terminal had been under construction for the last two years and was about to be officially opened. It has been ravaged as if hit by an F5 tornado. Everything was looted, from flight equipment to air conditioners. Even the glass doors were swiped.

On Wednesday, July 9, 1997, special commercial flights offer expatriates and NGO staff one-way flights to Bangkok at over $1,000 a seat. Many NGOs pay the full price to get their expatriate personnel out, leaving their Cambodian staff behind. France issues no instructions for its nationals to leave. Thailand and the United States, avowed enemies of the Hun Sen government, repatriate their citizens by military airlift. We watch the escorted convoys of families go by. Mothers clasp a few personal effects; children are crying, teddy bears in arms... It's the end for them, but not us.

I'm torn by this violent flare-up, but it seems that the whole thing just had to happen. Relations between the two prime ministers had been deteriorating and the verbal assaults spread in the media gave clear signs of such an outcome. The greatest impact was the immediate stoppage of investment and international aid, which plunges Cambodia into an economic slump, the last thing we need.

The government suffers from the suspension of international aid. A rapprochement with China is anticipated, and it reportedly advances funds to pay the salaries of the civil servants, many of whom disapproved of the fighting. The Taiwan representative office is ordered to pack up and go home. After years of pro-Vietnam policies, Prime Minister Hun Sen follows in Sihanouk's footsteps and adopts a one-China stance.

Although historically, I tended to support the CPP's opposition, my years in the field brought me into closer contact with Hun Sen's entourage, and the realism shines through. For many, the results of the 1993 elections were sure harbingers of hope. But once in power, the opposition did not feel it had to make any sacrifices. The first concern of many an elected representative was to make up for lost time with regard to personal advantages. Rather than seeing competence as paramount, they too went for family co-optations and cronyism, creating disillusionment and despair.

So the coup d'état (also known as the "counterattack") is perceived as a necessary evil. True, the methods are unacceptable, but the system of two diametrically opposed prime ministers and feuding co-ministers was not viable. A country with two heads loses its head. Too many development opportunities were lost and it was high time for a government capable of making decisions to take office. We had pressing social problems to care for and had no reason to flee Cambodia. Taking this stand drew me criticism, but I was obviously not politically motivated; I was simply being pragmatic. The big need was for political stability, without which no social development could take place. Confidence had to be restored so that corporate investors could feel at ease to do business. That is a prerequisite for society to develop and reach a higher level of solidarity. So in the days that follow, we show our concern for Cambodia's development by reopening all our schools and resuming our programs. Life goes on for those interested in working, regardless of their political leanings.

Nominally, a first prime minister is appointed, but it's only a charade. Power is now squarely in the hands of the CPP. In everyone's mind is the hope for development, for a successful fight against corruption, and a radical change in governance. A disarmament campaign is then launched. The prime minister is distrusted because of his takeover by force, but he exudes an image of firmness, stability, and security. He kicks off major campaigns to eliminate personal weapons and tries to keep a tighter rein on senior government officials. But there's a lack of concern for the common good. Each minister, each general feels that he's the king of his castle. A demonstration is even led by soldiers complaining that their general sold their barracks... and there was nothing in it for them. The sale raised no eyebrows, but the failure to divvy up the proceeds is unacceptable.

Little by little fewer bodyguards are seen armed with AK-47s or automatic rifles accompanying the vehicles of rich merchants who fear being kidnapped. For a time, kidnappings were a bonanza enterprise for bandits—often police or military personnel. Armed robbery was a daily affair. The first automatic teller machine in Phnom Penh was plundered by thieves using a military platform hoist. Since then, no guns are allowed in bars and night clubs... or at least if one believes the signs that advise gun-toting patrons that they cannot enter until relieved of their weapons. The police run night spot-checks. Violence does cool down, but remains palpable.

In late January 1998, I go down the Tonle Sap to meet my older brother and his family. To save time, I go in an outboard motorboat. A few plastic chairs are scattered in it. The boat scuds rapidly over the water and one has to hang on for dear life. It feels quite sporty. The boat barrels along and takes only three and a half hours instead of the usual six. Suddenly, we pass over some fishing nets and the fishermen rail vehemently at us. Our pilot gets fidgety. A military boat protecting the fishing lots gives chase. The pilot bolts ahead before the soldiers open fire. The passengers scream and drop flat. Three bullets hit the hull and a Cambodian is hurt by shrapnel. The pilot radios his base in Phnom Penh and relates what happened with gales of laughter, as if it was a routine incident. When I disembark, furious, I call the French embassy and report the incident. The embassies then join forces to pressure the authorities to improve security on the waterways.

The next week, we take the regular boat. My older brother, his wife Marie and their children Clément and Claire are along. They are surprised to see me so quiet. I wait tensely until we get there before telling them what happened only a week earlier. My nephew and niece learn a lot during their first trip to a developing country. Their parents have told them much about living conditions in Cambodia and they were very touched by my conferences every time I went through Chambéry. They saved a big chunk of their pocket money to donate to us, something I really appreciated. They'll long remember the trip, even though we have to set up a permanent safety barrier around Claire. Redheaded, very light skinned, and covered with freckles, she's forever being touched, squeezed, and pinched by Cambodians. It's torture for her. Vincent, my brother, sprains his ankle when getting off the boat. We go to Handicap International to borrow a pair of crutches and, when visiting the temples surrounded by crowds of crippled beggars, a British tourist in a gesture of dubious humor offers him a bill. Since my parents came in 1995, my older brother's trip is the second time family paid me a visit. I'm delighted to show them what we've accomplished despite the enormous challenges facing us.

The July 1997 events were not to the liking of all, even people in the winning party. To silence opponents, maintain unity, and keep hold of the leadership, it seems that concessions were made. A number of *oknhas*, or wealthy businessmen, form a sort of mandarin-like establishment linked to the high-ranking military powers. They decide to create a no man's land between the borders and build casinos on it. Thailand prohibits such dens of iniquity on its soil. Cambodians with ties to Thai speculators want to profit from the insatiable penchant Asians have for gambling. Cambodia's official border is moved back several hundred meters. The zone is developed and serviced. And while small-time crime is declining, big-time crime is prospering.

To fill in the low land between the borders, tens of thousands of truckloads of earth are brought in… Without ever asking us, one fine day a squadron of backhoes and trucks dig deep into the piece of our land that we've not been able to build on yet on due to lack of funds. We attempt to stop them, but gun-pointing soldiers keep us at bay. An endless stream of trucks extracts earth from our property to level off the casino zone. Despite many letters of protest to the governor, the king, the prime minister, and minister of interior, nothing happens.

By way of answer, one day I receive a visit from a Cambodian army general who claims that he was ordered to settle the matter out of court. He wants to take all of the land and transfer us several kilometers out of Poipet. He spits on our agreements with the Ministry of Social Affairs. Without the support of the king and prime minister, we would certainly have been steamrollered *manu militari* like the other buildings and thousands of inhabitants along the national highway. They don't seem to realize the war is over and, along with it, the almightiness of the army. Or maybe it's me that hasn't got the point that in fact nothing has changed.

Such a move is unthinkable as far as we're concerned. How will the women in our center be able to work if, in addition to caring for children, they have to travel several kilometers every day? How can children that far away get to school? How can we continue to work with the little waste pickers, the street children of Poipet, the trafficking victims, if our staff has to spend a lot of time on the road?

In Poipet, we find our school along the edge of the national highway already destroyed. The Ministry of Education has sold the land to a private company. Earlier, 4 km from there, a building was put up with a sign "School Built by Krousar Thmey"! That puts the neighborhood children several kilometers from their school. And, of course, without the least consultation. Once again, I decide to fight.

From one meeting to another at the Ministry of Defense or at the governor's office, from full files sent to the government to letters to the king or prime minister, my efforts are in vain. From field visits to intimidating walking tours over isolated areas, everything is done to crack me. The general records all of our conversations on mini-cassettes. The war of attrition goes on for months. He alternates between friendliness when he calls me "my friend" or flattery along the lines of "you're a very intelligent man," and then threatens or yells. But I refuse to sign. The pressure mounts.

During one such final attempt at reconciliation, the general promises me an acceptable agreement. We leave together for Battambang by plane. We arrive late at the airport because the general had to finish his nap. Royal Air Cambodge tells us there's been a change of aircraft and the number of passengers has to be reduced; the plane will be loaded first come first served. The enraged general grabs the company employee by the scruff of the neck and gives him a brutal shake. In the middle of the waiting room, he hollers that he has a meeting to go to in Sisophon that night and that he absolutely has to have two seats.

I whisper to him that without a third seat for my translator (who keeps an eye out for traps), I will not board the plane. I think he's going to explode. Luckily security had taken his weapon off him; otherwise he would surely have used it. The plane is jam-packed. I have no choice but to go alone. I'll look for a staff member in Sisophon who can translate properly for me. Ms. Makyom recently joined us and her involvement and devotion for children are unstinting. And there's Hahn, who's been working with us since the days of the refugee camps. He has no love for the soldiers and their daily acts of extortion. Neither of them will be intimidated by the general.

It's pitch black when we arrive in Battambang. Soldiers are waiting for us, their mugs furrowed with scars, their predatory smiles highlighted by gold teeth; they're wearing camouflage fatigues, their shirts wide open exposing heavy solid gold chains or necklaces. There's no shortage of B40 air rifles, M-16 assault rifles, and AK-47s. I try to look nonchalant, as if their staging doesn't intimidate me, but inside my heart is in my boots.

In Sisophon, we meet the deputy governor, who I feel is an ally. Like me, he's somewhat the hostage of these soldiers who, in just a few months, have taken over the border with fake registry documents and evicted the inhabitants. He knows that he has very little room to maneuver. He's listless, only confirming his tenuous position. The soldiers know that I'm banking on him and try to convince me to sign. On several occasions, the opposition has tried to politicize my endeavors. Although the soldiers fear the opposition, I also realize that asking the opposition to back me will not be good for our relationship with all the ministries. My position is uncomfortable. I'd prefer not to have to make a choice.

The general offers me a drink, but I want to be in full possession of my faculties. Despite his insistence that I stay in the nearby hotel cum brothel, which would have kept me under his control, I ask to be taken to the Krousar Thmey center in Sisophon, and keep myself on home turf. Ms. Makyom welcomes me, true to herself, her little purse over her arm. She's impeccably dressed, a real lady. She had long worked as a school principal, but rather than taking a well-deserved retirement, she's been running the Sisophon center since 1997 and cares for the orphans and abandoned children as if they were her own children. An adherent of the old school, she raises them with affection and discipline. She's up at 5:30 every morning for exercises. A woman of incredible self-sacrifice! The results speak for themselves. The children are well-behaved and the center is properly maintained. During the rainy season, they are given group work in our 11 ha of rice paddies. She was worried when I was late in arriving. I bed down reassured, but exhausted.

The next morning, instead of going to look around Poipet as planned, the general calls me to his hotel, a shabby-looking establishment. A guard keeps watch outside his room. I enter the bluish-green space, dully lit by a filthy fluorescent bulb. The general receives me in his briefs as he lies face down on dirty sheets while another soldier gives him a back rub. He reeks of body odor. The air conditioner rattles away loudly. It's one of those obstructed-view rooms common in Asian hotels. You open the electric blue or pink curtains and you look out at a wall. He mumbles that after last night's meeting, with the governor's okay, he has prepared an agreement that I just have to sign. It's all in Khmer. I have it translated in full. The agreement is unacceptable. Utterly furious, I state that I intend to go back to Phnom Penh without signing a thing. The pretense has gone on long enough. The general is raving mad. The door slams shut and I hear the click of an AK-47 being cocked. I feel very small, although I realize it'd be hard for him to do away with me right here. The place is in full view of the public and I'm well known here. He gets dressed. His eyes are bloodshot. The mixture of hangover and irritation compound his scruffy looks. He already looked bad, now downright ugly. Horrible, hideous, dreadful, beastly are words that come to my mind.

"Watch out for the candle! Don't go to the candle! And watch what you do! You'll regret it!" he bellows. The candle is the emblem of

Sam Rainsy, leader of the main opposition party. Since the events of July 1997, the soldiers feel all-powerful, but as the May 1998 elections approach, they know that the opposition is using their acts of extortion to win votes. Over the next few days, he calls me on my cell phone three or four times daily to spew threats. I can't talk to him anymore. I can't stand his voice. Every time he rings, it gives me a start and my heart thumps at a record pace. I'm afraid. I can't sleep. My house is at the edge of a stream. At night, fishermen come to set their nets. I listen for noises and keep on the lookout, afraid of a break-in at any moment. We already have an armed guard assigned to the office at night. I ask my house guard Yon to sleep in the neighboring room and to keep his AK-47 handy.

I've previously received death threats from some young ones from Krousar Thmey that we had to expel because they didn't want to go by the rules and others from pedophiles that we'd taken to court. That has never bothered me. For the first time, though, I'm confronted with imminent danger. With the general impunity prevailing in Cambodia, there's little reason to be optimistic. The general keeps calling and coming to the office. I don't want to see him again, ever. Maxime, in charge of our logistics, takes over. He is a jovial, baby-faced little fellow with a disconcerting look. He's the right man. Maxime listens kindly, calmly, and patiently to the general's abusive railing and promises him that he will report everything back to me. I don't show my face anymore and refuse his calls. He turns up the heat.

One evening, I get a call from a friend well connected with the military. He had heard about our situation in Poipet. He understands our position and my refusal to sign an agreement. But he advises me to get the word out that we won't be pressing matters with the high-ups in government circles anymore. If we don't turn down the heat, the military boys in this massive casino operation in Poipet won't hesitate to take it one step further. Not openly against me, but against some of my teams, such as by causing a road accident, by burning my house down, or by committing assaults to make me live in a state of acute paranoia.

I don't want to go out of my mind; I want to enjoy a peaceful sleep. It's crucial to keep the programs running. I need my energy for that and

I don't want to be gnawed away by fear. I capitulate. I don't sign, but I stop filing complaints. So the soldiers and their cronies, the Poipet *oknhas*, win. As they do everywhere throughout the country, they grab land, they expel the farmers, then speculate on the land they've snatched to buy a villa, a new Lexus, or another Hummer. We lose three quarters of our initial land holding and get a casino next door to boot.

The CPP wins by a clear majority in the 1998 elections. Irregularities are reported, but the majority of voters, disillusioned by the opposition, vote for stability. After several months of wrangling, an agreement is eventually reached that enables a new government to be formed. It almost feels like the country is at peace, although serious incidents occur. In March 2000, a tourist boat is taken hostage by a commando of five men. The passengers are stripped of everything. The ordeal goes on for hours. The tourists are tied and chair covers pulled over their heads. One of them who will be volunteering for Krousar Thmey tries to keep them calm. The pirates are extremely tense and just about finish him off. The boat trip turns into a nightmare. The tourists disembark traumatized in Siem Reap the next morning. Prime Minister Hun Sen orders the police to find the guilty parties. They're arrested with much of the booty, but the robbed tourists never see hide nor hair of it. The perpetrators commit suicide in jail.

In August 1998, the first three of our charges from the Ta Khmau welfare center graduate from high school. I'm very proud. Taken on board at Site II, they got through elementary and secondary school in Ta Khmau. They will soon enroll in a private business college. Just then, Matthew Leitner, a professor at the Graduate Institute of International and Development Studies in Geneva, happens to be visiting Cambodia. We met him at La Casa when it first opened and he's made regular trips to Cambodia to assist an NGO. He decided to join us and serves as deputy chairman of Krousar Thmey Switzerland. An economics professor, he tests our graduates. He asks the first one, who claims to love history, when Angkor Wat was built. Sokhum hesitates, then comes up with "Nineteen hundred... Nineteen hundred..." as his voice trails off, hoping his buddies will bail him out. I'm embarrassed. He can't answer.

Matthew throws him a line, asking him if it was before or after the First World War. Now he's certain. "After, of course!" Disaster! Matthew gives him an opportunity to make up for it by asking him the name of the king who built Angkor Wat. The answer is a matter of pure creativity. Between the name of the king that built Angkor Wat and the number of the sovereign that, years later, built Angkor Thom and a number of other temples, a new king is suddenly crowned: "Suryavarman VII," a mix of Suryavarman II and Jayavarman VII.

No rock to crawl under, no earth to swallow me up and hide my doleful countenance. Now it's the second one's turn, whose forte is geography.

"What are the countries along Cambodia's borders?"

"Thailand, Vietnam (easy, because of our border conflicts...), then Malaysia and Singapore!"

I burst out laughing. Matthew, like me, is dismayed. Happily it's agreed that things will get better! If school doesn't teach them the basics, how can we?

That gives birth to the idea of starting a board game along the lines of Trivial Pursuit: *Neak Na Doeung,* or "Who knows?" The game is developed in Khmer with such topics as culture, geography, history, sports, and leisure, specifically focusing on Cambodia and ASEAN. A writing and review committee is formed, and eventually over a thousand games are made in Cambodia and distributed to Krousar Thmey's facilities, as well as to nearby schools.

The years go by and the children grow up. Many of the street children started school very late. Despite remedial classes, they have a hard time catching up. So in many cases we work with other organizations to get them into vocational training. Friends, Hagar, Don Bosco, and many other organizations make quality technical courses available and are open to young people from Krousar Thmey. When they leave, it frees up room for new children, including those like Channa who are repatriated from prisons in Bangkok. For street children who have had little or no schooling, solutions are harder to come by. They cannot attend normal school. Something more is needed to get them involved, channel their energy, and present challenges to motivate them.

In 1995, I come across a project in Sihanoukville (Kompong Som) that teaches orphans seamanship, just the type of thing we're looking for. We partner up to get our project going, designed for certain street children old enough to work. Alain Courau, a former French navy commander, takes the lead. Of square build, businesslike, and efficient, he reminds one of Commander Cousteau… but a lot easier to get along with. Always good natured, snappy but friendly, he takes everything with a grin. There are sizable obstacles to overcome. Where can we find land with seafront access? How will we get permission from the fisheries authorities? How can we win the trust of the fishermen? The project is given a soft opening at the Sihanoukville port. After a few months of initial training, the young ones are put on small shrimp trawlers. The results are encouraging.

The project is then fleshed out. We get the use of a pontoon belonging to a project let go by Médecins du Monde and set up a seamanship training center with both academic and hands-on courses. Net repairs, boat piloting, trawler structure, engine repairs, the principles of offshore navigation and safety… The need is enormous. Given the traits of a fishing port community and its ancillary prostitution networks and high HIV rate, we even offer a course on AIDS and, with a small cucumber, explain how condoms are used! Under the guidance of Alain Courau, we partner up with the fishermen community. They are allowed access to the center where it's easier for them to repair their boats and, in return, they agree to hire people that are often considered to be good-for-nothings.

It must be admitted that some of the street youths transferred to Sihanoukville do give us trouble. Once, an altercation occurs after a local dance party and the Krousar Thmey boys come back with distress rockets that they proceed to light. Alain has many a negotiation session with the police to get these mad dogs out of the clink. The innovative project is featured on *Thalassa* (TV5Monde). When the courses end, graduates get jobs, but not necessarily on boats. Some of the young people, even after the training, prefer something more sedentary to the roughness and uncertainty of work on the sea. Traditionally,

Cambodians are not a mariner people and are glad to leave the trade to their neighbors. The media coverage enables us to purchase our own trawlers and we qualify for grants from the French Ministry of Foreign Affairs and the Brittany region in France. The project really becomes professional with assistance from our partners in Brittany, the summer school, and many other people who contribute their know-how to adapt the training to local needs as well as to make the fishermen aware of fisheries resources protection.

For Krousar Thmey, with Khmers now at the helm, the independence and financial weight of this project are challenging to manage compared to our other programs.

In June 2005, rather than discontinue this fine project, we decide to turn it over to someone else. The Guilde européenne du Raid and Pour un Sourire d'Enfant offer to keep it going. We are not necessarily on the same wavelength as Pour un Sourire d'Enfant, but the association has an excellent track record. The main thing is that it has sound financial backing that can be tapped into by the project.

But three years later, the project is broken away from the fishing community, ex-members are no longer welcome, and part of the staff is let go. There are rumblings of rage. Realizing that they can't get along without some of the managerial staff, the founders of Pour un Sourire d'Enfant take them back on, but too late. The teams are demoralized and the cooperation of the local fishermen is lost. The center shuts down. Some of the young ones feel they've been cast off, especially those who were having a rougher time of it and who felt that the human community associated with the project was their only family.

Vasa, not being the stick-to-itive type, always copped it more than the others. He took to drinking local alcohol, available for less than half a dollar a liter. He was found dead one morning on the pontoon. He was 27 years old. Alerted immediately by our faithful staff members, I leave for Sihanoukville with some older members to attend the funeral. Why didn't I give him a job at the hotel? Why didn't I find him work where he would've had more support? Why aren't we inculcating the desire to succeed? Why, after the years they spend with us, are some sucked into the downward spiral of failure? I take it personally. I appreciate that we can't go on mentoring them forever. The time comes when they have to face up to reality, life as it really is. Memories flood back. His arrival at the center, his antics to get attention. Vasa had never been able to overcome the brutal treatment he got from his step-father, nor being abandoned by his family. I cry like a baby. I'm not sure that I believe in reincarnation, but I can relate to these Khmers who have suffered excessively and who pray not to be reborn as Cambodians.

Orienting young people remains a thorny problem. We either push them on to higher education at the risk of nurturing unrealistic aspirations in them or we confine their ambitions to vocational training for a specific job, but without being sure it's the one for them. For blind students, the range of choices is even narrower.

In the mid-1990s, one organization employs a massage teacher to train blind adults and give them a trade. That's how Seeing Hands gets started. Very quickly, one of them sees how great it would be to have many establishments and, in turn, starts training blind workers that he puts on a salary.

When the first young blind students in our schools are old enough to work as masseurs, we contact one of these establishments about placing some of our young ones as trainees. But his conditions are unacceptable. After being trained, the new masseur will owe him ten years of work in a tourist massage parlor at a ridiculously low salary. It's slavery. We attempt to negotiate, proposing a couple of years instead of ten. He refuses. We then talk with a female physiotherapist who's staying at La Noria. She agrees to spend her next vacation to train a group of young people. Over the next several years, Charlotte spends her holidays with us to round out their training and teach new groups the techniques of relaxation massage. With her help, we now have twenty or so young blind people making a living from their work.

For deaf youth, Artisans d'Angkor proposes a smart partnership arrangement with us. After being trained in drawing, two successive groups of young deaf girls will be taught silk painting. To help with communication, the trainer learns sign language. These young deaf trainees learn how to copy traditional patterns and scenes from the

Reamker, Cambodia's version of the *Ramayana*. Their work is precise and their artistic sense awakened. The quality of the paintings is such that finished products are soon for sale—pillowcases, framed pictures, and a variety of other decorative items. The originality of the project and the happiness exuded by our young painters are such that Artisans d'Angkor decides to include this workshop on the visitor itinerary. This does wonders to boost the self-confidence of the artists.

FOSTERING RESPONSIBILITY AND PASSING ON OWNERSHIP
(1998 to the present)

In 2011, after 20 years of hard work, Krousar Thmey's activities are seated on three main pillars.

The social pillar involves four intake facilities for street children, three child welfare centers, 11 family shelters, and a village for single-parent families headed by women.

The education pillar includes four schools for blind children, five schools for deaf children, 44 integrated classes, the transcription and printing of all school textbooks in Braille and of all books for deaf children, a language committee for signs, and primary school classes in various locations.

The cultural pillar includes dance, music, shadow puppetry groups, and exhibitions on Khmer heritage.

Altogether, this makes 14 programs spread out over 81 activity centers, 1,100 children under our roofs, and an additional 3,000 receiving our support. This is all cared for by 400 salaried workers and only three European volunteers.

Implementation of the above has taken place gradually with the institutionalizing of our initiatives, team training, and turning responsibility over to Khmers. Dozens of different individuals, often volunteers, have helped pass ownership of this organization on to Cambodians who are now its directors.

Projects are developed at the rate of five or six a year. Thousands of children are managed in a number of provinces of Cambodia. Hundreds of Cambodians are working for Krousar Thmey, but aren't necessarily familiar with the other programs the foundation is caring for.

Starting in 1994, quarterly training and coordination meetings are held, which brings the program directors together. By rotating between the different centers, they get to know the other Krousar Thmey projects, compare how they are run, but especially benefit from a lateral interchange among the programs. There is a dual hierarchy: one regional and the other by project type (a little like ACCOR with its zones and different corporate images). The administrative teams travel together, have meals together, and thrash things out together, which knits them as one and promotes solidarity. But this way, only the leaders are involved.

So in 1998, the idea strikes me to organize big family gatherings, *Bon Prachum Nheat*, open to all. When I was a kid, I used to love these big family get-togethers where I mixed with my cousins, uncles, aunts, and distant relatives in a sort of community spirit. Couldn't these street children, these orphans, these disabled persons, often neglected or rejected, create their own family and feel closer to one another in active solidarity? After all, *Krousar Thmey* means new family.

After long preparations with everyone pitching in, notably to get the budget together—which I want the teams and the children to find locally in order to help them realize the challenge fundraising is—the big day comes. Transported from all the provinces of Cambodia, by bus or in the back of a truck, depending on funds available, all have been looking forward for months to these three days of celebration and competitions. After a bit of an official opening, there are singing contests, a general knowledge competition, sports events, poems, and many other activities to promote competition among individuals and among teams of the different centers. At night, there's dancing.

Everyone sleeps on location, piled into classrooms. Water distribution points, toilets, and makeshift showers are set up for the occasion. Near the cooking area with its huge caldrons of rice is a pen of animals: a beef animal, some pigs, and dozens of chickens. We don't have a refrigerator, so the meat is kept on the hoof and the animals slaughtered as needed. Phalla does a great job of managing the mindboggling logistics to feed nearly 2,000 persons. Bonds are created, exchanges developed. The children in the welfare centers and family shelters get to meet the disabled children and learn to accept them as members of their family.

The celebration ends with a ceremony. Assisted by the center leaders,

I give prizes to the winners of each event. When it's the turn of the blind, often hands-down winners of the singing and general knowledge competitions, emotions are at their peak. The grand prize, an Indra Devi sculpture, goes to the general knowledge winners.

Back in September 1993, Krousar Thmey France needed room to store promotional materials, photographs, and records relating to donors. To cut down on overhead, we look for a place free of charge. After years in Francis' veterinary office, Philippe Magnier takes the whole kit and caboodle to his place before coming up with a cool idea: get friends to buy a place and rent it to Krousar Thmey for one euro a year.

Mixing business acumen and generosity, our Captain Haddock thus makes available to us a place that keeps our overhead below 4 percent. These expenses mainly involve electricity, telephone, bank charges, and shipping. Volunteers donate much of their time and the association in France is soon recognized as a community and social service. Many volunteers make a valuable contribution by performing necessary tasks such as entering data, filing, selling kramas, kerchiefs, greeting cards, and other handicraft items that people have uncomplainingly brought back with them in their suitcases... Put together, the modest proceeds from such sales fund programs in Cambodia and allow us to operate independently.

From the "7 de la Cité" theater company to amateur soloists, from contributions to humanitarian forums to folding *Lettres de Famille* (Krousar Thmey newsletters), many others provide valuable support.

The display of so much self-sacrifice and courage to do often thankless tasks fills me with admiration, all the more so since the individual covers his own expenses; the association doesn't cover travel costs for members. Over 96 percent of donations received are transferred to Cambodia to support the children. What's in it for the volunteers? The success of our projects and the smiles of the children.

The same can be said of Switzerland where the association has been rooted since 1994. When Phnom Penh fell, Marie-Jo Duc, then International Committee of the Red Cross nurse in Cambodia, was made prisoner by the Khmer Rouge in the French embassy, then evacuated to

Thailand. Back home in Europe, that unforgettable experience left her wondering how she could help Cambodia. She heard of Krousar Thmey. A visit to its programs on location convinces her. She's joined by Jean-Luc Maurer, chairman of the Graduate Institute of International and Development Studies, Ivana, Marie-Edla, Thérèse, Mathiew, Renée, Ernst, Isabelle, and Anne to create Krousar Thmey Switzerland.

The association rises to prominence through gala dinners, highbrow concerts with Vadim Repin, Pascal Rogé, and les frères Capuçon, not to mention exhibitions, private showings, and movie premières, along with Cambodian food cooked by the Lo family. The job is not easy in a Geneva already bursting with all of manner of humanitarian organizations. But in the long run, our very low overhead and the long-term high performance of our programs are what make the difference.

After Krousar Thmey Switzerland, a branch is established in England with the help of Thérèse, Christel (the wife of Gilles who first introduced me to Site II), and Adam.

These extramural Krousar Thmey agencies, ex-officio members of Krousar Thmey Cambodia's board of directors, have a dual thrust: do most of the fundraising and create public awareness with regard to the problems of Cambodia. With no pathos intended, we wish to emphasize the need to train local stakeholders and build their sense of responsibility so that disadvantaged children find themselves among friends, loved, protected, and educated.

Besides fundraising, I feel that making people aware of humanitarian work and providing assistance to developing countries are paramount issues.

When I was in primary school, we got involved in a campaign run by the Committee Against Hunger and for Development in the Sahel. The money collected was used to dig wells. As we were able, we would slip coins into a piggy bank. Contributing this way gave us the feeling of doing something to stave off hunger and thirst in the desert. To me, it's crucial that children be aware of such things at an early age. With that in mind, for years now I have included primary, lower, and secondary schools in my conference tours.

So it has almost become a tradition that I make a presentation for eleventh graders at the Lycée français in Singapore, and I anticipate it as much as the students. I attempt to convey my concept of humanitarian work, its successes, and failures. All questions, all remarks, all criticisms are allowed. The audience is disappointed when I say to those who would like to join me that I don't need them. I'm then accused of being heartless, a humanitarian without human kindness, because I turn down volunteers who feel they have something to offer. In a country with such an abstruse language, what can they give in just a short time? Actually, it takes up precious time to receive them and help them adjust to the culture shock, thus adding to the problems to be handled. Opening one's heart and mind is possible without going off to the ends of the earth to look after children. They're the real beneficiaries.

In France, would we welcome volunteers from Burkina Faso for a couple of months, or from Bangladesh for six weeks, then a Mexican for four months, and so on? Why would we propose something to a developing country that we wouldn't agree to in France? Cambodians are capable of looking after their children. So let's give them the training they need, notably in liaison with neighboring countries of similar culture, and the resources to do so.

I don't need volunteers to work with the children, but I do need volunteers to communicate with donors and especially to manage the funds made available to us.

There are all kinds of volunteers doing humanitarian work. Here, some are semiprofessionals on a local allowance who had good-paying jobs in their home country; others are quasi-volunteers in organizations with small budgets.

In Krousar Thmey, until recently, the volunteers paid their own airfare. They are housed and insured by us, with help from the French government, and receive a monthly allowance of about $350. This may not look like much, but a person can live on it in Cambodia, moderately of course. Often, prior to their departure, I like to joke about this modest sum: "Your allowance is low, but the upside is that we ask you to work a lot. If you work a lot, you don't have time on your hands and therefore don't need much money!"

This type of clear-cut deal does not deter volunteers of very high caliber from pitching in for a year or two, no more no less. Why for a limited time? Because less than a year is not enough for the association, and over two years can be disruptive to the volunteer's career path.

In almost 20 years, I've seen over 150 volunteers come and go, and except for one or two cases, I've never been disappointed. Actually, we get over 150 applications a year for just three positions. I'm not very good at recruiting, so I leave the job to Rémi Duhamel, who has always handled it very insightfully.

We saw the pitfalls of individual sponsorships which led me to discontinue this form of fundraising. We therefore prefer program sponsorships, especially individual donations, if possible with no strings attached. Indeed, donations earmarked for a specific program tend to pour in when emotionally charged emergencies occur, while less dramatic initiatives are often overlooked. And an agency that respects the wishes of donors is unable to channel the donation elsewhere.

The 2004 tsunami speaks volumes in this regard, as it prompted exceptional displays of generosity to the detriment of other causes. But too much money is harmful. It encourages consumption of aid and is a deterrent for the local communities to get involved. Médecins Sans Frontières saw this and asked for donations to the tsunami disaster fund to be discontinued.

As for us, support for street children must stay linked to educational and cultural programs that enable personalities to be built or rebuilt. Yet, such programs are much more challenging to fund.

As for gifts in kind, we are not at all keen on them. The idea may be very well meaning, but used clothing, obsolete equipment, and the like can overwhelm the local people. When we were short of funds and accepted salvaged computers, we wasted so much time repairing them! Medication, fine, but batches of expired pills? Clothing, okay, but how many days spent to get them out of customs, then sort and transport them! It's better to buy new material, especially in Asia where most of the world's textiles are produced. And for a downhearted child, there's nothing like a gift of brand new, well-chosen clothes.

In the same vein, I'm reticent when it comes to grants from ponderous organizations or from certain governments that can tend to be straightjacketing. Such funds may be available to costly, large-scale projects, while little projects rarely interest public agencies because of the large input of work they require. The NGO has to put so much into it that it becomes discouraging—the time required to prepare the files, the trips back and forth to complete them, the wait for answers, finding the needed cash advances.

Sadly, government funds often serve a plethora of projects with a dependency effect. Although very valuable, such funds have perverse effects on the consumption of aid, because aid that comes in large amounts but late, with deadlines to be met, is counterproductive. This is illustrated by what happens in a computer or equipment store at year end. The managers rack their brains to find ideas for expenses in order to avoid budgets being frozen or not renewed. Projects are created as a function of the budget instead of the money being provided as a function of the need.

More subtly, government funds, because of the huge sums involved, put small NGOs at risk of subservience. Their very survival is at stake and, to meet the administrative requirements, these NGOs hire costly management professionals. Thus, government funds, a providential but dangerous manna, are to be handled with care. The same applies to funding from a little known agency that may turn out to be a proselytizing or politically oriented entity, creating all kinds of headaches.

In 1995, I agree to be in a story Serge Moati is shooting in Cambodia to mark UNICEF's 50th anniversary. It will mainly highlight our initiatives in partnership with UNICEF on child welfare issues. However, I refuse involvement in programs that may use our image but that do not support what we do or share our values.

The ideal situation is for major donors to share the philosophy of their beneficiaries. Thus, an exchange of street child educators with an organization in Morocco is arranged in partnership with Air France. Three Moroccans are to spend several weeks in Cambodia, completely immersed in our programs. In exchange, three Cambodians leave for

Morocco. The purpose of the exercise is to promote analytical thinking on local issues to improve one's own performance.

A similar process is instituted with a network of schools for blind and deaf children in India. The staff members who share in these exchanges are not the same persons when they return. From performers they become stakeholders, expanding their horizons and growing in maturity. We have always had a special place for regional training sessions in Thailand, in the Philippines, in Vietnam, or in Bangladesh. Experience confirms the rationale of this regional choice which is more seamless compared with European projects. The training is better perceived and more immediately usable. And the partners give us meaningful input for our activities.

Although we could get by without it, we have always had KPMG audit our accounts and I am grateful for their services. Far from fearing donor meddling in what we're doing, I consider it as a token of a sustainable partnership. Recently, with the support of the association IDEAS, we put some rules in place and made our website more transparent with regard to our activities and accounting.

While on the subject, I would like to see the governments and organizations develop a statement of standard accounting practices for humanitarian work, along with strict rules and regulations to make the accounts of the organizations understandable and available, to enable a comparison of expenses, and to make it easier to read how the funds are being used. What amount has actually been spent on overhead? What is included in overhead?

I sincerely hope that the competent government agencies will look into this. Because many NGOs that have expanded have seen their overhead or administrative expenses skyrocket and try to hide them by allocating the cost to operational budget lines.

In 1994, three years after I started, thinking about the future of the association and whether or not I could do something different, here in Cambodia or elsewhere, I want to put a Cambodian at the head of Krousar Thmey. I was advised by a woman with UNICEF to meet Boreth, a Cambodian who grew up in the United States. We hit it off relatively well and decide to try it out. But his involvement in the programs is not what I was hoping for. I ask him to put more into it than would be expected in other jobs available to him. He declines my offer to become director of Krousar Thmey. I have to look for someone else.

In 1995, I invite Sutheany, who formerly assisted Katell at SIPAR, to become my associate. Her strength of character, her ease with children, her ability to manage teams, and her tactfulness work wonders. She's nonplused by travel fatigue, lack of creature comforts, managing staff on a tight budget, or punchy discussions with government officials. Always there when she's needed, always good natured, she's the type of female leader I like. Actually, for some years now, I've preferred having women as program directors. They have a greater sense of responsibility and also more clout. I can delegate more, while keeping an eye on how our programs are doing.

Sutheany therefore seems to be the ideal candidate to take over my operational responsibilities and by 1996, she's co director. She's a domestic Cambodian, having never fled her country for the Thai border. She worked in a government factory. She's got the true grit we need. Despite many ups and downs, she's always worked hard, both to raise her son and help the small family cookie business.

So in early 1996, we agree that she will take over operational command starting January 1, 1997. The countdown begins, albeit with some hidden intentions.

On May 19, 1996, I end my semiannual round of conferences. Sometimes it's 20 cities in as many days. Fortunately, with the assistance of Rémi Duhamel's outstanding films and help from Philippe Magnier, I sometimes speak to packed halls of 200 people, at other times before distinguished groups of friends of the organizer, some of whom are firm believers, others who are strangers to be turned into firm believers. Even though the outcome is rarely worth the energy expended, even though the local media prefer headlines about the 30 boules competitors rather than schools for disabled Cambodians, I focus on my audience, try to get them to love Cambodia, appreciate what we're doing, and enjoy a pleasant evening.

When I get back, Sutheany comes to meet me at the airport and announces that she's leaving for Australia. She has family there and the news doesn't surprise me. Seeing me unperturbed, she lays her cards on the table. She's leaving for good. Nothing like an ice water dousing. For several years, she'd secretly been working on what she calls a family reunion. Actually, she's getting out of Cambodia so that her son can pursue his studies. I can't hold it against her. She lost her husband and several family members under the Khmer Rouge and courageously held up through those challenging times. Going abroad, as heartrending as it may be, is an opportunity not to be missed for her son.

A bolt out of the blue. As we talk on, I sink to the ground. When I ask her when she's leaving, she replies, "Next week." That finishes me. She leaves the office three days later. I was expecting to free myself of being director, but fail. I saw myself going in for some private-sector retraining, but no hope of that. Not only am I back at square one, but I have to assume again many responsibilities that she'd been handling over the last two years.

In 1996, Krousar Thmey already has a regular staff of 180 and it's a huge job. Before Sutheany left, we felt that Thary, an English teacher and her assistant, would make a good assistant director. He replaces her. In just a few weeks, he's at ease with the paperwork. Yet, a weakness appears. He doesn't like making tough decisions. He tends to leave me with the thankless role of the Whipping Father and the formal jobs. As I see it, it's not our money that we're managing but the children's. Although the human aspect is important, one has to work with one's head and make decisions, even if some toes get stepped on.

By 1997, it's already been six years since I left my management position with ACCOR to become a humanitarian officer, working seven days a week, 15 hours a day. I've no regrets over the energy and passion invested in this achievement, but I would like a break. My ACCOR friends and colleagues warn me of the increasing difficulty I would have if I returned to the corporate world. My time of involvement is inversely proportionate to my chances of landing a job in the private sector. But if I did get a job, I would rather work in Cambodia which would allow me to keep an eye on the programs.

Experience notwithstanding, my value on the labor market has shrunk considerably. Since 1996, I have seen that taking on a full-time job is out of the question. It would be too risky should Thary not pan out. And I'm tired of being the beggar who is always treated to meals when I'm in France. My friends are wonderful and know that going to a restaurant with me means they pick up the bill. I'm not comfortable with that.

The members of the board of directors of Krousar Thmey France would be happy if I stayed on as CEO for life, but I start pulling out to some extent. So as not to be a burden on the budgets, I staunchly refuse to increase my allowances and try to earn my own living. I started off as a volunteer, caring for many expenses out of my savings, then accepted a small allowance, and now I get a small salary from Krousar Thmey that doesn't go very far in Europe.

Given my management track record, I am contacted by the French embassy to teach at the Faculty of Law and Economics. And I do some auditing for Actif Cambodia. From 1997 to 2002, I do the quarterly audit of the accounts and activities of a European malaria control project. Seven well-paid days of work every three months is a start. And the hotel industry won't let go of me. Since the highway between Phnom Penh and Siem Reap opened in 1996, the number of temple tourists has been increasing. Siem Reap is still short of hotel capacity; it has only three or four good hotels, including the charming Angkor Village just built by a French-Cambodian couple. I believe in the future of temple tourism. The time is ripe, so six friends invest with me to buy a piece of land for a guesthouse.

Each of us puts in about $5,000 to buy 1,000 m² at the river's edge. A few months later, some refuse to increase their share; the events that shook Cambodia in 1997 are hardly confidence bolstering. In the western part of the country, we encounter fighting between the opposing troops of the two prime ministers on several occasions. Two of our volunteers get caught in some skirmishing. A rocket explodes less than 50 m away in the ditch down the road. Tension mounts between the two parties and it's feared that military confrontations will sweep through the rest of the country. Although I do earn a small income from teaching and auditing, I cannot cover the financial needs of the future La Noria buildings. I therefore open up the capital to nine other partners. Just after I apply for the building permit on July 4, 1997, fighting breaks out in Phnom Penh.

Starting in 1998, Thary becomes co-director of programs before taking on full senior management of the organization.

Meanwhile, the very go-ahead governor of Phnom Penh has undertaken an extensive plan to rebuild the main arteries of the city. Kampuchea Krom Avenue runs by La Casa. The constantly uneven asphalt has to be redone, along with the entire drainage system that is very quickly overwhelmed during the wet season. Whenever there's a heavy rain, the merchants pile up sandbags to keep the water from flooding their shops. Instead of taking in water, the manholes spew out foul-smelling black sewage. Rats emerge and swim in all directions. Cockroaches avoid drowning by climbing the walls. And the people just graciously accept this inexorable deluge of dirty water. They grin as they turn their pant legs or dress up their knees and slosh through. Cyclo drivers nonchalantly churn through the stream. Drivers of small cars slow down to avoid flooding their engines. The 4x4s and other high-chassis vehicles, without a care in the world, send water spraying and propel waves that give pedestrians an unasked-for dousing and destroy the improvised dams.

In early 2000, the governor therefore starts having all of Kampuchea Krom Avenue redone. He likes things that last, so he wants the asphalt and poor roadbed redone up to nearly a meter deep to prevent depressions and pavement heaving in the future. But once the road is dug up, why in the world would everything stop? There's nearly a 1 m drop from the main avenue to the adjoining streets. Our street is perpendicular to Kampuchea Krom Avenue so can no longer be accessed by car or motorbike. A complicated detour is needed to get to La Casa. The restaurant had already experienced a drop in patronage since the riverside was redeveloped and many new establishments went up in the downtown area and now this happens. Without further ado, I shut it down for good. We move our communications offices into it;

up till now they'd been sheltered in old sheet-metal lean-tos behind the restaurant. We demolished them to make room Krousar Thmey's permanent offices. Thus, everyone will have his or her own space. I repossess my house and Krousar Thmey has its own offices.

For heat and noise reduction, as well as to make the best use of light, I design a three-story building with a small inner open-air patio. The offices are placed around this central space to allow easy access between the accounting, communications, and management departments. The second floor has a wide open terrace for meetings. A kitchen and two bedrooms with bathrooms en suite complete this floor. The next story up has three more bedrooms and a bathroom for visitors passing through. I intentionally do not have an office put in for me. My idea is to mark the change and transfer of operational powers to Thary. If he's going to take over from me, he mustn't have me in the way. And no more table where people can dump files on for me to check.

In late December 2000, construction is completed. It's a beautiful building, white, clean lines, very open to the outside, and fits right in with the surroundings. To save energy, we have no plans for air conditioning, but have plenty of natural ventilation. The traditional terra cotta tiles give the place a touch of southern France. The inside temperature stays cool.

On moving day, I prefer to take my leave. I can't take it emotionally. When I return from Siem Reap, everything had been moved out during the weekend and set up in the new premises. There's not a thing left, absolutely not one thing. In all the commotion, my room hadn't even been cleaned. The posters had been torn off the wall, leaving strips of scotch tape shriveled by the heat. The walls preserve the blank memory of a few pictures now removed. The rooms are empty. My big desk, stripped bare, and a forlorn chair stand alone in the general abandon.

I feel a powerful stifling feeling come over me. I can hardly breathe. Right then, two volunteers walk in, delighted to pronounce the move over. They see me disheartened, wild-eyed. I can no longer stand and collapse onto the chair, gasping for breath. They look at me, stupefied. They can't understand. Strong emotion gets the best of me.

The painful memories of nine years come flooding back: the horrible roads, the AK-47 shots, the death of Vanna, the first of seven of our staff felled by AIDS, the discouraging times when facing the government steamroller, the threats of the Poipet military men... This move is agonizing, but as I sit behind my naked desk, I tell myself that I wanted it this way, and this is the way it is.

In 2000, by way of thanking me for my devotion and the work I've done, His Majesty King Norodom Sihanouk and Prime Minister Samdech Hun Sen grant me full Cambodian citizenship. Rare are those who get Cambodian citizenship without paying dearly. This permanent status allows me to hold property in my own name.

The next year, 2001, goes by without incident. I still do some fundraising and liaise with various institutions, but do ever less with the programs and nothing at all with regard to human resources. I depend a lot on Thary. When asked how much I spend with Krousar Thmey, I reply, "At the most, 30 percent of my time!" My volunteers joke, "That's true; Bénito gives 30 percent. Out of 24 hours, he spends eight at Krousar Thmey!"

Hiring and firing are Thary's job, except the extreme case of a guard who took advantage of the situation when the volunteers were away to smash open a desk where we lock the money, steal a motorbike, and flee. We publish his mug shot with promise of a reward. He's arrested, jailed, and sentenced. We hardly get a thing back, but it's a reminder that theft cannot be tolerated.

In 2002, while I'm away in France, my volunteers inform me that Thary has left for the United States. He wants to leave us and refuses our offers. We eventually accept his resignation and appoint Kosal, his assistant, as his successor. Her official appointment is announced to the staff. She has a harder time getting accepted, but takes a fresh look at the programs, notably education for young disabled persons. She also maintains a tighter grip. She serves as director of Krousar Thmey from 2002 to 2010 before stepping down.

Since then, while making enough to live on in hotel management, I spend about a fifth of my time helping Krousar Thmey. The work involves finding new donors, meeting with organizations, sharing in small operations that, when combined, provide the money needed for our activities in Cambodia. Like a herd of unruly farm animals, funds have the bad habit of not coming in on their own.

Despite all manner of frustrations, the moments of despair and disenchantment, I sometimes light-headedly tell myself that I could well have missed out on it all. When I think back to the first children, the decimated state of the country, the lack of roads and electricity, the misery and hopelessness of the camps, I see that Krousar Thmey has contributed to a profound change.

Attending the wedding of a young man who was found as a child wandering the streets proves that the efforts have paid off. Walking into a public school classroom and seeing blind or deaf children at ease, viewed as equals by their classmates, prompts me to clasp my hands in front of me and salute with a deep bow the teams of Cambodian teachers, drivers, cooks, the many professionals in so many fields, and the smiling, devoted directors. Chatting in English with blind students, now in university, concerned about their future and the integration of the disabled into a work environment fills me with elation. In 2010, this patient job of educating blind and deaf children was crowned with the Wenhui Award, conferred by the National Commission of the People's Republic of China for UNESCO in recognition of innovation in education.

On this sixth day of April 2011, in the presence of the prime minister celebrating his 60th birthday and the 20th anniversary of Krousar Thmey in the courtyard of our most recent school for blind and deaf children, the effort takes on its full meaning. All the more so since a few months ago, the prime minister accepted one of our proposals—the inclusion of all our teachers on the staff lists of the Cambodian Ministry of Education. Ownership of these programs by Cambodians and by the various levels of government is now on the right road.

Actually, I never thought of my life in terms of the projects we developed. I did not want to be a founder chained to "his work." Krousar Thmey exists, not as a personal project, but as an institution. I am happy to have been able to achieve this with hundreds of Cambodians who are going on without me. I have two reasons to feel proud: Krousar Thmey is the first Cambodian child welfare foundation and I'm no longer necessary. I can still lend a hand, but I'm no longer indispensable.

There is a butterfly on our emblem. May the fluttering of its wings continue to have far-reaching effects and give others the desire to flutter their wings too. Without going to the ends of the earth, right here, wings are just waiting to start fluttering. It's a pleasure to be an inspiration for some of them.

May this book impel the reader to support new families and experience the joy deriving therefrom…

Phnom Penh, April 6, 2011

AFTERWORD

Outcast—a word that is easy to say, easy to understand, that conjures up a clear image in the minds of each one. Paradoxically, though, if you ask around exactly what an outcast is, likely the answers would be quite stereotypical.

Some would say that outcasts are the poor, or perhaps the tramps, the mentally challenged, the elderly... Rarely would one mention street children or even less so disabled children... A group of outcasts among outcasts.

Their lot is particularly poignant, for, even if they were to be noticed, the next perplexing question is, "What can be done?"

Benoît Duchâteau-Arminjon visited a refugee camp on Thailand's border with Cambodia and immediately zeroed in on things. It was like a bolt out of the blue, because really nothing destined him to look into the lot of these kids. He had no background in health care, psychology, or social work. Up to that point, he had been a financial controller, a job that he took seriously and professionally, but one that would never have led him to encounter firsthand the problems and suffering of the children.

And yet, deeply moved, he realized that he was now being "called" to get involved in helping abandoned children. And with his intuition and talent, but more importantly with his heart, he looked for ways that he could help them.

Thus, out of the setting of refugee camps, the Krousar Thmey Association was founded in 1991 by Benoît Duchâteau-Arminjon, a man who related to the distress of the children, a man profoundly committed by this encounter. His purpose was rescuing these children, seeing to their integration into Cambodia, they who, long after the capsizing and destruction of their country, were the ultimate victims of that disaster.

These children were not just social and emotional outcasts; some of them—the deaf or blind—also had sensory disabilities, and were developmentally challenged.

I am in a position to attest to the faith and force that Benoît Duchâteau-Arminjon had to display in order to convince others of the need for, to construct, and to support these shaky new structures in the health care, social welfare, and educational world that a Cambodia undergoing rebirth was attempting to put in place. Deaf, blind, disabled, and abandoned children were certainly not a matter of urgency, a priority, for the country.

The work done over these 20 years must be acclaimed with respect and friendship.

Appalled by the unjust and unbelievable suffering of which the children were victims, Benoît Duchâteau-Arminjon started with just a small facility. Twenty years later, it has become a high-performance institution. It is the work of a man who never purported to be a professional humanitarian worker. His motivations sprung from a duty of brotherhood, a duty of human kindness and, let's say it, of love…

Dr Xavier Emmanuelli

TIME LINE

1990   • First visit to Site II.

       • Operation School Uniforms.

1991   • Opening of the Dangrek orphanage, followed by the O'Bok orphanage, on Site II.

1992   • Exhibition *Rizières: deux cultures à découvrir* put on in all the border camps.

       • Construction of first child welfare center in Cambodia and first Site II repatriation to Siem Reap.

       • Opening of La Casa restaurant in Phnom Penh.

1993   • Construction of second child welfare center and second Site II repatriation to Ta Khmau.

       • Construction of third child welfare center and final Site II repatriation to Sisophon.

       • Construction of 11 classrooms in Siem Reap, Sisophon, and Ta Khmau to promote integration of the child camp returnees into their new environment.

       • Elections in Cambodia.

       • Construction and opening of first center for street children in Psar Depot.

       • Second traveling exhibition: *Cambodge, un peuple, une culture*.

1994   • Construction and opening of first school for blind children. Start up of Khmer Braille and first workshop for the production of books in Khmer Braille.

       • Construction of first school in Poipet.

       • Construction of school in Wat Krabaeu.

       • Co-founding of ECPAT.

1995   • Seamanship training started for street children using trawlers at Sihanoukville and construction of intake center.

- The exhibition *Cambodia, mémoire vive* presented at Albert-Kahn Museum in Boulogne-Billancourt.

1996
- Construction and opening of first family shelter in Teuk Thla.
- Construction of a second center for street children in Poipet and first repatriations of children from prisons in Bangkok.
- Construction of Poipet village for single-parent families headed by women.
- Construction of arts and cultural center in Sisophon and rebirth of shadow puppet theater.

1997
- Construction of third intake center for street children in Chamkarmon.
- Construction of first school for deaf children in Chbar Ampov and startup of Khmer Sign Language.
- Forces of the two prime ministers engage in violent street fighting.

1998
- Startup of campaign for the prevention of child trafficking and prostitution.
- Construction of a primary school complex in Prum Nimith, Poipet.
- First large family celebration, *Bon Prachum Nheat*, an event subsequently held every two years.

1999
- Construction of two family shelters in Kpop Veng and Preah Kat.

2000
- Opening of second school for deaf and blind children in Battambang.
- First blind children admitted to public school.
- Construction of Krousar Thmey's offices and closure of La Casa.

2001
- Construction of school for blind and deaf children in Siem Reap.
- Startup of first seven integrated classes, to be followed by 37 others in subsequent years.
- First blind students to be trained as masseurs.

- Construction of two new family shelters in Siem Reap.
- Traveling exhibition: *Tonle Sap, source de vies*.
- Launch of board game *Neak Na Doeung*, a type of Cambodian Trivial Pursuit.
- Construction of an exhibition hall in Siem Reap.
- First hearing aids for hearing-impaired children.

2002
- Construction of fourth school for blind and deaf children in Kompong Cham.
- Opening of second workshop for production of Braille textbooks in Battambang.
- Construction of two more family shelters in Kompong Cham.
- Fourth intake center for street children in Siem Reap.

2003
- Launch of speech therapy program.

2004
- Construction of two new family shelters in Sihanoukville.
- First translation of national television news in sign language.
- Opening of first kindergarten for deaf children.

2005
- Awareness-raising campaigns on education of disabled children.

2006
- First three blind students from Krousar Thmey obtain high school diplomas.
- Construction of two more family shelters in Battambang.

2008
- Digital sign language dictionary put online.

2009
- Two temporary exhibitions: *Le braille au Cambodge* and *Sans un regard*.
- Construction of most recent school for blind and deaf children at Phnom Penh Thmey.
- Opening of hearing aid workshop.

2010
- Agreement to have all teaching staff of schools for blind and deaf children included on Cambodian Ministry of Education lists.

2011
- Krousar Thmey celebrates its 20th anniversary.

Royalties from this book are remitted in full to Krousar Thmey. Your donations to help Cambodian children may be sent directly to the foundation by check or bank transfer, or made by direct payment via our website.

Krousar Thmey
ក្រុសារថ្មី

www.krousar-thmey.org

Krousar Thmey is an association recognized as a community and public service in France, Switzerland, and the United Kingdom, which may qualify donations for tax advantages in these countries. In order to minimize bank charges, kindly send your donations directly to the support committee of the entity in your home country.

For further information, please contact Krousar Thmey:

>> In Cambodia: **communication@krousar-thmey.org**
Krousar Thmey – Acleda Bank Plc.: 0001-20-441353-1-3;
SWIFT: ACLBKHPP

>> In France: **france@krousar-thmey.org**
Krousar Thmey France, CCP 36 969 80 X 033
For donations eligible for ISF consideration, kindly contact us first.

>> In Switzerland: **switzerland@krousar-thmey.org**
Make money orders payable to "Krousar Thmey Suisse"
Account No.: 17-762996-2; IBAN: CH15 0900 0000 1776 2996 2;
BIC: POFICHBEXXX

>> In the United Kingdom: **uk@krousar-thmey.org**
Bank of Ireland Berkeley Square, London, Account No.: 69730386
Sort Code 301607

Our overhead accounts for less than 4 percent of donations. Our accounts are scrupulously transparent and are audited yearly by KPMG. They are available upon request or can be downloaded from our website.

A donation to Krousar Thmey is a way of directly helping the children of Cambodia.

We thank you in advance for your support.

ACKNOWLEDGMENTS

For the original French edition, I would like to thank all my proofreaders, especially Michel d'Orgeval for the tremendous job he did, along with Xavier Puéchal, Alain Courau, Rémi Duhamel, Béatrice Le Guay, and François Bourdoncle, as well as Marie-Claude, Didier and Valérie Millet for their valuable contributions.

For the English version, I would like to deeply thank David Rorke for the translation from French, James Pham for the meticulous proofreading job he did of the translated manuscript, along with Ed and Linda Blow, and Matthew Leitner for their valuable contribution. In addition, I would like to thank for their energy and dedication Emmanüelle Bucaille and Elizabeth Turchi and for their kind support SDV Singapore, Raffles Hotel Singapore, and the team of Éditions Didier Millet, without whom this English version would never have come into print.